AF867598

UK TAXATION

A SIMPLIFIED GUIDE FOR STUDENTS

12th Edition

FINANCE ACT 2026 EDITION

Twelfth edition
Published September 2026 by
Spiramus Press Ltd
102 Blandford Street
London
W1U 8AG

www.spiramus.com

Paperback ISBN 9781913507350
Digital ISBN 9781913507367

FSC www.fsc.org MIX Paper | Supporting responsible forestry FSC® C007915

PREFACE TO TWELFTH EDITION

As I sit and finalise this, my eighth edition of this text, I have looked back to my first preface dated July 2018. Over that time so much of the contents of this textbook has changed but you do notice some rates and allowances that have remined static. Take rent a room relief – unchanged since 2016 and the IHT annual exemption of £3,000 – no change since 1981! With this year's announcement that the main income tax allowances and rate bands are frozen until 5 April 2031, it seems clear that this fiscal drag remains every Government's favoured method of increasing the tax take.

However, the Tax Gap has increased slightly and it would be helpful if more targeted action could be taken to shrink this to give taxpayers more faith in the fairness of the tax system.

My laptop is currently threatening to melt, on this the hottest June day on record. Perhaps a few more sustainability changes could help too!

Since my first edition, we have seen seven different Chancellors, each with their own view of the direction of change (or lack of change) of UK taxation. Another new Chancellor AND a new Prime Minister) were announced last week – will this lead to a few surprises in the Autumn Budget?

As in previous editions, I have attempted to use a clear style throughout this text to make it easy to read and follow and I hope that students find this book accessible and helpful in their studies.

To make this book as useful as possible, I have included worked examples throughout and have tried to keep chapters short and easy to read in one session. Appendices 2 and 3 contain further practice questions.

This text is not intended to be used by tax practitioners or as a tax advice guide but is for students of taxation. It is aimed primarily at undergraduate students; however, students on professional courses, for example, AAT, ICAEW, ACCA and perhaps ATT, may also find this helpful.

The text does not attempt to be a comprehensive guide to the entire UK taxation system but concentrates on the key areas that a student should know.

As usual, I thank my colleagues and students at Birmingham City University for their helpful input.

Mark Hunt

Solihull

July 2026

IMPORTANT NOTICE TO STUDENTS

This publication is based on tax law up to and including the Finance Act 2026. This book is to assist students with their studies and is not intended to provide comprehensive tax planning advice.

CONTENTS

2026/27 TAX RATES AND ALLOWANCES

Income tax

	Income bands	Normal rates	Dividend rates
2026/27			
Basic rate	1-37,700	20%	10.75%
Higher rate	37,701 - 125,140	40%	35.75%
Additional rate	Over 125,140	45%	39.35%

Savings income nil rate band:	
- Basic rate taxpayers	£1,000
- Higher rate taxpayers	£500
Dividend nil rate band:	£500

A starting rate of 0% applies to savings income where it falls within the first £5,000 of taxable income.

Personal allowance

Personal allowance	£12,570
Income limit	£100,000
Transferable Marriage Allowance	£1,260

Car benefit

Zero emissions	4%
1g/km to 50g/km:	
Electric range: *130 miles or more*	4%
70 -129 miles	*7%*
40 -69 miles	*10%*
30-39 miles	*14%*
Less than 30 miles	*16%*
51g/km to 54g/km	17%
55g/km to 59g/km	18%
60g/km to 64g/km	19%
65g/km to 69g/km	20%
70g/km to 74gkm	21%
75g/km to 79g/km	21%
Each additional 5g/km	+1%
Diesel supplement (not RDE2)	+4%
Maximum charge	37%
Car fuel benefit amount	£29,200

Van benefit (Emissions above 0%)	£4,170
Van fuel benefit	£798

Authorised mileage rates

	Rate per mile
Annual business mileage up to 10,000 miles	55p
Each additional mile over 10,000 miles	25p

Official rate of interest

2026/27 3.75%
(At the time of publication)

Pension contribution limits

Annual allowance	£60,000
Minimum annual allowance	£10,000
Income limit	£260,000
Lifetime allowance abolished	

National insurance contributions 2026/27

Class 1 Employees	£1 - £12,570 per year	0%
(Annualised rates)	£12,571 - £50,270 per year	8%
	Over £50,270 per year	2%
Class 1 Employers	£1 to £5,000 per year	-
	Over £5,000 per year	15%
	Employment allowance	£10,500
Class 1A	Employers only	15%
Class 2	Weekly rate	£3.65
	Small profits threshold	£7,105
Class 4	£1 to £12,570	-
	£12,571 to £50,270	6%
	Over £50,270	2%

Capital gains tax

Annual exemption	£3,000
Lower rate	18%
Higher rate	24%

Business asset disposal relief	
- Lifetime limit	£1,000,000
- Rate	18%

Corporation tax

Corporation tax rates are fixed for financial years:

Financial year 2026 and 2027

Main rate	25%
Small profits rate	19%
Small profits rate limit	£50,000
Marginal relief limit	£250,000
Marginal relief fraction	3/200
Large Company Profit threshold	£1,500,000

Capital allowances

Plant and machinery

FYA – Main pool from 1 January 2026	40%
Main pool WDA	14%
Special rate pool WDA	6%

Motor Cars

New cars with Zero CO_2	100%
CO_2 emissions between 0 and 50 grams per km	14%
CO_2 emissions over 50 grams per km	6%

Annual investment allowance

Rate of allowance	100%
Expenditure limit	£1,000,000

Full expensing (Companies only)

New main pool assets	100%
New special rate pool assets	50%

Structures and buildings allowance

From April 2020	3%
Previously, from 29 October 2018	2%

Value added tax

Standard rate	20%
Reduced rate	5%
Registration limit	£90,000
Deregistration limit	£88,000

Inheritance tax

Nil rate band	£325,000
Residence Nil Rate Band	£175,000
Tax rates : Lifetime rate	20%
Death rate	40%

Taper relief

3 to 4 years	20%
4 to 5 years	40%
5 to 6 years	60%
6 to 7 years	80%

CHAPTER 1

Introduction

Tax can be a "Marmite" subject for students and many qualified accountants too – some love it, others hate it!

Often, the problem, however, is that many tax textbooks use complex language and introduce too many new facts at the same time, leaving students confused. This book tries to avoid this, where possible and the wording tries to be clear with each new key issue followed by an illustrative example.

Many students believe that learning tax is simply about doing multiple examples. This can be true for some parts but to pass any tax examination well, you need to understand the basic underlying principles. Understanding the basics means that you can cut down the need to simply memorise all the facts and will not be caught off guard by a different style of question. This book concentrates on the basics. Understanding the *basic principles* at an early stage can pay dividends later.

Tax can be both fascinating and enjoyable and can possibly offer the student a rewarding future career in the accountancy profession, industry or with HMRC (His Majesty's Revenue and Customs).

Tax is dynamic

The UK tax system does not stand still. Each year brings changes introduced by the latest Finance Act and new cases sometimes give surprising outcomes or just seem bizarre (Try an internet search for "Is a Pringle a crisp"!). The question of tax avoidance remains a hot topic in the news, particularly where celebrities or Tech giants are involved. During 2025-6, HMRC collected £938.8 billion in taxes. The latest estimate, published by HMRC in June 2026, shows that 6.4% of the total theoretical UK taxes remain unpaid each year ("the tax gap"), a slight increase on the previous year. In cash terms, this is estimated at £59.2 billion. Small businesses are responsible for 62% of the tax gap.

Tax is not a difficult subject to study

In studying this text, it may help to skim-read the brief "Summary" at the end of each chapter; then read the whole of the chapter slowly, pausing to try to work through the examples, before moving on to the next part of the chapter.

If understanding any particular part of a chapter proves a little too difficult, move on and come back to it later in your studies. You will be surprised at how often something that you found difficult at one stage of your studies becomes straightforward when you return later.

For ease of understanding, throughout the text, any pence have been dropped from examples. In strictness, most taxes should be calculated to the penny!

This book assumes absolutely no prior knowledge of UK taxation.

This text is completely self-contained, covering the fundamental areas of taxation studied at undergraduate level and initially for many professional exams. It can be used to support other texts and includes all the various allowances, tax rates, etc., that a student may need at the front of the book.

I hope that you find this book to be written in a user-friendly manner. It includes numerous examples throughout the text designed to illustrate specific points and then provides further examples for you to try in Appendix 2 with the solutions available online. Appendix 3 includes multiple-choice questions for each chapter for you to dip into at any time to test your understanding.

I have tried to avoid "tax jargon", and wherever possible, plain, straightforward English is used. But I am a self-confessed "Tax Nerd" and may not always achieve this as well as I hope. In Appendix 1, I have suggested some tips for studying tax.

This book covers the main UK taxes: income tax (paid by individuals), capital gains tax (paid by individuals), corporation tax (paid by companies), value added tax (levied on consumers by businesses), inheritance tax (normally payable on the death of an individual) and National Insurance Contributions.

Although primarily aimed at students studying at undergraduate level, these are the taxes that typically form the core of the syllabus for most of the UK's professional examinations in taxation such as those of the ICAEW, ACCA, AAT and possibly ATT, although no specific professional syllabus has been followed.

In general, each of the chapters should be read through in the order in which they are arranged, as later chapters often assume knowledge from earlier chapters. Having said this, the Value Added Tax and Inheritance Tax chapters could be studied at any point, as a standalone, as both are quite different from the other taxes studied.

Tax can be a career in its own right and these initial studies could eventually lead you to study for membership of the Association of Taxation Technicians or the Charted Institute of Taxation. Some believe that tax is the engine that drives the accountancy profession and there is no doubt that if you choose a career in accountancy or finance, whatever the role, taxation will cross your path, in some way, at some point.

It may be that tax is not your favourite subject, but I hope that this text will help you to get through your taxation module and at least equip you with the ability to check the income tax and NIC deductions from your first pay!

So, enjoy the read. Pick up the book when you are in the mood and good luck with your studies!

One thing is for certain – taxation is not going to disappear!

Finally, this book is for students. It is not for tax advisers – this text does not attempt to be a comprehensive tax guide to use for tax planning.

(see also **Appendix 1 – How to study taxation**).

What's New – Summary of main changes introduced by the Finance Act 2026 and other changes from 6th April 2026

Income tax

The personal allowance remains at £12,570. The basic rate band limit stays at £37,700 and the additional rate starts after £125,140. The personal allowance and basic rate band are frozen until 5 April 2031. These will have remained unchanged for 10 years.

The basic and higher rates of income tax on dividends are both increased by 2% to 10.75% and 35.75%, respectively.

From 6 April 2027, the income tax rates on savings will increase by 2% across all bands and new separate tax rates will apply to property income of 22%, 42% and 47%, in line with the increased savings rate bands.

Making Tax Digital for Income Tax Self-Assessment

This new quarterly online only return system is introduced from 6 April 2026 for self-employed individuals and property landlords with a combined income from these sources above £50,000.

Capital allowances

From 6 April 2026 (1 April 2026 for Corporation tax), the rate of writing down allowance for the main pool is reduced to 14%, requiring a hybrid rate for periods straggling 6 April 2026.

Capital gains tax

The rate of tax on gains qualifying for Business Asset Disposal Relief and Investors' relief increases to 18% for disposals made on or after 6 April 2026.

Corporation tax

There are no changes to Corporation tax.

National Insurance Contributions

The rates of Class 1 and Class 4 NIC remain unchanged.

VAT

There are no VAT changes.

Inheritance tax

The main IHT rate bands are frozen until 5 April 2031.

A new limit of £2,500,000 is introduced for 100% IHT Business property relief and Agricultural property relief, with 50% relief above this limit. Qualifying shares listed on AIM will now only qualify for 50% BPR.

From 6 April 2027, most pension assets will be included in the value of the death estate for IHT.

CHAPTER 2

Income Tax: General Principles and Tax Rates

Introduction

This chapter will introduce various concepts, including:

- an introduction to the administration of the UK tax system
- how income is taxed
- the rates of tax that apply
- the categories of income

The following chapters will introduce further aspects of the income tax computation so that by the end of Chapter 4 you should be able to calculate any individual's income tax liability. We will then look at the calculation of specific sources of taxable income and other income tax aspects through to Chapter 12.

HM Revenue and Customs

The UK tax system is managed by HM Revenue and Customs (HMRC). HMRC is responsible for the administration and collection of both direct and indirect taxes in the UK. HMRC has various additional duties, including the collection of student loan repayments and the enforcement of the National Living Wage.

HMRC has five strategic objectives:

- close the tax gap;
- improve day-to-day performance and the overall customer experience;
- reform and modernisation of tax and customs administration;
- build a high-performing organisation with a skilled and engaged workforce; and
- support wider government economic aims through HMRC's work.

(https://www.gov.uk/government/organisations/hm-revenue-customs/about)

UK tax law

UK tax legislation is comprised of several specific tax acts, for example, the Corporation Tax Act 2010 (referred to as CTA2010), supported by annual Finance Acts. The Finance Acts put into law the announcements made by the Chancellor of the Exchequer in the annual Budget statement to the House of Commons. This text has been updated to include the Finance Act 2026 (referred to as FA 2026), but older Finance Acts may be referred to in this text where still relevant. The Chancellor announced her proposed changes to the tax system in her Budget speech on 26 November 2025, and, after various parliamentary reviews, these were passed into law as the Finance Act 2026 on 18 March 2026.

In addition to the statute law, there is a large body of tax case law that guides the interpretation of tax legislation. All case law originates from a disagreement between HMRC and a taxpayer.

Finally, HMRC provides technical guidance via its website, although it must be considered that this only represents HMRC's view of the law!

Tax Planning, avoidance and evasion

One of HMRC's roles is to "make it easy to get tax right and hard to bend or break the rules".

Tax planning involves making use of available tax reliefs for the purpose the law intended. For example, this may include claiming tax relief on certain qualifying investments or saving tax by way of ISAs or approved pension plans in the manner that the legislation sets out.

In the view of HMRC, tax avoidance "involves bending the rules of the tax system to try to gain a tax advantage that Parliament never intended". Often, this will involve a complex scheme that may involve artificial steps simply to try to gain a tax advantage. HMRC has successfully challenged many such schemes through the courts in recent years.

Finally, tax evasion encompasses all deliberate attempts not to pay tax by deliberately bending or breaking the law. This could include smuggling items into the UK without paying duties or under-declaring income to avoid direct taxation. Tax evasion can lead to financial penalties, criminal convictions or imprisonment (See Chapter 21).

HMRC can reward individuals if they provide information that leads to the collection of at least £1.5 million in unpaid tax,

Self-Assessment

For individuals and companies, the UK takes a self-assessment approach to taxation, where taxpayers are usually required to calculate their own tax liability when they are required to submit a tax return, with HMRC reserving the right to review the return and calculations. Most UK individuals are not required to submit a Self-Assessment tax return; their tax deductions are deducted from their pay under the PAYE system.

Making Tax Digital

Making Tax Digital is a plan to gradually introduce personalised digital tax accounts for individuals and will greatly change the procedures across the UK tax system. HMRC believes that this will help small businesses to benefit from modern accounting software and will reduce tax loss due to unintentional errors. Making Tax Digital for Income Tax Self-Assessment (MTD-ITSA) is introduced from 6 April 2026 for many Self-employed individuals and landlords, requiring quarterly online information submissions. This is explained in further detail in Chapter 21.

Who pays income tax?

An *individual* who is resident in the UK will pay UK income tax on their worldwide income (this is explored further in Chapter 11). As we shall see later in the book (Chapter 16), a company does not pay income tax but corporation tax on its profits.

What is income?

Income can include, for example:

- salary or wages from employment;
- trading profits from an individual's business carried on as a sole trader;
- bank interest;
- dividends from companies; and
- rental income.

Generally, capital receipts, such as the proceeds from the sale of a house, are not subject to income tax but may be subject to capital gains tax.

Exempt income

Some income is specifically exempt from income tax. Common examples of exempt income include:

- Income from an Individual Savings Account (ISA);
- Lottery, Premium bond or gambling winnings;
- Interest on NS&I Savings Certificates;
- Scholarship awards and educational grants;
- Up to £1,000 trading income (The trading allowance – see Chapter 6).

What is an income tax liability?

An individual's *income tax liability* is the tax liability on their *taxable income.*

To calculate an individual's income tax liability, it is necessary to aggregate all of their taxable income to which they are entitled in a tax year (see below) from all sources (referred to as Total income) and to then make certain deductions. Two types of deduction can be made:

- a deduction for reliefs; and
- a deduction for the personal allowance.

The effect of these calculations is to produce the following definitions:

Total income less reliefs = Net income

Net income less personal allowance = Taxable income

More will be said about these terms in Chapter 3.

Tax year

In the UK, the tax year runs from 6 April in any year to the following 5 April.

The tax year beginning on 6 April 2026 and ending on 5 April 2027 can be referred to as 2026/27.

A tax year can also be referred to as a *year of assessment*.

Calculating the income tax liability

Although an individual's income to which they are entitled is aggregated, it also needs to be allocated to one of the three following categories:

- Non-savings income
- Savings income
- Dividend income

This categorisation is needed as these different sources of income are taxed at different rates of income tax and in a specific order.

Categories of income

Non-savings income includes:

- rent from letting out a property;
- business profits from the carrying on of a trade;
- income from employment and pensions; and
- any income that does not fall into one of the other categories.

Savings income comprises:

- interest income (e.g. from a bank or building society deposit).

Dividend income comprises:

- dividends from shareholdings.

Order of taxing

Taxable income is taxed on a cumulative basis:

1. Non-savings income (NSI) is taxed first
2. then, Savings income (SI) is taxed
3. then, Dividend income (DI) is taxed.

Rates of income tax for the year to 5 April 2027 (2026/27)

		Main rates	*Dividend rates*
Basic rate	£1 – £37,700	20%	10.75%
Higher rate	£37,701 – £125,140	40%	35.75%
Additional rate	Over 125,140	45%	39.35%

These tax rates are applied on a cumulative basis to all taxable income. Any rate band or part of a rate band used up by, say, Non-savings income is then not available for Savings or Dividend income. The three types of income can be considered to stack on top of each other, using up the basic rate band, then the higher rate band and then moving into the Additional rate band if taxable income exceeds £125,140.

- For *Non-savings income (NSI)* the first £37,700 of Taxable Income is taxed at the basic rate of 20%; the next £87,440 (i.e. income up to £125,140) is taxed at the higher rate of 40% and everything above £125,140 is taxed at the additional rate of 45%.

- For *Savings income (SI),* which is taxed after Non-savings income (i.e. on top of it), any amount falling in the first £5,000 of Taxable Income is taxed at 0% (referred to as the starting rate for savings). Each £1 of non-savings income reduces the starting rate for savings by £1. Therefore, as is often the case, if non-savings income exceeds £5,000, this starting rate will not be available.

  Then, for basic rate taxpayers, the next £1,000 savings income is taxed at 0%, reduced to £500 for higher rate taxpayers (these limits are referred to in the legislation as the savings nil rate). Additional rate taxpayers do not receive a savings nil rate band.

  Otherwise, savings income is taxed at the same rates as non-savings income using the unused balance of the rate bands.
- For *Dividend income (DI),* which is taxed after both Non-savings and Savings income (i.e. on top of both), the first £500 is taxed at 0% (the dividend nil rate). Then any dividend income falling within the unused basic rate band is taxed at 10.75%, at 35.75% within the higher rate band and 39.35% within the additional rate band.

It should be remembered that there is only one set of rate bands. For example, if NSI uses up the full basic rate band, then any SI or DI will be taxed at the higher or additional rates as appropriate.

The 20% rate is referred to as the *basic rate* of income tax. An individual with a top rate of income tax of 40% or 35.75% on dividends is referred to as a higher rate taxpayer. An individual who is liable to pay income tax at 45% or 39.35% on dividends is referred to as an additional rate taxpayer.

Let us look at how all this works in practice. At this stage, reliefs and the personal allowance will be ignored (these items will be looked at in more detail in Chapter 3) and can be assumed to have already been deducted.

First, we will assume that all of an individual's income is Non-savings income. All calculations in this chapter assume that the figures given are <u>after deducting any available personal allowances and reliefs.</u>

Example 2.1

Wolf has taxable Non-Savings income of £25,000 for 2026/27. He has no other taxable income.

Income tax due:

£25,000 @ 20%	=	£5,000
Therefore, total income tax liability	=	£5,000

Example 2.2

Emily has Non-Savings income of £40,000 and no other income for 2026/27.

Income tax due

First	£37,700 @ 20%	=	£7,540
Next	£2,300 @ 40%	=	£920

Therefore, total income tax liability			=	£8,460

Example 2.3

Hafiz has taxable Non-Savings income of £170,000 for 2026/27. He has no other taxable income.

Income tax due

First	£37,700	@ 20%	=	£7,540
Next	£87,440	@ 40%	=	£34,976
Next	£44,860	@ 45%	=	£20,187
Therefore, total income tax liability			=	£62,073

Emily in Example 2.2 is therefore taxed on a part of her income at 20% (i.e. up to £37,700); with only the excess over £37,700 then being taxed at 40%. Hafiz in Example 2.3 has part of his income taxed in each of the three "tax brackets"

Let us now look at the position if all the income is Savings income.

Example 2.4

Georgia has taxable Savings income of £25,000 and no other income for 2026/27.

Income tax due

First	Savings starting rate	£5,000	@ 0%	=	£0
Next	Savings nil rate	£1,000	@ 0%	=	£0
Balance		£19,000	@ 20%	=	£3,800
Therefore, total income tax liability				=	£3,800

Example 2.5

Jenny has taxable Savings income of £40,000 for 2026/27 and no other income

Income tax due:

First	Savings starting rate	£5,000	@ 0%	=	£0
Next	Savings nil rate	£500	@ 0%	=	£0
Next	Up to limit of basic rate	£32,200	@ 20%	=	£6,440
Balance		£2,300	@ 40%	=	£920
Therefore, total income tax liability				=	£7,360

Note that both the savings rate band and savings allowance, although taxed at 0%, use up part of the basic rate band of £37,700. The savings allowance is reduced to £500 as Jenny is a higher rate taxpayer. For an additional rate taxpayer this would be £nil. In many calculations involving multiple sources of income, NSI will use up the first part of the basic rate band, so the savings starting rate is usually not available.

Compared to Example 2.2 above, Jenny's tax liability is some £1,100 lower (i.e. £8,460 - £7,360). This is explained by the fact that £5,500 of taxable income has been taxed at 0% rather than 20%.

It should be noted that the examples 2.4 and 2.5 are uncommon, as it is unusual for an individual to only receive Savings income. It should be remembered that the £5,000 Savings starting rate is reduced by any taxable Non-savings income and if taxable NSI exceeds £5,000, the Savings starting rate of £5,000 will disappear.

Let us now assume all the income is dividend income.

Example 2.6

Alfie has taxable Dividend income of £25,000 for 2026/27 and no other income.

First	Dividend nil rate	£500	@ 0%	=	£0
Balance		£24,500	@ 10.75%	=	£2,633
Therefore, total income tax liability				=	£2,633

Example 2.7

Helen has taxable Dividend income of £40,000 for 2026/27 and no other income.

Income tax due:

First	Dividend nil rate	£500	@ 0%	=	£0
Next	Balance of basic rate	£37,200	@ 10.75%	=	£3,999
Balance		£2,300	@ 35.75%	=	£822
Therefore, total income tax liability				=	£4,821

In this case, Helen is taxed on a part of her income at 0% up to £500, then 10.75% (up to £37,700); the balance is taxed at 35.75%.

Note that the dividend allowance, although taxed at 0%, uses up part of the basic rate band of £37,700.

Finally, we can look at some examples where there is a mixture of Non-savings, Savings and Dividend income.

Example 2.8

Alex has the following taxable income for 2026/27 *after* deducting their personal allowance:

Non-savings income of	£20,000	
Savings income of	£2,500	
Dividend income of	£17,500	
Taxable income	£40,000	(Alex is, therefore, a higher rate taxpayer)

Non-savings income:	£20,000	@ 20%	=	£4,000
Savings income:				
Savings nil rate	£500	@ 0%	=	£0
Balance of savings income	£2,000	@ 20%	=	£400
Dividend income:				
Dividend nil rate	£500	@ 0%	=	£0
Balance of basic rate band	£14,700	@ 10.75%	=	£1,580
Balance of dividend income	£2,300	@ 35.75%	=	£822
Taxable income	£40,000			
Income tax liability				£6,802

This example illustrates that although each category of income is taxed at different rates of income tax and in a specific order, in working out the total income tax liability, each category is stacked on top of the other to ascertain which rate of income tax should apply and to how much of that category of income.

Thus, the non-savings income of £20,000 is taxed at 20%. This is so because the amount of non-savings income is not more than £37,700 and therefore the 40% rate does not apply.

With taxable income totalling £40,000, Alex is a higher rate taxpayer. Therefore, the first £500 of savings will be taxed at 0%. However, this amount utilises part of the available basic rate band. None of the savings income falls into the first £5,000 taxable income, as this was fully used by NSI, so the Starting rate for savings is not available. The balance of the savings income, £2,000, falls within the basic rate band.

Therefore, of the £37,700 basic rate band, £22,500 has been used, leaving a balance of £15,200.

The first £500 of dividend income is taxed at 0%. However, this reduces the available basic rate band to £14,700. After this has been used, the remaining £2,300 of dividend income falls into the higher rate band and is taxed at 35.75%.

Example 2.9

Bev has the following taxable income for 2026/27 *after* deducting her personal allowance:

Non-savings income of	£40,000
Savings income of	£600
Dividend income of	£8,000
Taxable income	£48,600 (Bev is, therefore, a higher rate taxpayer)

Non-savings income:	£37,700	@ 20%	=	£7,540
Balance of Non-savings income	£2,300	@ 40%	=	£920
Savings income:				
Savings nil rate	£500	@ 0%	=	£0
Balance of savings income	£100	@ 40%	=	£40
Dividend income:				
Dividend nil rate	£500	@ 0%	=	£0
Balance of dividend income	£7,500	@ 35.75%	=	£2,681
Taxable income	£48,600			
Income tax liability				£11,181

Again, this example illustrates that although each category of income is taxed at different rates of income tax and in a specific order, in working out the total income tax liability each category is stacked on top of the other to ascertain which rate of income tax should apply.

In this case, the full basic rate band of £37,700 is used by Non-savings income, leaving both Savings income and Dividend income subject to tax at the higher rate.

As a higher rate taxpayer, the first £500 Savings income is taxed at 0%.

The first £500 of dividend income is taxed at 0%. After this has been used, the remaining £7,500 of dividend income falls into the higher rate band and is taxed at 35.75%, the higher rate of tax on dividend income

SUMMARY

- Different income tax rates apply to different sources of income.
- Non-savings income (NSI) is taxed at 20%, 40% and 45%
- Savings income (SI) is taxed at 0%, 20%, 40% and 45%
- The starting rate for savings will only be available where non-savings income is less than £5,000
- Dividend income (DI) is taxed at 0%, 10.75%, 35.75% and 39.35%
- Non-savings income is taxed first; then Savings income; then Dividend income
- There is only one set of rate bands. For example, if NSI uses up the full basic rate band, then any SI or DI will be taxed at the higher or additional rates.
- Each category of income is added to the earlier category of income to ascertain the tax rates to apply.

APPENDIX

Since 6 April 2019, the Scottish Parliament has used its powers to set income tax rates for individuals resident in Scotland. For 2026/27, for non-savings income, these are as follows:

Starter rate	£1 – 3,967	19%
Scottish basic rate	£3,967 - £16,956	20%
Intermediate rate	£16,957 - £31,092	21%
Higher rate	£31,093 - £62,430	42%
Advanced rate	£62,431 - £125,140	45%
Top rate	Above £125,140	48%

However, throughout this text, the tax rates applicable to the remainder of the United Kingdom have been applied.

Although Wales has similar powers, for 2026/27 the tax rates for Welsh taxpayers are the same as those applying to England and Northern Ireland residents.

CHAPTER 3

Income Tax Computations

Introduction

This chapter explains how an individual's taxable income is calculated for a tax year (6 April to the following 5 April) and introduces tax reliefs and the personal allowance.

Taxable Income

Chapter 2 identified that:

Net income = Total income less reliefs
Taxable income = Net income less personal allowance

Total income

Chapter 2 referred to three categories of income:

- Non-savings income
- Savings income
- Dividend income

An individual's total income is simply the aggregate of these three categories of income for a particular tax year.

Non-savings income ("NSI") includes income from carrying on a trade (i.e. trading profit), employment income and income received from a property business (e.g. rent).

Savings income comprises interest income typically earned on cash deposits with banks and building societies.

Dividend income simply refers to dividends received from shares (excluding Real Estate Investment Trust (REIT) dividends – these are treated as non-savings income).

Each type of income has its own set of rules to determine both how it is to be taxed (e.g. accruals or receipts basis) and how the appropriate amount to be taxed is to be calculated. The rules for each type of income may vary. For example, any profit from a property business is usually determined by offsetting certain expenses paid (e.g. repairs to the property) from the rental income received. On the other hand, dividend income from companies is taxed when paid by the company, without any deductions.

In summary:

Type of income	Basis of assessment
Property income	Normally receipts basis (see Chapter 5)
Trading income	Cash or Accruals basis (see Chapter 6)
Interest income	Receipts basis (i.e. when received or credited)
Employment income	Receipts basis
Dividend income	Receipts basis

Later chapters will consider the detailed computational rules for some of these income categories.

Reliefs

Having ascertained an individual's total income for a tax year, any available reliefs are then deducted to arrive at net income. By deducting the reliefs from total income in this manner, an individual will obtain a reduction in their income tax liability.

Reliefs mainly comprise of:

- interest payments on qualifying loans; and
- trading losses (see Chapter 8).

Interest on qualifying loans

Not all interest payments qualify for income tax relief and therefore not all interest payments can be deducted in computing net income.

Only interest paid on the following qualifying loans may be deducted:

- loans to purchase shares in an employee-controlled company or invest in a cooperative;
- loans to purchase ordinary shares in a close company or to lend money to a close company. The taxpayer must own at least 5% of the close company's ordinary shares or spend the majority of their time working in the company's management;
- loans to purchase an interest in a partnership or contribute money to the partnership;
- loans to buy equipment for employment or partnership use; or
- loans to pay inheritance tax.

There is a cap on the maximum income tax reliefs that may be deducted, as detailed in Chapter 8.

Example 3.1

Sally has Total Income of £39,000 for the tax year 2026/27.

She pays interest on a qualifying loan (i.e. a relief) of £3,000.

Her net income = total income – reliefs

Net income = £39,000 - £3,000 = £36,000

Personal allowance

Having subtracted any reliefs from total income to obtain net income, it is then necessary to deduct the available personal allowance to find the taxable income.

The personal allowance represents the amount of income which an individual may be entitled to "tax-free", i.e. without being liable to income tax on that income.

The personal allowance for an individual is fixed for a tax year and for the 2026/27 tax year it is £12,570. Every individual is entitled to this personal allowance regardless of age, including in the year of birth and death.

Example 3.2

For 2026/27, Eva has a salary of £40,600, bank interest of £800 and dividends received of £1,200.

What is Eva's taxable income for 2026/27?

Non-savings income – salary	40,600
Savings income – bank interest	800
Dividend income	1,200
Net income	42,600
Less: Personal allowance	-12,570
Taxable income	30,030

If an individual has adjusted net income ("ANI") above £100,000, the personal allowance is reduced by £1 for every £2 ANI above this limit. ANI is calculated as net income less the gross amount of any allowable personal pension contributions and gift aid donations (see Chapter 4).

Example 3.3

For 2026/27, Noah has net income of £105,000 and paid £800 to charity under gift aid. The gift aid donations are paid net of basic rate tax and must be grossed up to £1,000 (£800 x 100/80). Noah, therefore, has ANI of £104,000 (£105,000-£1,000).

As this is greater than £100,000, Noah's personal allowance will be reduced by £1 for every £2 ANI above £100,000. As Noah's ANI is £4,000 above the limit, his personal allowance of £12,570 will be reduced by £2,000 (1/2 x (ANI less £100,000)) to £10,570.

Noah's taxable income will, therefore, be £105,000 - £10,570 = £94,430 (Net income less personal allowance – the gift aid donation does not reduce taxable income).

In addition, the gross gift aid donation will extend the income tax rate bands – see Chapter 4.

Marriage allowance or transferable personal allowance

An individual can, by election, transfer 10% (rounded up to the nearest £10) of their personal allowance to their spouse or civil partner, but only if neither is a higher or additional rate taxpayer.

This relief is given as a 20% "tax reducer" by reducing the individual's tax liability and the transferred personal allowance is not deducted from their income. This election must be made within four years of the end of the tax year of the claim.

This claim is useful where one spouse or civil partner is not fully utilising their personal allowances, which, therefore, would otherwise be wasted.

Example 3.4

Peter has net income of £6,000 for 2026/27. Part of his personal allowance is not being utilised. Peter is married to Pat. Pat has net income for 2026/27 of £27,500 (all non-savings income). Peter can transfer 10% of his personal allowance to Pat. This will reduce Peter's personal allowance to £11,310 (12,570-1,260) and therefore Peter will still be a non-taxpayer.

Pat's income tax liability will be:

Non-savings income	£27,500
Less: personal allowance	(£12,570)
Taxable income	£14,930
Income tax	
NSI £14,930 @ 20%	£2,986
Less: marriage allowance £1,260 @ 20%	(£252)
Income tax liability	£2,734

Note

10% of Peter's personal allowance is 1,260 (12,570 x 10% - rounded up to the nearest £10). If Pat is a higher or additional rate taxpayer, Peter would not be able to transfer the marriage allowance.

Income Tax Computation

It should now be possible to calculate an individual's income tax liability for a tax year.

However, before doing so, a set of steps is set out below which should be followed whenever working out an individual's income tax liability.

Step 1

Calculate the various amounts of income that are taxable and categorise the individual incomes into one of three categories:

- Non-savings income (i.e. property business income, trading income and employment income)
- Savings income (i.e. interest received)
- Dividend income (i.e. dividends)

Step 2

Add up the amounts under each of these three categories to give three separate sub-totals. The total of the three categories will comprise total income.

Step 3

Deduct from the total for non-savings income under Step 2 the amount of any reliefs, such as allowable interest and loss reliefs.

If total reliefs exceed the total for non-savings income, then deduct the surplus from savings income and then any remaining balance from dividend income.

The total of the three categories will comprise net income.

Step 4

Deduct from non-savings income (arrived at under Step 4) the personal allowance to give non-savings taxable income. If net income is less than £100,000, the full personal allowance is available. Otherwise, a separate calculation of ANI and available personal allowance will be necessary.

If the personal allowance exceeds the total for non-savings income, deduct the surplus from savings income and then any remaining balance from dividend income.

The total of the three categories after the personal allowance gives the taxable income.

Step 5

Compute the income tax liability by applying rates of income tax to each of the three taxable income figures obtained under Step 4. The tax rate bands may be extended by gift aid and personal pension payments (see Chapter 4).

Step 6

Deduct the marriage allowance tax reducer, if applicable, and any other tax reducers to calculate the *income tax liability*.

Step 7

Deduct from the total in Step 6 any income tax which may have been deducted at source from income *received* (e.g. PAYE on salary) to get the *income tax payable*.

In strictness, the deductions under Steps 3 and 4 can be applied to income in any order to give the lowest tax liability, rather than the strict order of NSI, then SI, then DI. However, this can require several "what if" type calculations. The ACCA Tax-UK examination assumes the set off as per steps 3 and 4 and this text has adopted this convention for simplicity.

Example 3.5

Jaz has the following income for tax 2026/27:

Property business profit	£4,000
Trading profit	£15,000
Employment income (salary as an employee before PAYE)	£25,000
Interest income	£12,000
Dividends	£3,000
Interest paid on qualifying loan	£3,500

Income tax of £5,400 has been paid under PAYE from Jas' salary.

Calculated Jaz's tax liability and tax payable for 2026/27.

Answer

	Non-Savings	Savings	Dividends	Total
Steps 1 and 2	£	£	£	£
Property business profit	4,000			4,000
Trading profit	15,000			15,000
Employment income	25,000			25,000
Interest income		12,000		12,000
Dividends			3,000	3,000
Total income	44,000	12,000	3,000	59,000
Step 3				
Less Qualifying interest	(3,500)			(3,500)
Net income	40,500	12,000	3,000	55,500
Step 4				
Less personal allowance	(12,570)			(12,570)
Taxable income	27,930	12,000	3,000	42,930

Step 5

Tax liability:

Non-Savings income		
27,930	@ 20%	5,586
Savings income		
500 (Higher rate taxpayer)	@ 0%	0
9,270 (37,700-27,930-500)	@ 20%	1,854
2,230 (12,000-500-9,270)	@ 40%	892
12,000		
Dividend income		
500	@ 0%	0
2,500	@ 35.75%	893
3,000		
Income tax liability		9,225
Step 6 – Not applicable		
Step 7		
Less:		
PAYE deducted		(5,400)
Income tax payable		£ 3,825

Notes - *Important*

The above proforma should be applied to all income tax computations.

The total column is very useful. Firstly, it allows for a cross-check to avoid simple addition errors. The Net income total gives you an indicator as to whether the full personal allowance is available or not. Finally, total Taxable income gives an indicator of the highest rate of income tax and can be used to establish the savings income tax rates.

The total at step 3 is a useful checkpoint – if it exceeds £100,000 you will need to review ANI and the personal allowance.

The total at step 4 is another useful checkpoint that can be used to establish the highest tax rate and therefore, the savings nil rate amount.

When working out the income tax liability, the above layout should be used but do not include the references to the various "Steps" as they have been included for illustration purposes only.

Some important points to note:

- all figures included in a tax computation are *gross;*
- it is necessary to keep three separate columns, one for each category of income;
- deduct the reliefs from the non-savings income column first;
- deduct the personal allowance against the non-savings income column first;
- the personal allowance may be reduced if adjusted net income exceeds £100,000;
- the personal allowance is deducted from net income to give taxable income;
- non-savings income, then savings income and then dividends are taxed in that order; and
- income tax *liability* is different from income tax *payable.*

High Income Child Benefit Charge

Although universal child benefit is income tax free, as part of the austerity measures, this stand-alone charge was introduced to claw back up to 100% of the benefit received by high earners.

Introduced by Finance Act 2012, the charge applies where the taxpayer is entitled to child benefit and they or their partner have adjusted net income (ANI) above £60,000 (the individual must be living with their partner, which includes a spouse, civil partner or unmarried partner).

The charge is calculated as a percentage of the child benefit, calculated as (Adjusted net income – 60,000)/200. The resulting percentage is rounded down to the nearest whole number. If ANI is greater than £80,000, the child benefit will be clawed back in full.

Example 3.6

Kate has ANI of £66,520 and received child benefit of £2,212 for 2026/27. What is her High income child benefit tax charge?

Answer

(66,520-60,000)/200 = 32.6 rounded down to 32%

The charge is therefore £2,212 x 32% = £707

Notes

The High income child benefit tax charge is added to the income tax liability (at Step 6 of the tax computation, as shown above) for the year and collected under self-assessment.

High income individuals, with ANI greater than £80,000, may elect not to receive the benefit, in which case the charge would not apply.

Income tax liability and income tax payable

An individual's income tax *liability* is the liability based on aggregate income less certain deductions. However, some income may be received after tax at source has been deducted (usually under PAYE from a salary). This tax deduction represents a partial settlement of the individual's ultimate income tax liability on this income. This is why any tax deducted from income received must be deducted from the income tax liability calculated (see Step 7), as only the balance is *payable.*

It should be remembered that the income tax liability is always calculated on gross income (i.e. the amount before deduction of tax paid).

SUMMARY

- Reliefs and allowances reduce the income taxable on an individual.
- Most individuals are entitled to deduct the personal allowance of £12,570 from their *net income* to calculate their *taxable income.*
- The basis of assessment for each category of income is very important (as will be seen later in the book), as is the order in which categories of income are taxed.
- Each step of the tax computation should be worked through in order.
- The proforma layout used to calculate an individual's income tax liability is very important and should be used for all income tax computations.
- The income tax liability is before the deduction of any tax deducted at source.
- The income tax payable is the income tax liability less any tax deducted at source.

APPENDIX

Blind persons allowance

An individual who is registered blind or severely sight-impaired is eligible to claim this additional allowance of £3,250 for 2026/27. Effectively, this increases the individual's personal allowance. If the claimant cannot fully utilise the allowance, it may be transferred to their spouse or civil partner.

Married couple's allowance

Note that this is not the same as the marriage allowance detailed above.

This is now of limited application and only applies to married couples or civil partners where at least one spouse was born before 6 April 1935. The maximum married couple's allowance is £11,700 for 2026/27. This is reduced by £1 for every £2 of adjusted net income above £39,200, to a minimum allowance of £4,530. Relief is given at 10% of the allowance as a "tax reducer".

Any unused element of the married couple's allowance on the part of the claimant can be transferred to the spouse or civil partner.

The claim is made by the husband for marriages before 6 December 2005 and the spouse or civil partner with the higher taxable income for marriages or civil partnerships after that date.

CHAPTER 4

Extending the Rate Bands

Introduction

This chapter will look at the concept of the extended basic and higher rate bands which will apply when an individual makes either charitable donations under gift aid and/or personal pension payments.

What is the extended rate band?

The extended rate band refers to how higher and additional rate income tax relief is obtained on the following payments made by an individual:

- payments to charity under gift aid; and
- personal pension contributions.

Gift aid payments are donations to registered charities where a gift aid declaration has been made.

Personal pension contributions are payments by an individual made to provide for a pension, usually on retirement (certain employees may make payments under an occupational pension scheme rather than as personal pension payments (see Chapter 12)).

Payments made net of basic rate tax

Payments to charity under gift aid or into a personal pension are made net of basic rate income tax (20% for 2026/27).

For example, if a payment of £400 is made under gift aid to a charity, a gross payment of £500 has actually been made as income tax at 20% (i.e. £100) is deducted. The person making the payment only pays £400 and has, therefore, received basic tax relief at source (£500 @ 20% = £100). The charity receiving the payment only receives £400 (i.e. £500 less £100) from the payer and can obtain a refund of the £100 tax deducted from HMRC.

To calculate the gross payment from the net, the net amount is multiplied by the fraction 100/80.

Example 4.1

Chloe makes a personal pension contribution of £1,200 and a gift to charity under gift aid of £20. Calculate the gross payments made.

Answer

Personal pension contribution	1,200 x 100/80	= 1,500
Gift aid payment	20 x 100/80	= 25

As a consequence of the tax deducted at source, immediate basic rate tax relief has been obtained for the payment.

However, in working out an individual's Net income, *no* deduction is made in the computation for either the gift aid or personal pension payment.

However, if the taxpayer is a higher rate or additional rate taxpayer, additional income tax relief is due.

Extended rate bands

Higher and additional rate tax relief is obtained by extending the basic rate and higher rate bands.

As a result, the level of taxable income at which income tax at the higher rate (i.e. 40%) applies (currently £37,700 for 2026/27) is increased. The increase is equal to the "gross" amount of the Gift aid or Personal Pension contributions (PPC) (or the aggregate of both if both payments are made).

The effect of extending the basic rate band is that the 20% rate applies to this extension rather than the 40% rate, which would normally apply. The impact is to produce a tax saving of 20% (i.e. 40% minus 20%) on this extra amount or extension.

Example 4.2

For 2026/27, John has taxable non-savings income of £40,000, after deducting his personal allowance. John makes a payment to charity under gift aid of £1,600 (net). Calculate John's income tax liability.

Answer

The net gift aid payment must be "grossed up". The gross amount is equal to 1,600 x 100/80 =2,000.

The basic rate band is extended by £2,000 from £37,700 to £39,700. The 40% rate will now only apply to taxable income above this figure.

It can be helpful to draw up a table to show the extended rate bands as follows:

	Basic rate band	*Higher rate band*
Basic rate limit to	*37,700*	*125,140*
Add: Gross gift aid	*2,000*	*2,000*
Add: Gross PPC	*0*	*0*
Extended rate bands	*39,700*	*127,140*

We can now use these extended rate bands to calculate John's income tax liability:

	Taxable income	**Tax rate**	**Income tax**
	£	%	£
First	39,700	20	7,940
(representing the basic rate band plus extension for gross gift aid)			
Next	300	40	120
Total	40,000		8,060

John's tax relief is therefore obtained by deducting income tax at the basic rate (20%) when actually making the payment, amounting to 20% of £2,000 (i.e. £400), and an extra 20% of tax relief is obtained by the rate band extension.

Overall, this provides total tax relief of £400 + £400 = £800 (i.e. 40% of the gross gift: £2,000 x 40% = £800).

Example 4.3

For 2026/27, after deducting her personal allowance, Sarah has taxable non-savings income of £33,000, savings income of £5,000 and pays £300 to charity under gift aid and £900 into her personal pension. Calculate Sarah's tax liability.

Answer

The gross gift aid payment is equal to 300 x 100/80 =375 (gross)

The gross personal pension contribution is equal to 900 x 100/80 =1,125 (gross)

It can be helpful to draw up a table to show the extended rate bands as follows:

	Basic rate band	*Higher rate band*
Basic rate limit to	*37,700*	*125,140*
Add: Gross gift aid	*375*	*375*
Add: Gross PPC	*1,125*	*1,125*
Extended rate bands	*39,200*	*126,640*

We can now use these extended rate bands to calculate Sarah's income tax liability:

	Taxable income	**Tax rate**	**Income tax**
	£	%	£
Non-savings income			
First	33,000	20	6,600
Savings income			
First	1,000	0	0
Next	4,000	20	800
Total	38,000		7,400

Note that by extending the basic rate band, Sarah is no longer a higher rate taxpayer and receives the £1,000 savings allowance. Without the basic rate band extension, Sarah would have been a higher rate taxpayer and therefore only £500 savings income would have been taxed at 0%.

Both the basic rate and higher rate bands are extended.

Example 4.4

For 2026/27, Sam has taxable non-savings income of £200,000 and pays £2,400 into his personal pension. Sam has no other income.

Answer

The gross personal pension contribution is 2,400 x 100/80 =3,000 (gross)

Sam's extended rate bands are as follows:

	Basic rate band	*Higher rate band*
Basic rate limit to	*37,700*	*125,140*
Add: Gross gift aid	*0*	*0*
Add: Gross PPC	*3,000*	*3,000*
Extended rate bands	*40,700*	*128,140*

We can now use these extended rate bands to calculate Sarah's income tax liability:

	Taxable income	**Tax rate**	**Income tax**
	£	%	£
First	40,700	20	8,140
Next	87,440	40	34,976
	128,140		

Next	71,890	45	32,337
Total	200,000		75,453

Sam is not entitled to a personal allowance due to the level of his income.

It should also be noted that the gross amount of gift aid and personal pension payments also reduces Adjusted Net Income when calculating the available personal allowance (See Chapter 3).

Clawback of tax deducted at source

Where an individual's total income tax liability is less than the amount which has been deducted from a gift aid payment, a payment may be due to HMRC to fully cover any shortfall.

On the other hand, for personal pension payments, no such clawback occurs in such circumstances.

Example 4.5

Trevor's income tax liability for 2026/27 is £500. Trevor made a gift aid payment during the tax year of £2,400 (net).

On making the payment, Trevor will have deducted tax at source of 20% x £3,000 = £600 and thus will have received tax relief of £600.

In this case, Trevor's additional income tax liability will be £100 (i.e. £600 - £500).

The gift aid scheme can apply to any cash donation to charity, both one-off and regular payments (unless covered by the payroll giving scheme).

For the charity to be able to recover the income tax which has been deducted by the donor at source, the donor must give an appropriate declaration to the charity concerned that the gift is made under the gift aid scheme.

Comprehensive example

The following example brings together many of the elements of an income tax computation explained in Chapters 2 to 4.

Example 4.6

Kim has the following income for 2026/27:

- Business profits £34,700
- Property business profits £19,100
- Dividends £7,500
- Building Society interest £3,750

Kim makes the following payments:

- Interest on a qualifying loan of £2,000
- Gift aid payment of £780 (net)

Calculate Kim's income tax liability and his income tax payable for 2026/27.

Answer

Kim's extended rate bands are as follows:

	Basic rate band	*Higher rate band*
Basic rate limit to	*37,700*	*125,140*
Add: Gross gift aid 780 x 100/80	*975*	*975*
Add: Gross PPC	*0*	*0*
Extended rate bands	*38,675*	*126,115*

	Non-Savings	**Savings**	**Dividends**	**Total**
Trading profit	34,700			
Property business profits	19,100			
Building Society interest		3,750		
Dividends			7,500	
Totals	53,800	3,750	7,500	
Less: Interest paid	(2,000)			
Net income	51,800	3,750	7,500	63,050
Less: PA	(12,570)	-	-	(12,570)
Taxable income	39,230	3,750	7,500	50,480

Income tax calculation

The extended rate bands, as calculated above, are used.

Non-savings	
£38,675 @ 20%	7,735
£555 @ 40%	222
£39,230	
Savings	
£500 @ 0%	0
£3,250 @ 40%	1,300
£3,750	
Dividends	
£500 @ 0%	0
£7,000 @ 35.75%	2,502
£7,500	
Tax liability	£11,759

SUMMARY

- Where an individual makes charitable donations under gift aid or personal pension payments, neither payment is deducted in working out an individual's taxable income.
- Tax relief at the higher and additional rates of tax is obtained by extending the basic and higher rate bands by the gross amount of the gift aid and/or personal pension payment, basic rate income tax relief having been obtained by deducting basic rate income tax at source.

- The gross amount is calculated by grossing up the net payment (net x 100/80).
- If an individual makes both types of payment, then the rate bands are extended by the aggregate amount of both payments.
- Basic rate tax deducted at source when making a gift aid payment may be clawed back if the individual has not suffered sufficient income tax. This is not the case for personal pension payments, where any tax relief is retained by the individual.
- The comprehensive example (Example 4.6) above provides a good illustration of the various computational elements that make up the calculation of the income tax liability for 2026/27.
- Remember that any amounts that extend the rate bands are deducted when calculating Adjusted Net Income, for example, when calculating the restricted personal allowance.

Questions for students

See Appendix 2 for practice questions relating to Chapters 1 to 4. Answers are available online at https://spiramus.com/uk-taxation-for-students-20267-answers.

CHAPTER 5

Income from a Property Business

Introduction

This chapter identifies the key issues associated with the taxation of income from land and buildings, more correctly referred to as property business profits.

Description

Profits from land and buildings are treated, for tax purposes, as arising from a property business. For each individual, the income and expenses from all properties are combined as one property business. In addition, an individual may have an interest in one or more property business partnerships. For individuals, property business profits are taxed as non-savings income.

Whilst property business income primarily consists of rental income, it may also consist of the receipt of lease premiums.

A lease premium is a "one-off" lump sum payment that the person renting the property (i.e. the tenant) pays to the person from whom the property is being rented (i.e. the landlord) and may be payable in addition to any rent. It is usually only payable in respect of commercial (offices, warehouses etc.) rather than residential properties.

Other receipts from the use of land, for example, fishing or sporting rights, are assessed as property income. However, commercial farming or running a hotel would be considered trading.

Basis of assessment and expenses

The profits of a property business are calculated in a similar way to the profits of a trade (see Chapter 6). The amount assessable is the total aggregate property income less allowable expenses for the tax year under consideration.

For most individuals, the cash basis is now the normal basis of assessment for property business profits.

Cash basis

The cash basis will apply to individuals unless the cash receipts exceed £150,000 during the year, the property business is carried out by or jointly with a company, LLP or trust, or the individual elects for the accruals basis to apply.

Under the cash basis, rent is taxable in the tax year of receipt and allowable expenses are deducted in the tax year that they are paid.

Accruals or GAAP basis

Where the cash basis does not apply, the accruals basis is used in ascertaining the amount of rental income to be assessed or expenses allowed, for a tax year. Therefore, the actual date of payment or receipt of rent is irrelevant.

Example 5.1

Kulvinder owns a furnished flat which he lets to a tenant for a rent of £700 per month payable in advance from 6 April 2026. However, the rent due in January, February and March 2027 was not paid until after 5 April 2027.

Calculate Kulvinder's property business income for 2026/27.

Answer

Kulvinder is assessed on his property business profits on a cash basis.

For the tax year 2026/27, he is assessed on 9 months x £700 = £6,300

The three months of rent received later in 2027, i.e. in the next tax year (i.e. 2027/28) will be taxed in that year.

If Kulvinder were required to use the accruals basis or had elected to do so, then the full 12 months' rent due during 2026/27 would be assessed for that year.

Real Estate Investment Trusts (REITs)

Dividends received on an investment in a REIT are assessed as property business income on the date of payment.

Expenses

Expenses are also deductible on a cash or accruals basis as appropriate.

Deductible expenses are those allowable under the normal rules for trades/businesses (see Chapter 6) e.g. the expenses are of a revenue nature and must have been wholly and exclusively incurred for the purpose of the property business (for example, not for private purposes). Typical items include:

- insurance of the property;
- estate agents' fees (e.g. for finding tenants and rent collection);
- property maintenance (e.g. redecorating, repairing the roof or broken windows, gardening etc.); and
- bad debts written off (but this could only apply when using the accruals basis).

Examples of expenditure that are *not* deductible would include:

- capital expenditure on the property (e.g. the initial cost of the property, a kitchen extension, or expenditure on fitting a new and improved roof rather than simply repairing it or replacing it with a similar one);
- expenditure incurred repairing a newly acquired property *before* it could be let out (e.g. having to repair several broken windows to make the property secure (in this case the expense is treated as capital expenditure, not revenue expenditure and thus not deductible against rental income);

- expenditure incurred for private purposes (e.g. landlord lives in a flat above a shop which he rents out. If the whole of a building was redecorated, some part of this cost would be disallowed as relating to the landlord's private flat. The percentage of cost allowed would need to be agreed with the tax authorities);
- depreciation of assets (e.g. furniture in furnished letting); and
- interest on loans to buy or improve let residential property (see below).

Example 5.2

Shaista owns an unfurnished house which she lets out. The house was let out for the whole of the tax year 2026/27. Shaista has no other rental income and the cash basis applies.

Rent of £8,750 was received during the year.

Expenses paid by Shaista during the tax year are as follows:

	£
Buildings insurance	375
Repairs (i.e. painting/decorating and roof repair)	500
Estate agent commissions	1,000
Water rates	250
Council tax	775
Loft conversion	4,250

Calculate Shaista's property business profit assessment for 2026/27.

Answer	£	£
Gross rents		8,750
Less: Expenses:		
Insurance	375	
Repairs	500	
Commissions	1,000	
Water rates	250	
Council tax	775	
		(2,900)
Property business profit		5,850

Notes

1. The loft conversion is capital and therefore not deductible (only revenue expenses are deductible).
2. If the accruals basis applies, any items such as the insurance paid may be required to be spread over the period of the cover.

Other capital expenditure

As previously mentioned, no deduction is allowed for the purchase of a building or land and any improvements.

Under the cash basis, certain capital expenditure is allowable. Broadly, deductions for expenditure of a capital nature are allowed for some depreciating assets used in the property business, provided it is of a type which would qualify as plant and machinery for capital allowances, for example, integral features in a commercial building, but not cars. No deductions are allowed for capital expenditure on, or assets used in, residential properties – instead, replacement of domestic items relief is available (see below).

Under the accruals basis, capital expenditure is not a deductible expense in computing the profits of a property business. Capital allowances (a form of tax allowable depreciation on capital assets purchased; see Chapter 7) are sometimes available for certain assets connected with commercial properties where the accruals basis applies, including qualifying integral features.

Replacement of domestic items relief

In the case of a *residential* property letting, capital allowances are not available on these items but a deduction is permitted for the cost of *replacing* domestic items used in the property. This includes items such as moveable furniture, curtains, carpets, moveable household appliances and kitchenware. Fixtures, for example, baths or fitted wardrobes, do not qualify.

There is no deduction for the original cost of the item but the cost of replacing an item is allowed. The deduction is limited to the cost of replacement with an asset of a similar type and standard. Any sale proceeds for the original item reduce the claim.

Example 5.3

Stuart buys a new refrigerator costing £800 for his let furnished property. He trades in the old refrigerator which is given a value of £300 and meets the rest of the cost with £500 in cash. The amount of the deduction for replacement domestic items would be £500 (£800 less £300).

He also buys a new television for £600 to replace an existing one. The new television is much larger and has many more features than the original one. It would have cost £350 to have bought a television of similar quality and standard, therefore his claim is limited to £350.

Finally, Stuart buys a coffee maker for the property for £200. There was not previously one of these in the property. Therefore, it is not a replacement and a deduction is not allowed.

Finance costs for residential property (income tax only)

Since April 2017, there has been a restriction on the amount of income tax relief allowed for interest on loans to buy or improve let residential property. Loans to buy let commercial properties or land are not affected by this restriction.

There is no deduction from property business profits for interest paid on loans in connection with let residential property. The finance costs are instead allowed as a tax reducer at the basic rate of tax, 20%. The tax reducer is limited to 20% of the lower of the finance costs, the net property business profit (after deducting any losses brought forward) and the non-savings income. Any unrelieved disallowed interest cost can be carried forward to the following year.

Example 5.4

Paula's only income is from her property letting business. Her results for 2026/27 are as follows:

Rents received	£64,400
Allowable expenses	£9,500
Finance costs	£8,800

Her assessable property business profits are therefore

Rental income			64,400
Allowable expenses			(9,500)
Property business profits			54,900
Paula's income tax liability will be			
Property business profits		54,900	
Less: Personal allowance		(12,570)	
Taxable income		42,330	
Income tax	37,700	@ 20%	7,540
	4,630	@ 40%	1,852
Less: Tax reducer	£8,800	@ 20%	(1,760) (Finance costs tax reducer)
Income tax liability			7,632

Notes

The finance costs tax reducer is calculated as 20% of the finance costs.

More than one property

Where more than one property is owned, the property business profit is simply the aggregate of the profit or loss arising from each property treated as part of a single property business producing one single profit or loss figure.

This means that any loss which might arise on one property is automatically offset against the profit on any other property.

Example 5.5

Ellie rents out several residential flats. For 2026/27, her income and expenses for each property are as follows:

	Flat 1	**Flat 2**	**Flat 3**	**Flat 4**	**Flat 5**
Rent received	4,000	7,000	2,500	4,250	1,600
Expenses paid	1,000	1,250	4,000	6,000	4,600

Calculate Ellie's property business profit assessment for 2026/27.

Answer

	Flat 1	**Flat 2**	**Flat 3**	**Flat 4**	**Flat 5**
Gross rent	4,000	7,000	2,500	4,250	1,600
Less:					
Expenses	1,000	1,250	4,000	6,000	4,600

Profit/loss	3,000	5,750	(1,500)	(1,750)	(3,000)

Assessable profit = 3,000 + 5,750 + (1,500) + (1,750) + (3,000) = 2,500

Note

The property business profit is the net total for all properties - profits and losses are automatically offset. There is no need to calculate the profit or loss for each property.

If an individual is also a member of a property business partnership, any profit share is not aggregated with their own property business.

Premiums received for the grant of a short lease

As mentioned earlier, the income from a property business not only includes rents but also lease premiums (i.e. a lump sum payable by a tenant to the landlord, normally on commencement of a lease). However, premiums paid in respect of the grant of long leases (i.e. for more than 50 years) are not taxable as income.

For income tax purposes, only part of a "short" lease premium is treated as rental income for the landlord.

Basis of assessment

A premium is assessed in the tax year in which the lease is granted.

Income element of a premium

Only a part of the premium is assessable as income.

The income element of the premium is computed as follows:

Amount assessable =

Premium – [2% x Premium x (duration of the lease (in years) – 1)]

Note: premiums for an *assignment* i.e. where the entire property interest is sold, are treated as a capital receipt.

Example 5.6

Jack received a premium of £10,000 on 1 June 2026 when he let out a property under a 10-year lease. Monthly rent of £500 is payable in advance, on the first day of each month. All of the monthly rent due had been received by the end of 2026/27.

Calculate Jack's property business income for 2026/27.

Answer

Property business income comprises both the rent and a proportion of the premium.

Taxable element of premium	= 10,000 – [2% x 10,000 x (10 – 1)] = 8,200
Rents received	= 500 x 11 months = 5,500
Property business income	= 8,200 + 5,500 = 13,700

11 months' rent would be received – the first on 1 June 2026 and the last on 1 April 2027 (Under the accruals basis, most of the rent received in advance on 1 April 2027, would fall into the following tax year).

Any allowable expenses could then be deducted to arrive at the assessable property business profits.

Grant of a sub-lease

Where a tenant grants a sub-lease to a sub-tenant, any premium paid by the sub-tenant to the tenant is assessed on the grantor tenant as above.

However, if that tenant had paid a premium on receiving their own lease, then a measure of relief from the assessment on the sub-lease premium is available. The relief is:

$$\frac{\text{Duration of sublease}}{\text{Duration of head lease}} \times \text{Taxable premium for the head lease}$$

Example 5.7

Ayesha granted a lease to Bev for 40 years on 1 March 2019 with a premium of £16,000 paid by Bev to Ayesha.

Bev grants a sub-lease to Carl on 1 June 2026 for 8 years with Carl paying Bev a premium of £30,000.

How is Bev taxed for 2026/27?

Answer

Taxable element of the Premium received by Bev on sub-lease =
30,000 – [2% x 30,000 x (8 – 1)] = 25,800

Less:
Allowance for the premium paid by Bev to Ayesha =
[16,000 – [2% x 16,000 x (40 – 1)]] x 8/40 = (704)
Premium taxable on Bev for 2026/27 = 25,096

Trading expense deduction

Part of the *receipt* of a lease premium, as indicated above, is taxable as part of the profits from a property business. However, a deduction is also available to the payer of the premium as a trading expense if the payer is carrying on a trade (see Chapter 6) and the property is used in the trade. This does not apply to businesses using the Cash basis to calculate their trading profits.

The amount allowable/deductible is equal to the amount assessable on the landlord, as calculated above, divided by the number of years of the lease. This amount is then deductible for each year for the life of the lease.

Rent-a-room scheme

Gross receipts up to £7,500 for 2026/27 are exempt from income tax if they relate to the letting of furnished accommodation within the landlord's main residence, for example, where a lodger rents a room in a house. The receipts can include both rent and other services, such as the provision of meals. However, the taxpayer can instead ignore the above exemption and calculate the property income assessment under the normal rules. This would only be helpful if a loss arises under the normal rules.

If gross receipts exceed £7,500, the normal property business rules apply. However, the taxpayer may elect to be assessed instead on the excess of gross receipts over £7,500 with no expense deductions.

Example 5.8

Matt rents out a room in his house for £6,000 for the tax year 2026/27. His allowable expenses are £1,000.

As the rent is below £7,500, it will be exempt. It would not make sense for Matt to claim to be assessed on £6,000 less £1,000 i.e. £5,000 under the normal rules.

If, however, he let the room for £8,500 with expenses of £2,000, under the normal rules, Matt would be assessed on £8,500 less £2,000 i.e. £6,500. In this case, an election to be taxed on the excess of £8,500 over £7,500 should be made reducing the assessable income to £1,000.

Property allowance

Since 6 April 2019, an annual property allowance of £1,000 has been available. Individuals with gross rental receipts, excluding Rent-a-room scheme lettings, of up to £1,000 in total will be exempt from income tax on their rental income. If gross rental income exceeds £1,000 the individual may elect for partial relief. This means that they will be assessed on their gross rental income less £1,000 instead of gross rental income less allowable expenses.

Furnished holiday lettings

The special rules that previously applied to Furnished Holiday Lettings are abolished from 6 April 2025. Income and expenses from such properties are now included as part of the property business and are calculated as for any other residential property.

Property business losses

Any loss arising from a property business can only be carried forward to be offset against future profits of the same property business.

In certain circumstances, to the extent that losses are related to capital allowances, a claim to offset against general income may be available (ITA 2007 section 120).

Companies

It may be appropriate to read this section after having studied Chapter 16.

The tax treatment of rents, whether received by an individual or a company, is very similar.

However, there are some differences. For a company in receipt of rental income and/or lease premiums:

1. the accruals basis of assessment will always apply;
2. relief for interest on loans for the purchase or improvement of property is dealt with under the loan relationship rules;

3. the restriction on allowable interest for residential let property does not apply;
4. the basis period for assessment is the *accounting period* of the company, not the *tax year* which applies to an individual;
5. for a company any losses arising from a property business can be claimed against total profits (before qualifying charitable donations) of the same accounting period (see Chapter 19); and/or group relieved (see Chapter 20); any surplus loss then remaining is eligible to be carried forward for offset against future profits of the company.

SUMMARY

- Rental income and a proportion of lease premiums from land and buildings in the UK, less allowable expenses, are taxed as property business profits.
- Property business profits for individuals are taxed as non-savings income.
- Rental income is normally taxed on individuals on a cash basis and for companies on an accruals basis.
- Part of a lease premium granted for 50 years or less is taxed as income in the tax year of the grant of the lease.
- Rental income and expenses of more than one property are simply aggregated to produce one assessable property business profit.
- Interest payable on loans to acquire or improve let residential property is not allowable when calculating the profits of a property business for an individual. However, the interest will be treated as a 20% tax reducer.
- The property allowance can exempt a property business from income tax with receipts of up to £1,000.
- Rent-a-room relief can exempt receipts from letting furnished accommodation in an individual's own home of up to £7,500 per year.
- For individuals, losses arising from a property business can, generally, only be relieved by carrying forward for offset against future profits of that property business.
- Certain rules differ for rental income received by companies.

Questions for students

See Appendix 2 for a practice question relating to Chapter 5. Answers are available online at https://spiramus.com/uk-taxation-for-students-20267-answers.

CHAPTER 6

Trading Profits

Introduction

This chapter looks at how the business profits of a sole trader are calculated and assessed for income tax purposes. This chapter comprises three parts: firstly, to consider if a trade is being carried on, then looking at the calculation of taxable trading profits and finally explaining the rules to identify the basis period and the actual assessable amounts to be included in the calculation of income tax and Class 4 NIC.

The Badges of trade – is it a trading transaction?

At times, it is necessary to consider whether a transaction should be treated as trading, with the appropriate income tax and NIC liabilities or perhaps should be treated as a capital gain. For example, the sale of a rental property after nine years of ownership and generating rental income for the owner, would not normally suggest trading as a property dealer. However, a property purchased, renovated and sold after a short period of letting may be more indicative of trading.

To determine if a trade is being carried on, the usual starting place is by reference to the "badges of trade" as listed by the Royal Commission in 1955. Each badge should be considered in turn and a decision made based on the overall picture that they present.

The badges are:

1. The subject matter – is the item sold something that could be used or enjoyed by the owner or realistically is the only reason to own the item to sell it?
2. Length of ownership – acquiring an asset and selling it shortly afterwards can suggest trading.
3. The frequency of transactions – a one-off transaction may not suggest trading, but a volume of transactions can indicate trading.
4. Additional work – improvements or repairs to an item with a view to a sale may increase the probability of trading.
5. Circumstances for the sale – a forced sale due to a change of circumstances may not suggest trading.
6. Motive – the purchase of an item with a clear intention to sell it on can be a pointer to the conclusion that a trade is being carried on.

Over the decades since the Royal Commission, a number of other considerations have been adopted by the courts including:

- The source of finance – a short term loan may suggest trading, particularly if the terms of the loan can only be met with a sale.

- Similar or existing trade–trading can be suggested if the individual is involved in a similar business.
- Method of acquisition – the acquisition of an asset by inheritance, or as a gift, is less likely to suggest trading.

In conclusion, when considering whether a specific transaction has the character of trading income or not, all the above factors should be considered and weighed up to give an overall picture of the transaction. The decision will be based on the specific facts for each transaction. Some factors may not be present in every case.

Even a one-off transaction may be deemed to be "an adventure in the nature of trade" if the circumstances support this conclusion.

(The badges of trade are Subject matter, Length of ownership, Frequency, Circumstances, Additional work, and Profit motive – *more than twenty years ago, I used the mnemonic* ***S****am* ***L****ikes* ***F****ish* ***C****hips* ***A****nd* ***P****eas to remember this for my final exams and it's still there!*)

Sole trader versus limited company

A sole trader carries on a trade, business or profession on their own and is entitled to all of the profits.

For example, Jill Green may carry out her consultancy business in her own name or she may use a trading name such as "The Green Consultancy". In either case, there is no limited company involved and Jill is trading as a sole trader. Therefore, Jill will be subject to income tax as non-savings income (and NIC – see Chapter 20) on any profits of the business.

It is, of course, open to Jill to form a limited company as her trading style and then any profits would belong to the company and be subject to Corporation tax (see Chapter 16).

Trading allowance

The trading allowance was introduced from 6 April 2017, to help very small businesses. The trading allowance provides an exemption from income tax for traders with trading receipts of £1,000 or less in a tax year, in total from all of their businesses.

Alternatively, partial relief is available where trading income exceeds £1,000. In these circumstances, the trader has the choice to deduct their allowable business expenses when calculating their taxable profits or elect to deduct the £1,000 trading allowance instead.

The trading allowance cannot be claimed by partnerships and cannot be claimed if any of the trading income is received from an employer, spouse, civil partner, partnership in which they are a partner or a close company in which they are a participator.

Cash basis or traditional accounting principles?

All businesses are required to prepare business accounts showing their results based on their income and expenses for the period. These accounts or financial statements have historically been prepared using the traditional accruals method, recognising income and expenses in the period that the item is related to, rather than looking at receipts and payments. However, from 6 April 2024, the cash basis has been the default basis for calculating the profit or loss for all unincorporated businesses with the option to use the traditional accruals method. When announcing this change HMRC stated that "the cash basis is a simplified regime that reduces the complexity of reporting income....while still providing an appropriate measure of trading profits for many businesses".

Cash basis

Until 5 April 2024, small, unincorporated businesses with a turnover of up to £150,000 could opt to calculate their profits using the cash basis. However, from 6 April 2024, this becomes the default for all unincorporated businesses.

This means that income is recognised when received, rather than the invoice date, and expenses are allowed when they are paid, including most capital items such as plant and machinery, but excluding land, buildings and cars (but capital allowances can be claimed on cars – see Chapter 7).

Unless otherwise stated, it should be assumed that the cash basis applies in all sole trader examples in this book. Limited companies cannot use the cash basis.

Traditional accounting or accruals method

Alternatively, when preparing the financial statements or accounts for an unincorporated business, the business may opt for the accounts to be prepared using the traditional accruals method (GAAP/accruals rules).

Example 6.1

Marsha is preparing her accounts for the year to 31 March 2027. She raised an invoice to a customer on 13 March 2027 for £5,000 but did not receive this until 10 April 2027. Marsha purchased a new computer for her business in June 2026, paying £800 cash.

How would these items be treated under the cash basis and using the traditional accruals method?

Answer

Under the cash basis, the invoice would be recognised on receipt, 10 April 2027 and therefore be included in the accounts to 31 March 2028.

However, with the traditional accruals method, the invoice date is important and the £5,000 would be included in sales for the year to 31 March 2027.

Using the cash basis, the cost of the computer is deducted as an allowable expense.

Under the traditional accruals method, the cost of the computer would not be deducted when calculating the trading profit. The cost would be capitalised and depreciation calculated. Adjustments would be required to disallow tax relief on the depreciation but capital allowances would be available (see later in this chapter).

Accounting date

Financial statements or accounts for a sole trader may be prepared for any date, referred to as the accounting date. Typically, accounts are prepared for 12 months to the same date each year but may be for a longer or shorter period. These will need to be apportioned or allocated to the relevant tax year or years as detailed later in this chapter.

Adjusted Trading Profits

Under both methods, *for tax purposes*, the rules for calculating the profit may not be the same as those applying *for accountancy purposes*, and as a result, the profit as shown on the profit and loss account is likely to be different from the taxable profit for the same period.

Where there is a specific tax rule which is different from the accountancy rule, the tax rule prevails. An example would be client entertaining expenditure. In determining a sole trader's accounts profit for a period, the costs of entertaining business clients would be deducted. However, for tax purposes, such costs are *not* deductible. It is necessary in this case to disallow these costs and add back this item to the accounts' profit to arrive at the correct taxable profit of the business.

As we will see below, other adjustments to the accounts' profit may also be necessary to obtain the taxable profit.

The starting point in ascertaining the taxable profit for a period is always the accounts' profit i.e. the net profit as shown by the accounts.

Tax adjusted profit

To calculate the tax adjusted profit, four types of adjustments may need to be made to the corresponding net profit shown in the accounts.

Two adjustments involve *adding back* items to the net profit per the accounts and two adjustments involve *deducting* items from the net profit shown in the accounts.

Add back items

- *expenditure* deducted in the accounts but not deductible for tax purposes
- *income* assessable as trading income but not shown in the accounts.

Deduction items

- *expenditure* not shown in the accounts but deductible in arriving at the trading profit

- *income* shown in the accounts but not assessable as trading income, for example, interest received on the business bank account (this is taxable as savings income).

Typically, most adjustments will arise from the need to disallow and add back expenses that have been deducted in arriving at the net profit for accounting purposes but, for various reasons, are not tax deductible.

Allowable expenses for tax purposes

In calculating the tax adjusted profits of a trade, under the traditional basis, no deduction is allowed for items of a capital nature.

However, under the cash basis, capital expenditure on most depreciating assets is deductible except for the cost of land, buildings and cars.

In addition, for an expense to be allowable in computing a sole trader's taxable business profit it must be:

> *wholly and exclusively incurred for the purpose of the trade.*

In other words, if an expense has a private purpose, it is not a tax-deductible business expense. For example, travel expenses paid from the business bank account incurred by a sole trader for a private holiday would not be deductible.

However, if the expense is incurred for more than one purpose, any identifiable proportion of the expenditure may be allowable. As an example, where a sole trader uses a motor car for both business and private purposes it is possible to agree with the tax authorities on an appropriate percentage split between business and private usage so that the business proportion of the costs of running the car can be deducted in computing the taxable profit (ITTOIA 2005[1] section 34 sets this out in a surprisingly clear and understandable manner!).

If the expense has a dual purpose and cannot be easily separated, then no relief is due. The leading example would be an item of clothing purchased to wear for business. As well as being suitable for work, the clothes also provide normal "warmth and decency" and therefore would not be allowable expenditure.

Finally, certain expenditure is specifically disallowed as a deduction by the tax legislation and will need to be added back to find the tax adjusted profit.

Examples of disallowed expenses

The following is a summary of some of the main items of expenditure deducted in the accounts but ***not deductible*** for tax purposes either due to the

[1] Income Tax (Trading and Other Income) Act 2005

general rules above or specifically detailed by legislation (All references are to ITTOIA 2005). These items are disallowed and added back to the profit.

Donations: no deduction is allowed for political or charitable donations. Trade subscriptions are generally deductible, e.g. an accountant's subscription to the ACCA; small donations to a local charity are also normally deductible. Note, however, if the payment to charity constitutes a gift aid payment, then higher and additional rate relief may be available (see Chapter 4).

Fines and/or penalties: e.g. fines for breach of health and safety regulations; car parking fines for a sole trader; (however, car parking fines paid by a sole trader on behalf of an employee whilst on the employer's business are usually allowable). Fines would cover illegal payments and payments for bribery.

Entertaining: only employee entertaining is deductible; disallow client or supplier entertaining.

Gifts to clients: for a gift to a customer to be deductible the gift must cost less than £50 per client per year, the gift must carry a conspicuous advertisement for the business *and* the gift must not be of food, drink or tobacco (although gifts to employees are normally deductible) (sections 45-47).

Capital expenditure – cash basis: the cost of new equipment and other plant and machinery is deductible under the cash basis, except for the cost of land, buildings and cars. Any disposal proceeds from the sale of such items are brought into charge as a trading receipt. Capital allowances may be available on the cost of cars as detailed in Chapter 7.

Capital expenditure – traditional accruals accounting: under the traditional accruals basis, the cost of a capital asset is not allowable (e.g. the cost of equipment, machinery or buildings). However, capital allowances may be available (see Chapter 7).

Capital expenditure – property improvements: under both the cash and accruals basis, improvements to buildings would be considered as disallowable capital expenditure. The replacement of part of a building rather than a repair may be allowable, for example, where it is found to be cheaper to replace an entire roof rather than repair it. However, if replacing the roof substantially improved it at the same time then such expenditure would be regarded as capital and therefore not deductible. Repairs to a property purchased that are required before the property can be used are also treated as capital.

Depreciation: the depreciation of a capital asset is not deductible. However, capital allowances may be available (see Chapter 7). It should be noted that depreciation would not apply where cash basis accounting is used.

Legal and professional fees: Disallow fees in connection with a capital transaction e.g. solicitors' fees etc incurred in relation to the acquisition of capital or non-trading items unless the cost of that item is deducted under the cash basis rules.

Other legal and professional fees charged concerning trading (e.g. legal fees for the collection of trade debts, accountants' fees for the preparation of accounts and tax computation) are deductible. Legal costs associated with the *renewal* of a lease of 50 years or less are also deductible.

General provisions of any sort: disallow general provisions for potential future costs.

Unpaid remuneration: no deduction is allowed for unpaid employee remuneration (e.g. a bonus) unless it is paid within nine months from the end of the period of account (section 36).

Salary or interest on capital paid to the sole trader: Disallow - this should be treated as drawings. In addition, a salary paid to the sole trader's spouse or child, as an employee, is deductible if it is at the same rate as would be paid to an unconnected employee – disallow any excessive proportion of such payment.

Private expenses of the sole trader: disallow payments by the business of the sole trader's private expenses or private proportion if this can be ascertained, for example, the private proportion of a mobile phone bill (such payments on behalf of employees are deductible. However, see Chapter 10 for impact on employee's tax position).

Interest: disallow interest payable on loans not incurred for trade purposes e.g. a loan which the sole trader used to buy a property for renting to third parties (see Chapter 5).

Expenditure incurred more than seven years before the commencement of trading: expenditure incurred within seven years before the commencement of the sole trader's trade is deductible if it would have been deductible if it had been incurred after commencement; it is assumed to have been incurred on the first day of actual trade.

A proportion of any car hire payments paid in relation to the lease of a car with CO_2 emissions of more than 50 g/km. When using the accruals basis, 15% of such car hire or lease charges are disallowed. There is no restriction for lower-emission motor cars (section 48) or when the cash basis is used.

Training course costs where the course is in relation to the sole trader acquiring new skills or knowledge are disallowed. However, if the course merely updates or develops existing skills or knowledge, the cost will be deductible. The cost of training courses for employees is deductible.

Income assessable as trading income but not shown in the accounts

Under the accruals basis, an addition to profit is necessary where the sole trader takes items from the inventory of the business for personal consumption and either does not pay for the stock or pays less than the full value. For example, a wine trader may take some of his stock of wine for his personal consumption without paying for it.

In such cases, the full market value of the items taken (basically, their selling price) must be added to the net profit as shown by the accounts (i.e. increase income by this amount) less any amount actually paid by the owner (which may be nil).

Under the cash basis, the cost of such goods would be disallowed with no other adjustment required.

Deductions from trading profit

Income shown in the accounts but not assessable as trading income

This refers to any item of *non-trading* income.

Typically, such items would include:

- interest income, rental income and dividend income (these items are assessable but not as trading income); and
- certain capital profits (e.g. profit on the sale of business premises is normally a capital gains tax, not an income tax issue).

Expenditure not shown in the accounts but deductible in arriving at the trading profit

Two types of expenses fall into this category:

1) Capital allowances (see Chapter 7) which may be claimed on items of plant and machinery. Under the cash basis, capital allowances will only be available in respect of the cost of cars.
2) A part of any premium payable under a lease of 50 years or shorter (see Chapter 5). This deduction is not available when the cash basis is used.

Therefore, to work out a sole trader's taxable profit for a period of account, the net profit shown in the accounts for that period must be adjusted for each of the above potential adjustments. Not all adjustments will be necessary in every case.

Remember, the purpose of this exercise is to arrive at the taxable trading profit of the sole trader for the period of account. The fact that, for example, bank interest is deducted does not mean that such interest is not liable to income tax but merely that it is not liable to tax as trading profit.

The following example highlights many of the issues just raised.

Example 6.2

Omar started trading as a wine merchant on 1 April 2015, preparing annual accounts to 31 March each year. His profit and loss account for the year ended 31 March 2027, calculated using the cash basis rules, shows the following:

			£
INCOME			
Sales			485,000
Purchases			(235,000)
Gross profit			250,000
Bank interest received			8,000
Dividends received			3,500
Rental income			4,000
Receipt from sale of capital items			2,500
			268,000
EXPENSES			
Salaries:	staff	65,000	
	Omar's wife	25,000	
Shop premises:			
	repairs and maintenance	6,600	
	rent & business rates	7,500	
	council tax for flat	850	
	water rates	225	
	buildings insurance	1,500	
	gas and electricity	2,600	
	telephone	1,275	
Motor expenses		9,000	
Professional charges		1,000	
Advertising, promotion and gifts		7,600	
Sundry expenses		12,000	
			(140,150)
Net profit			127,850

Notes

1. Omar's wife only works part-time for the business and if Omar were to employ someone other than his wife, he would only need to pay a salary of £15,000.
2. Omar and his wife occupy a flat above the shop. It has been agreed that this flat represents 40% of the overall premises (i.e. flat plus shop). Business rates are £2,500.
3. Repairs and maintenance of the premises include £1,600 for improvements and the redecoration of Omar's flat at a cost of £750.
4. The telephone charge of £1,275 includes private non-business calls of £650.
5. Omar is leasing his car. The car has CO_2 emissions of 155 g/km. His private use has been agreed as 30%. The leasing cost included is £3,000. The balance of motor expenses, £6,000, represents normal running costs.
6. Professional charges include legal fees of £375 in connection with a new 5-year lease; accountancy fees of £500 and £125 for legal fees in connection with pursuing a trade debt.

7. The gifts amounted in total to £1,200 and consisted of food hampers for clients.
8. Sundry expenses include client entertaining of £5,000; a donation to a local charity of £350; car park fines of £250 for Omar. The balance of the expenses is in connection with printing costs for business cards, stationery and invoices plus postage costs.
9. Over the Christmas period, Omar took wine from the inventory for his family's consumption which cost £800.

Calculate Omar's adjusted trading profit for the year ended 31 March 2027.

Answer

Omar Adjusted trading profit		*Year ended 31 March 2027*	
		£	£
Net profit per accounts			127,850
Less:			
Bank interest		8,000	
Dividends		3,500	
Rents		4,000	
Capital profit (Taxable under cash basis)		0	
			(15,500)
Add:			
Excessive Wages for wife	(25,000 – 15,000)		10,000
Premises:			
repairs & maintenance	(1,600 + 750)		2,350
rent & rates	40% x (7,500 – 2,500)		2,000
council tax	(wholly private)		850
water rates	40% x 225		90
insurance	40% x 1,500		600
gas and electricity	40% x 2,600		1,040
telephone	private calls		650
Motoring:			
Car leasing costs	Private use 3,000 x 30%		900
	Restriction 2,100 (3,000 - 900) x 15%		315
Running costs	Private use (30% × 6,000)		1,800
Professional charges	(New lease = capital)		375
Advertising, gifts etc.			1,200
Sundry expenses	(5,000 + 250)		5,250
Goods for own use			800
Adjusted trading profit			**£140,570**

Notes

1. Omar's wife's salary exceeds a normal arm's length amount by £10,000, which is therefore added back.
2. Repairs and maintenance include improvements of £1,600 which are not repairs but capital (Improvements) and are therefore not deductible. The repairs attributable to the private flat are not business expenses and so are not deductible.

3. Only 60% of the costs of the premises are deductible. All the council tax has been added back as this is a personal cost for Omar and not a business cost.
4. The telephone call costs can be split; only the business-call costs are deductible.
5. 30% of the car leasing cost is added back for private use. The 15% restriction applies to the balance as the car has CO_2 emissions greater than 50 g/km.
6. Legal charges in connection with a new lease are capital and therefore not deductible.
7. The gifts comprise food and are therefore not deductible.
8. Client entertaining and car park fines for Omar are not deductible.
9. The cost of goods taken for own use is disallowed and added back.
10. Although bank interest, dividends and rent received have been deducted, these items may still be taxable but not as trading income. Similarly, the capital profit may be subject to capital gains tax.

Basis periods

We now move on to the final part of the chapter to look at how the assessable profits are calculated and "matched" with a tax year.

A sole trader may choose any accounting date to prepare their annual accounts to. Having calculated the taxable adjusted trading profit for a period it is then necessary to identify and determine the taxable profit which falls liable to income tax for a particular tax year. This requires a set of rules to determine the basis period for the relevant tax year. If accounts are prepared to 5 April (or 31 March) each year then this is straightforward, but other year ends require some calculations.

From 6 April 2024, the Tax year basis applies. To 5 April 2023, the current year basis was used with the year to 5 April 2024 as a transitional year. The rules for these earlier years are included as an appendix at the end of this chapter.

Tax Year Basis – tax years from 6 April 2024

Under these rules, a sole trader may select any year end but the profits are simply apportioned between the relevant tax years. Any apportionments necessary should be made in proportion to the number of days in the relevant periods.

Example 6.3

Martha's tax adjusted trading profits are as follows:

Year to 30 June 2026: £36,000
Year to 30 June 2027: £50,000

Calculate Martha's assessable profits for the year ending 5 April 2027.

Answer

This will be the profits falling between 6 April 2026 and 5 April 2027-

Year to 30 June 2026: £36,000 x 86/365 days =	8,482
Year to 30 June 2027: £50,000 x 279/365 days =	38,219
Total assessable for 2026/27	46,701

Example 6.4

Alec commenced self-employment as a civil engineer on 1 October 2026 and prepared his first accounts to 30 September 2027 showing tax-adjusted trading profits of £79,600. What is his assessable profit for 2026/27?

Answer

This will be the profits falling between 1 October 2026 and 5 April 2027. Therefore, we simply apportion the profits:

Profit to 30 September 2027 £79,600 x 187/365 days = 40,781

Example 6.5

Irina ceased trading on 10 January 2027. She normally prepared her accounts to 30 November each year. Her tax adjusted trading profits were

Year to 30 November 2026: £24,600

Period to 10 January 2027: £1,900

What is Irina's assessable profit for the 2026/27?

Answer

This will be the profits falling between 6 April 2026 and 10 January 2027-

Year to 30 November 2026: £24,600 x 239/365 days =	16,108
Period to 10 January 2027: £1,900 x 41/41 days =	1,900
Total assessable for 2026/27	18,008

Businesses with a 31 March year end will be treated as being the same as 5 April (i.e. there will be no requirement to apportion 5 days' profits from the following year).

SUMMARY

- Cash basis is now the default basis for calculating the taxable trading profits for most unincorporated businesses.
- However, the business may opt for the traditional accruals accounting method.
- In either case, a calculation of tax adjusted trading profits will be necessary. The starting point for calculating a sole trader's taxable profit for a period of account is the profit as calculated in the profit and loss account.
- Adjustments are necessary to the accounts' profit as in certain cases there is a clash between the rules for tax and those for accountancy; where this arises the tax rules prevail.
- In all cases, expenses that are not *wholly and exclusively incurred for the purpose of the trade,* are disallowed and added back to calculate tax adjusted trading profits.
- In addition, a number of specific rules disallow certain other expenses and any non-trading income must be deducted.
- Where profits are calculated using the cash basis, income and expenses are recognised when received or paid and the cost of most depreciating

capital items can be deducted, with the main exception of cars (capital allowances may be available on the cost of cars used in the business).

- Where the traditional accruals basis of accounting is used, expenses of a capital nature are disallowed. Capital allowances may also be available to reduce taxable profit.
- Before the taxable profits for a tax year can be determined it is necessary to establish the basis period and match the period of account to the appropriate tax year.

APPENDIX

Current Year Basis – tax years up to 5 April 2023

The normal rule

A sole trader was normally assessed on the trading profit to the accounting date (i.e. the date to which accounts have been prepared) ending in the relevant tax year. If the accounts are prepared to 5 April or 31 March each year, then this will match the tax year, but it is more complicated for other year ends.

Example 6.6

Tracey has been trading for many years and prepares her accounts for the 12 months to 30 June each year. Which profits are assessable to income tax for the tax year 2022/23?

Answer

For the tax year 2022/23, the assessable trading profit is based on the accounting period ending between 6 April 2022 and 5 April 2023, therefore, the profit for the 12 months ended 30 June 2022. The basis period is from 1 July 2021 to 30 June 2022.

Tax year of commencement of trading

The taxable profit for the tax year in which a sole trader starts to trade was the taxable profit from the date of commencement of the trade to the end of that first tax year (i.e. the following 5 April).

Example 6.7

Eve commenced trading on 1 September 2022 and prepared her first set of accounts for 12 months to 31 August 2023 showing a tax adjusted profit of £36,000.

Therefore, the tax year to 5 April 2023 (2022/23) is the tax year in which Eve started to trade and her basis period for 2022/23 is 1 September 2022 to 5 April 2023. Her assessable profits for 2022/23 will be £36,000 x 7/12 months = £21,000.

Second tax year of trading

Identifying the basis period for the second tax year can be more difficult.

For the second tax year, the amount of the taxable profit depends upon:

- whether or not there are accounts prepared to a date ending in the second tax year; and
- the length of the accounting period.

Taking each scenario in turn:

No accounting date ends in the second tax year

The basis period is the tax year itself (i.e. 6 April to the following 5 April)

Accounting date ends in the second tax year and accounts are for less than 12 months

The basis period is the first 12 months of trading.

Accounting date ends in the second tax year and accounts are for exactly 12 months

The basis period is the period of 12 months to the end of the accounting period.

Accounting date ends in the second tax year and accounts are for a period longer than 12 months

The basis period is the period of 12 months to the end of the accounting period.

Example 6.8

Geri started to trade on 1 January 2021. What are the basis periods for Geri's first two tax years of trading, assuming that she prepares her first accounts as follows:

(a) 16 months to 30 April 2022;

(b) 9 months to 30 September 2021;

(c) Year to 31 December 2021; or

(d) 15 months to 31 March 2022.

Subsequent accounts will be prepared for 12 months. (i.e. to the end of the same month in the following year).

Answer

In each of the above four options (a) to (d), the commencement year or *first* tax year is **2020/21** i.e. the tax year in which Geri started to trade.

Therefore, in all four cases, the basis period for the tax year 2020/21 is the period 1 January 2021 (i.e. the date trading started) to 5 April 2021 (i.e. the end of that tax year in which the trade started). However, the actual profits apportioned may be different depending on the overall tax adjusted profits shown in the first accounts.

The basis period for the second year of trading, **2021/22**, will be different in each scenario due to the choice of accounting date.

(a) 2021/22 is the second tax year of trade. In this case, there is no accounting date ending in 2021/22. Therefore, the basis period for the tax year 2021/22 is the period from 6 April 2021 to 5 April 2022.

(b) In this case, there is an accounting date ending in the tax year 2021/22 but it is for a period of less than 12 months. Therefore, the basis period for the tax year 2021/22 is the period 1 January 2021 to 31 December 2021, the first 12 months of trading.

(c) Here, there is an accounting date ending in the tax year of exactly 12 months and this will form the basis period. Therefore, the basis period for 2021/22 is the period 1 January 2021 to 31 December 2021.

(d) In this case, there is an accounting date ending in the tax year but the accounts are for more than 12 months. Therefore, the basis period for the tax year 2021/22 is 12 months to the end of the accounting period, 1 April 2021 to 31 March 2022.

Third tax year of trade

The basis period for the third year of trading was 12 months to the accounting date ending in this tax year.

Example 6.9

Continuing from 6.8 above, Geri started to trade on 1 January 2021. She prepared her first set of accounts as follows:

(a) 16 months to 30 April 2022;
(b) 9 months to 30 September 2021;
(c) Year to 31 December 2021; or
(d) 15 months to 31 March 2022.

Subsequent accounts will be prepared for 12 months. (i.e. to the end of the same month in the next year).

What are the basis periods for the third year of trading, **2023/24**?

(a) 2022/23 is the third tax year of trading. The accounting period to 30 April 2022 ends during this tax year. Therefore, the basis period will be 12 months to 30 April 2022.
(b) In this case, there will be accounts for the year to 30 September 2022. As this ends during 2022/23 and is for 12 months, this will form the basis period.
(c) Here there will be accounts for the year to 31 December 2022. As this ends during 2022/23 and is for 12 months, this will form the basis period.
(d) In this case, there will be accounts for the year to 31 March 2023. As this ends during 2022/23 and is for 12 months, this will form the basis period.

Overlap profit

It may have become clear from the examples above that in most cases some taxable profit is in fact assessed twice. Such profits are referred to as *overlap profits*. Relief for overlap profits was provided when a business ceased, possibly on a change of accounting date or under the transitional rules. As a result, *over the life of a business, the tax adjusted profits arising will be equal to the profits taxed,* although the timing may differ.

Example 6.10

Returning to Geri in examples 6.8 and 6.9, let's show the tax adjusted profits for each accounting period and then we can calculate the assessable profits for each tax year and overlap profits.

Geri started to trade on 1 January 2021. You will recall that we examined four possible year end scenarios. Her *tax adjusted profits* as per her accounts are as follows:

(a)	16 months to 30 April 2022	Profit £24,600
(b)	9 months 30 September 2021	Profit £11,100.
	Year to 30 September 2022	Profit £24,300.
(c)	Year to 31 December 2021	Profit £16,500.
	Year to 31 December 2022	Profit £25,800.
(d)	15 months to 31 March 2022	Profit £22,500.
	Year to 31 March 2023	Profit £27,000.

For each scenario, calculate Geri's assessable profits for 2020/21, 2021/22. 2022/23 and her overlap profits.

Answer

(a)

2020/21 Basis period 1 January 2021 to 5 April 2021
Profits £24,600 x 3/16 months = £4,613

2021/22 Basis period 6 April 2021 to 5 April 2022
Profits £24,600 x 12/16 months = £18,450

2022/23 Basis period 12 months to 30 April 2022
Profits £24,600 x 12/16 months = £18,450

Overlap profits:

Period 1 May 2021 to 5 April 2022 11 months = £16,913

(Reconciliation £4,613+£18,450+£18,450-£24,600 = £16,913)

(b)

2020/21 Basis period 1 January 2021 to 5 April 2021
Profits £11,100 x 3/9 months = £3,700

2021/22 Basis period 1 January 2021 to 31 December 2021
Profits to 30/9/20 £11,100 plus to 30/9/21 £24,300 x 3/12 months = £17,175

2022/23 Basis period 12 months to 30 September 2022
Profits £24,300

Overlap profits:

Period 1 January 2021 to 5 April 2021 and 1 October 2021 to 31 December 2021 (To 30/9/21 x 3/9 months plus to 30/9/22 x 3/12 months) = £9,775

(Reconciliation £3,700+£17,175+£24,300-£11,100-£24,300 = £9,775)

(c)

2020/21 Basis period 1 January 2021 to 5 April 2021
Profits £16,500 x 3/12 months = £4,125

2021/22 Basis period year to 31 December 2021
Profits £16,500

2022/23 Basis period year to 31 December 2022
Profits £25,800

Overlap profits

Period 1 January 2021 to 5 April 2021 3 months = £4,125

(Reconciliation £4,125+£16,500-16,500 = £4,125)

(d)

2020/21 Basis period 1 January 2021 to 5 April 2021
Profits £22,500 x 3/15 months = £4,500

2021/22 Basis period 1 April 2021 to 31 March 2022
Profits £22,500 x 12/15 months = £18,000

2022/23 Basis period year to 31 March 2023
Profits £27,000

Overlap profits

None

(Reconciliation £4,500+£18,000-22,500 = £0)

Notes
The overlap profit can be reconciled (or calculated) by adding the assessable profits for each of the tax years and deducting the adjusted profits for the accounting periods involved.

Overlap profit relief

There was no relief for overlap profits until either the sole trader changed their accounting date or ceased to trade (see Example 6.7 below).

Overlap profit relief was obtained by deducting some or all of the overlap profit from the taxable profit of the tax year of cessation or accounting date change and may create a trading loss.

Cessation of trading

In the tax year in which the trade ceases the taxable trading profit is the taxable profit for the period from the end of the basis period of the tax year before the tax year of cessation to the date of cessation. When calculating the assessable profits for the year of cessation, any unused overlap profits may be deducted.

Example 6.11

Henry has been trading for several years. He prepares his accounts to 30 November each year. He ceased to trade on 31 December 2023. He has overlap profits brought forward of £50,000. His taxable profits for his last three accounting periods of trading are as follows:

Year to 30 November 2022: £400,000
Year to 30 November 2023: £500,000
1 December 2022 to 31 December 2023: £10,000

What is the assessment for the tax year of cessation?

Answer

The tax year of cessation is 2023/24.

The basis period for the tax year before cessation (2022/23) is 1 December 2021 to 30 November 2022 (Normal current year basis).
The taxable profit for the tax year 2023/24 (the tax year of cessation) is therefore for the period 1 December 2022 to 31 December 2023
i.e. £500,000 + £10,000 = £510,000

However, relief for the overlap profit is available in the tax year of cessation.
Therefore, the assessable profit for 2023/24 is £510,000 - £50,000 = £460,000

Transitional Year – year to 5 April 2024

Any new business commencing after 5 April 2023 will use the Tax year basis.

For existing businesses to move from the Current year basis to the Tax Year basis, a transitional year is necessary. This has the effect of "stretching" the profits under the Current Year Basis to 5 April 2024 and relieves any unused overlap relief. To reduce the impact of this, further transitional relief is available allowing the transition profits to be spread over 5 years.

Example 6.12

Harry has traded for many years, preparing his annual accounts to 30 September each year. His recent results were as follows:
Year to 30 September 2023 £42,000
Year to 30 September 2024 £60,000
Harry has overlap profits brought forward of £8,500.

What are his assessable profits for 2023/24 under the transitional rules?

Answer

Under the Current Year basis, Harry would be assessed on the profits for the year to 30 September 2023 of £42,000.

However, the transition profits must also be calculated

Profits 1 October 2023 to 5 April 2024 =

£60,000 x 187/365 =	30,739
Less Overlap profits	(8,500)
Transition profit	22,239

The transition profits will be spread over 5 Years, commencing with the year to 5 April 2024. Therefore, his assessable profits for 2023/24 would be:

Year to 30 September 2023:	42,000
Transition profits £22,239 x 1/5 =	4,448
	46,448

In addition, £4,448 will be added to Harry's profits for each of the following four tax years.

Alternatively, Harry could elect to be assessed in 2023/24 on £64,239 being his "normal" profits of £42,000 plus the full transition profit of £22,239.

The spreading of transition profits will automatically apply. However, a taxpayer may elect to disapply this spreading rule. Where a trader permanently ceases to carry on their trade before the start of the fifth year, the balance of the transition profits is treated as arising in the tax year of cessation. In addition, the rules are slightly more complicated when losses are involved.

Finally, the transition profits are not included in certain income calculations, namely, the calculation of income for the High Income Child Benefit charge and the Pension's annual allowance restriction. In strictness, two income tax calculations are required, with and without the transition profits to calculate the additional tax due, but this text has taken a more simplified approach.

Basis period examples covering 2022/23 to 2024/25

Example 6.13

Sal commenced her business in 2010 and has always prepared her accounts to 31 March and therefore has no overlap profits. Her results are as follows:

Year to 31 March 2022	Profit £44,800
Year to 31 March 2023	Profit £55,100
Year to 31 March 2024	Profit £61,200
Year to 31 March 2025	Profit £70,650

Show Sal's assessable profits for the years 2022/23, 2023/24 and 2024/25.

Answer

2022/23 Current year basis - Year to 31 March 2023 Profit £55,100
2023/24 Transitional year – Year to 31 March 2024 Profit £61,200
2024/25 Tax year basis – Year to 31 March 2025 Profit £70,650

As accounts have always been calculated to 31 March, there is no impact of the change to the basis period rules.

Example 6.14

Rufus commenced his business in 2014 and has always prepared his accounts to 30 June and has overlap profits available of £18,400. His results are as follows:

Year to 30 June 2022 Profit £32,800
Year to 30 June 2023 Profit £41,500
Year to 30 June 2024 Profit £53,200
Year to 30 June 2025 Profit £61,800

Show Rufus' assessable profits for the years 2022/23, 2023/24 and 2024/25.

Answer

2022/23 Current year basis - Year to 30 June 2022 Profit £32,800

2023/24 Transitional year

This will comprise the "normal" profits under the current year basis plus the "transition" profits to 5 April 2024 less any overlap profits.

Year to 30 June 2023 Current year basis	Profit £41,500
Year to 30 June 2024 Profit £53,200 x 279/365 days =	40,665
Less: overlap profits	(18,400)
Transition profit	22,265

The transition profit will be spread over 5 years, giving 2023/24 assessable profits of 41,500 + 4,453 = 45,953. £4,453 (22,265/5) will also be added to the assessable profits for each of the next four tax years.

However, Rufus can elect to be assessed in 2023/24 on the "normal" profits plus the transition profit in full (41,500 + 22,265 = £63,765).

2024/25 Tax year basis

Year to 30 June 2024 Profit £53,200 x 86/365 days =	12,535
Year to 30 June 2025 Profit £61,800 x 279/365 days =	47,239
	59,774

Under the spreading option, £4,453 transition profit will also be assessable for 2024/25.

CHAPTER 7

Capital Allowances

Introduction

This chapter considers the tax equivalent of the accountant's depreciation - capital allowances. Capital allowances allow the cost of certain capital assets to be written off over time against taxable profits.

As noted in Chapter 6, depreciation charged in a sole trader's accounts is not an allowable expense in computing taxable trading profit as it is capital in nature. Instead, capital allowances are claimed which are treated as a trading expense, allowing the cost of certain assets to be claimed against taxable profits over time. This provides a uniform rate of deduction for all businesses and can be used by Governments to incentivise investment in new machinery and equipment. There are two types of capital allowance claims – on plant and machinery and for structures and buildings (SBA).

Trading expense

Capital allowances are deducted when computing taxable trading profits using the traditional method.

Remember that most sole traders and partnerships will use the cash basis of accounting where the cost of most items of equipment used in the business is fully deductible as an expense, except for cars, where the capital allowances rules apply.

Therefore, Capital allowances may be more relevant when using the traditional accruals method of accounting. As this will always be the case for limited companies, you may wish to skip this chapter now and return to it when looking at Chapter 16, Corporation Tax: General Principles.

Chargeable period

Capital allowances are computed for a chargeable period which, for income tax purposes, is any period of account (assuming such period is 18 months or shorter).

Capital expenditure

Capital allowances are available for qualifying plant and machinery and on construction expenditure on buildings and structures incurred on or after 29 October 2018. Related professional fees and installation costs are also considered as a part of the eligible expenditure for the plant and machinery.

Plant and machinery

Plant and machinery (P&M) are items or apparatus used by a sole trader in carrying out their business, but not the setting in which the business is carried on. Such apparatus is of a permanent nature and therefore does not include the sole trader's inventory or trading stock, which is bought and sold.

Typical P&M items include:

- cars
- other motor vehicles such as vans and lorries
- office furniture
- fixtures and fittings
- computers
- production machinery
- fire alarm systems.

Items that have been held by the Courts not to qualify as P&M include:

- football stand
- a canopy over a petrol station forecourt
- false ceilings used to hide electrical wiring.

Rates of allowance

Capital allowances are available to a sole trader who incurs capital expenditure on P&M which is used for their business.

There are three main types of capital allowance:

- writing down allowance;
- annual investment allowance; and
- first-year allowances.

For Corporation tax only, "full expensing" for certain new unused plant and machinery is introduced from 1 April 2023 and these rules are explained in Chapter 16.

All of the rates detailed are the maximum claims and a trader or company may claim a lower amount if more suitable, for example, where the full claim would create unusable losses.

Writing down allowance (WDA)

A writing down allowance (WDA) is available for *each* period of account *including* in full for the period of account in which the expenditure on the P&M is first incurred. Normally, no account is taken of when the expenditure is incurred during the period – the full WDA would apply if the expenditure were incurred on the first or the last day of the period. The annual rate of WDA from 6 April 2026 (or 1 April 2026 for Corporation tax) is 14% on the main pool and 6% on the special rate pool (see below). Previously the main pool rate was 18% and where an accounting period straddles 6/1 April 2026 it will be necessary to calculate a "hybrid" rate of main pool WDA using a daily basis.

Example 7.1

Suleman purchases a car for use in his business. The car qualifies for the main pool rate. Suleman prepares his accounts to 30 June each year.

What will be the rate of Writing Down Allowance on his main pool for the year to 30 June 2026.

Answer

1 July 2025 to 5 April 2026	18% x 279/365 days	=	13.758
6 April 2026 to 30 June 2026	14% x 86/365 days	=	3.298
Hybrid rate (rounded up to 2 decimals)		=	17.06%

A WDA is an allowance *per annum* and therefore depends upon the length of the period of account. If the period of account is shorter or longer than 12 months the WDA is then adjusted either down or up respectively.

Most expenditure on P&M is aggregated and allocated to the main pool. However, expenditure on the following items is allocated to a separate special rate pool:

- P& M that form part of a building – referred to as 'integral features';
- items with a long life (25 years or more);
- thermal insulation of buildings; and
- motor cars with CO_2 emissions of more than 50g/km.

Integral features include items such as:

- lifts, escalators and moving walkways;
- space and water heating systems;
- air-conditioning and air-cooling systems;
- cold water systems;
- electrical systems, including lighting systems; and
- external solar shading.

All other expenditure on P&M is allocated to the main pool.

The WDA for each period of account for P&M is based on each pool's *tax written down value* (TWDV) (i.e. original cost less allowances claimed previously) at the end of the previous period of account and is calculated on what is referred to as a *reducing balance basis.* For the first period of trading, there will be no brought forward amount and any allowances will be based on the asset cost.

The value of the pool of P&M expenditure may be increased when items of P&M are purchased and decreased when items of P&M are sold. The WDA for any period of account is calculated on the balance of the pool i.e. after considering asset purchases and sales.

Example 7.2

Ben prepares his business accounts to 31 March each year using the traditional accruals basis. He can therefore claim capital allowances. As at 31 March 2026, the TWDV on the pools are as follows:

Main pool	£24,000
Special rate pool	£10,000

Calculate Ben's capital allowances (CA) for each of the years ended 31 March 2027 and 31 March 2028, assuming no new purchases or sales of P&M.

Answer

Hybrid rate of Main pool WDA:

1 April 2026 to 5 April 2026	18% x 5/365 days	=	0.25
6 April 2026 to 31 March 2027	14% x 360/365 days	=	13.81
Hybrid rate (rounded up to 2 decimals)		=	14.06%

Year ended 31.3.27

	Main Pool	**Special Rate Pool**		**Allowances or Claim**
TWDV brought forward	24,000	10,000		
WDA @ 14.06%	(3,374)			3,374
WDA @ 6%		(600)		600
			CA claimed	3,974
TWDV carried forward	20,626	9,400		
Year ended 31.3.28				
WDA @ 14%	(2,887)			2,887
WDA @ 6%		(564)		564
			CA claimed	3,451
TWDV carried forward	17,739	8,836		

Notes

1. The WDA for the year ended 31 March 2027 is calculated based on the TWDV carried forward.
2. From 1 April 2026, the rate of WDA is reduced to 14%. The WDA is, therefore, lower as it is based on a reducing tax written-down value.
3. Capital allowances of £3,974 would be deducted from tax adjusted trading profits to 31 March 2027 and £3,451 for the following accounting period.
4. Note the basic template used for calculating capital allowances. Usually, the calculation will only cover one period of account.
5. If Ben had used the cash basis method to prepare his accounts, the full cost of the assets would have been deducted from his income for the year when purchased – he would only claim capital allowances on the cost of motor cars.

Annual Investment Allowance (AIA)

AIA was introduced as an incentive for businesses to invest in additional plant and machinery (P&M).

AIA of 100% can be claimed for additions of P&M in an accounting period totalling up to the lower of the total expenditure on P&M and the annual maximum, currently £1,000,000. If the accounting period is less than or greater than 12 months, a pro rata AIA will be available.

AIA is available on all P&M whether main pool or special rate pool except for motor cars.

If the expenditure on new P&M exceeds the annual limit, the balance of the expenditure falls into the appropriate pool and WDA may be claimed. If expenditure exceeds the annual limit, then the maximum claimed should be made for items falling into the special rate pool in priority to main pool items to maximise the capital allowances claim. If the expenditure is new and unused, 40% FYA may be available on the balance or full expensing may be available for limited companies (See Chapter 16).

Example 7.3

Jasmeen, a sole trader, has been trading for several years and prepares her accounts to 31 December each year using the traditional accruals method. During the year to 31 December 2026, Jasmeen purchased a new unused machine, an item of P&M falling into the main pool, for £1,300,000. As at 31 December 2025, the TWDV on the pools are as follows:

Main pool	£40,000
Special rate pool	£8,000

Calculate the capital allowances to which Jasmeen is entitled for the accounting period to 31 December 2026.

Answer

Hybrid rate of Main pool WDA:

1 January 2026 to 5 April 2026	18% x 95/365 days	=	4.685
6 April 2026 to 31 December 2026	14% x 270/365 days	=	10.356
Hybrid rate (rounded up to 2 decimals)		=	15.05%

		Main Pool	**Special Pool**		**Allowances or Claim**
TWDV brought forward		40,000	8,000		
Additions qualifying for AIA					
Main pool	1,300,000				
AIA (Maximum)	(1,000,000)				1,000,000
Balance		300,000			
		340,000			
WDA @ 15.05%		(51,170)			51,770
WDA @ 6%			(480)		480
				CA Claimed	1,051,650
TWDV carried forward		33,980	7,520		

Notes

1. Note the template used for calculating capital allowances involving AIA.
2. Compare this to example 16.13 for corporation tax, including full expensing.

First-Year Allowances

In place of AIA, certain assets qualify for 100% First Year Allowances (FYA). Therefore, a business may claim 100% allowances on items qualifying for AIA up to the annual maximum plus an unlimited amount on items qualifying for 100% FYA. The following items can qualify for FYA if purchased new and unused:

- cars with Zero CO_2 emissions;
- electric vehicle charging points;

- gas, biogas and hydrogen refuelling equipment; and
- zero-emission goods vehicles and vans.

From 1 January 2026, a new First year allowance of 40% is introduced for expenditure on new unused main pool expenditure, excluding motor cars. For most businesses this will have little impact due to the availability of Annual Investment Allowance and Full expensing for companies.

Example 7.4

Stephen, a sole trader, has been trading for many years and prepares his accounts to 31 May each year using the traditional accruals method. In the year to 31 May 2026, Stephen purchased a new machine, a piece of P&M falling into the main pool, for £1,175,000 (not qualifying for 40% FYA) and a new car (CO2 emissions 115g/km) for £15,500. In addition, he acquired new zero-emission goods vehicles costing £54,000. As at 31 May 2025, the TWDV on the pools are as follows:

Main pool	£10,000
Special rate pool	£27,000

Calculate the capital allowances to which Stephen is entitled to for the accounting period to 31 May 2026.

Answer

Hybrid rate of Main pool WDA:

1 June 2025 to 5 April 2026	18% x 309/365 days	=	15.238
6 April 2026 to 31 May 2026	14% x 56/365 days	=	2.147
Hybrid rate (rounded up to 2 decimals)		=	17.39%

		Main Pool	**Special Rate Pool**	**Allowances or Claim**
TWDV brought forward		10,000	27,000	
Additions not qualifying for AIA				
Car (to SR pool due to emissions level)			15,500	
Additions qualifying for AIA				
Main pool	1,175,000			
AIA	(1,000,000)			1,000,000
Balance		175,000		
		185,000	42,500	
WDA @ 17.39%		(32,171)		32,171
WDA @ 6%			(2,550)	2,550
Additions qualifying for FYA				
Main pool	54,000			
FYA	(54,000)			54,000
CA Claimed				1,088,721
TWDV carried forward		152,829	39,950	

Notes

Note the template used for calculating capital allowances involving AIA and FYA.

Small Pools Allowance

If the balance on the main pool or special rate pool before calculating WDA is £1,000 or less, then a WDA up to the entire balance may be claimed. This was introduced to simplify calculations by avoiding the requirement to calculate ever reducing small amounts of WDA.

Non-pooled assets

Some assets do not form part of the pool of P&M.

These assets are:

- assets with any private use by the sole trader; and
- short-life assets.

In each of these cases, each asset is treated separately and all allowances are computed separately.

Assets with private use

Any asset which is used partly for business and partly for private purposes by the owner (i.e. the sole trader) of the business is not pooled.

Capital allowances are computed individually for each such asset. However, although the capital allowances computation is carried out as normal, the amount of allowance which can be claimed is reduced by the private usage, i.e. only the percentage usage attributable to business can be deducted as a trading expense. The WDA is calculated and deducted from the pool in full but the amount claimed is reduced for private use.

If the asset is used partly privately by an employee of the business (i.e. not the business owner) there is no restriction of allowances.

Note that if there is more than one asset used privately, each asset with private use is treated separately i.e. privately used assets are not pooled together.

Example 7.5

Gloria, a sole trader, has been trading for many years and prepares her accounts to 31 March each year using the cash basis. Gloria claims capital allowances on two cars – one used by an employee and included in the main pool and another that she uses personally. In the year to 31 March 2027, Gloria made no acquisitions or disposals of P&M. As at 31 March 2026, the TWDV are as follows:

Main pool	£24,600
Car with private use	£16,800

30% of Gloria's use of the motor car is private. The car has CO_2 emissions of 125 g/km.

Calculate the capital allowances to which Gloria is entitled to for the accounting period to 31 March 2027.

Answer

Hybrid rate of Main pool WDA:

1 April 2026 to 5 April 2026	18% x 5/365 days	=	0.25
6 April 2026 to 31 March 2027	14% x 360/365 days	=	13.81
Hybrid rate (rounded up to 2 decimals)		=	14.06%

	Main Pool	Asset with Private Use		Allowances or Claim
TWDV Brought forward	24,600	16,800		
WDA @ 14.06%	(3,458)			3,458
WDA @ 6% (Note)		(1,008)	(less 30%)	705
			CA Claimed	4,163
TWDV Carried forward	21,142	15,792		

Note

The WDA for the car with private use is calculated at the full rate of 6% applicable for a high-emission motor car. However, the allowances *claimed* for the car are reduced to reflect the 30% private use.

Short-life assets

Some assets wear out or depreciate very quickly. An election may be made for such an asset to be treated as a short-life asset where it is anticipated that it is likely to be sold or scrapped within eight years of the end of the period of account in which the asset is acquired (cars and special rate pool assets cannot be subject to a short-life assets election).

The advantage of short-life asset treatment is that a balancing allowance (see below) can arise on sale, which would not be the case if the asset had simply been added to the general pool.

If the asset is not in fact sold by the end of the period of account eight years after the end of the period when it was purchased, its tax written down value as at that time (i.e. end of eight years) is transferred to the general or special rate pool, as appropriate, at the commencement of the next period of account.

Note that if there is more than one short life asset, each asset is treated separately i.e. short life assets are not pooled together.

Sales of assets

Balancing allowances and balancing charges

In the year of purchase AIA or FYA will normally be available on P&M and thereafter, a WDA will be available. If the asset is not sold, eventually its original cost will be written down to zero.

If, however, an item of P&M is sold then in the period of account in which the sale occurs, a deduction will be required from the pool. On sale, the amount deducted from the pool is *the lower of* the actual sale proceeds or the asset's original cost.

Ongoing Businesses

Main or special rate pool

On the sale of an asset out of the main pool or special rate pool, *the lower of* sale proceeds and the original cost is deducted from the pool i.e. the pool will decrease. However, if the amount brought into account on disposal exceeds the balance of the pool, then a balancing charge will arise, effectively clawing back any excessive allowances previously provided. A balancing charge reduces the capital allowances claim and if it exceeds the allowances, it increases the taxable trading profit.

Assets with private use or short-life assets

In these cases, the sale of the asset will close the pool and lead to a balancing allowance or balancing charge, depending upon whether the sale proceeds are respectively less than or more than the tax written down value of the asset at the time of sale. For assets with private use, any balancing adjustment is reduced for private use.

Note that where an asset is sold, the amount deducted from the pool is the *lower of the original cost and sale proceeds.* This is because it is not possible to claw back more allowances than have been given for the asset.

Example 7.6

Malcolm, a sole trader, has been trading for several years and prepares his accounts to 31 March each year using the traditional accruals method. In the year to 31 March 2027, Malcolm made no acquisitions. As at 31 March 2026, the TWDV are as follows:

Main pool	£18,500
Car with private use	£15,250

An item in the main pool, which originally cost £1,000, was sold during the year for £1,500.

The car was also sold during the year for £12,000.

25% of Malcolm's use of the motor car is private. The car has CO_2 emissions of 105 g/km.

Calculate the capital allowances to which Malcolm is entitled to for the accounting period to 31 March 2027.

Answer

	Main Pool	Asset with Private Use		Allowances or Claim
TWDV Brought forward	18,500	15,250		
Disposals	(1,000)	(12,000)		
Balancing allowance		3,250	(Less 25%)	2,437
	17,500			
WDA @ 14.06%	(2,460)			2,460
			CA Claimed	4,897
TWDV Carried forward	15,040			

Notes

1. As the car with private use was sold during the year, there is no WDA.
2. On the sale of an asset with private use, a balancing allowance or charge can arise. In either case, the balancing amount is reduced for private use.
3. The disposal from the main pool does not create a balancing charge as there remains a balance to calculate WDA.
4. The deduction is the lower of proceeds and original cost. Therefore, £1,000 is deducted from the main pool and not the proceeds of £1,500.
5. See previous examples for calculation of Hybrid WDA rate

Example 7.7

During the accounting year to 5 April 2027, Marie, a sole trader using the cash basis sold her existing car for £18,000. This car had originally cost £24,000 and had a tax written down value of £16,138 at the start of the period. It was replaced by a new car costing £34,000. This new car had CO2 emissions of 105g/km. Both cars have 30% private use.

Calculate the capital allowances to which Marie is entitled to for the year to 5 April 2027.

Answer

	Old Car	New Car		Allowances or Claim
TWDV Brought forward	16,138			
Additions – new car		34,000		
Disposals – old car	(18,000)			
Balancing charge	(1,862)		(Less 30%)	(1,303)
WDA @ 6%		(2,040)	(Less 30%)	1,428
			CA Claimed	125
TWDV Carried forward		31,960		

Notes

1. As the sale proceeds of the old car exceed the TWDV, there is a balancing charge.
2. The deduction is the lower of proceeds and original cost. Therefore, £18,000 is deducted and not the original cost.
3. Both the balancing charge of the old car and WDA on the new car are reduced by the 30% private use.

Cessation of a business

For the accounting period of cessation, there is no FYA, AIA or WDA. Additions are simply added to the appropriate pool. Disposal values are deducted from each pool and on each, a balancing charge or allowance can arise. If the business owner keeps any assets on cessation, they are treated as sold to them at market value at the cessation date.

Remember that when an asset is sold, the amount brought into account *is the lower of the original cost and sale proceeds.* This is because it is not possible to claw back more allowances than have been given for the asset.

Example 7.8

Paula, a sole trader, has been trading for many years and prepares her final accounts to cessation on 14 August 2025 using the traditional accruals method. During the period to 14 August 2025, Paula purchased additional Main pool P&M for £3,000. At the start of the accounting period, the TWDV are as follows:

Main pool	£6,200
Special rate pool	£12,090
Car with private use	£8,800

The sale proceeds for each pool were as follows:

Main pool	£8,000

Special rate pool	£14,000
Car	£6,000

In each case, the disposal proceeds were less than the original cost. 10% of Paula's use of the motor car is private.

Calculate the capital allowances to which Paula may claim for the accounting period to 14 August 2025.

Answer

	Main Pool	Special Rate Pool	Asset with Private Use		Claim
TWDV Brought forward	6,200	12,090	8,800		
Additions	3,000				
Disposals	(8,000)	(14,000)	(6,000)		
Balancing allowance	1,200				1,200
Balancing allowance			2,800	less 10%	2,520
Balancing charge		(1,910)			(1,910)
			CA Claimed		1,810

Notes

1. As this is the period of cessation, there are no FYA, AIA or WDA.
2. On the sale of the asset with private use, the balancing allowance has been reduced for the 10% private use.
3. The disposal from the special rate pool creates a balancing charge which reduces the overall claim.

Hire purchase and leasing

Hire purchase

An asset bought on hire purchase is treated as if it had been purchased outright. Consequently, capital allowances are available based on the purchase price.

Leased assets

Under a lease, the lessee merely hires the asset over the leased period. The hire charge is treated as a normal trading expense/deduction.

However, for leased motor cars with CO_2 emissions of more than 50g/km, a 15% restriction is placed on the amount of the leasing costs which are eligible for treatment as a deductible trading expense (see Chapter 6).

Comprehensive example

The following example brings together many of the elements of the capital allowances computation described earlier in this chapter.

Example 7.9

Aida, a sole trader, has been trading for many years and is preparing her accounts to 31 May 2026 using the traditional accruals method. During this year, Aida made the following purchases of plant and machinery:

New car for employee (CO2 125 g/km)	£22,000
New machine	£80,000
New electric van	£24,000

She also sold an item from the main pool for £6,000 (It had originally cost £18,000)

At the start of the accounting period, the TWDV are as follows:

Main pool	£14,800
Special rate pool	£8,200
Car with private use (CO2 85 g/km)	£12,000

25% of Aida's use of the motor car is private.

Calculate the capital allowances to which Aida may claim for the year to 31 March 2026.

Answer

Hybrid rate of Main pool WDA:

1 June 2025 to 5 April 2026	18% x 309/365 days	=	15.238
6 April 2026 to 31 May 2026	14% x 56/365 days	=	2.147
Hybrid rate (rounded up to 2 decimals)		=	17.39%

		Main Pool	Special Rate Pool	Asset with Private Use		Claim
TWDV Brought forward		14,800	8,200	12,000		
Additions- no AIA – car			22,000			
Additions – AIA	80,000					
AIA @ 100%	(80,000)					80,000
Balance		0				
Disposals		(6,000)				
		8,800	30,200	12,000		
WDA @ 17.39%		(1,530)				1,530
WDA @ 6%			(1,812)			1,812
WDA @ 6%				(720)	-25%	540
FYA additions – Van	24,000					
FYA 100%	(24,000)					24,000
Balance		0				
TWDV Carried forward		7,270	28,388	11,280		
Total capital allowances claim						**107,882**

Notes

1. The capital allowances claimed on Aida's car are reduced for the 25% private use.

Structures and buildings allowance

Finance Act 2019 introduced a new type of capital allowance in respect of qualifying construction expenditure on new buildings and structures incurred on or after 29 October 2018. Structures and Buildings Allowance

(SBA) was introduced as the government believed there was a gap in the existing capital allowances system, where relief had not been given for buildings and structures other than for integral features. Relief is given for eligible expenditure at an annual rate of 3% on a straight-line basis per year until the full cost has been relieved (The rate increased from 2% per annum from 6 April 2020/1 April 2020 for corporation tax). There is no balancing allowance or charge on the disposal of a building on which SBA has been claimed – the purchaser will simply be entitled to continue to claim 3% of the original cost for the balance of the unrelieved cost. However, when calculating the capital gain on the seller, the cost is reduced by the SBA claimed.

SBA is not available to businesses using the Cash basis. Relief is available for new commercial buildings and structures, including costs for conversions or renovations. Relief is available for UK and overseas buildings and structures where the business is subject to UK tax. Relief is limited to construction costs and does not include the cost of land. Expenditure on integral features will qualify as P&M and will not be included in an SBA claim.

SBA is available when a structure or building is first brought into use for a qualifying activity. This includes a trade, profession, vocation or a property business. Relief is not available for residential property or other dwellings, such as student accommodation at a university, but is available for hotels and care homes.

Example 7.10

PWZ Limited buys a new office building from a developer at a cost of £12 million, of which £2 million has been identified as relating to integral features and £3 million relates to the land. PWZ Limited prepares accounts to 31 December each year and starts to use the building in its trade on 1 May 2026.

Calculate the SBA for the years to 31 December 2026 and to 31 December 2027.

Answer

The expenditure eligible for SBA is calculated as follows:

Total expenditure	£12 million
Less: P&M - integral features	(£2 million)
Cost of land	(£3 million)
Eligible expenditure for SBA	£7 million
Annual SBA @ 3%	£210,000

Year to 31 December 2027

As the building is used from 1 May 2027, the claim is reduced to 8 months

Claim £210,000 x 8/12 = £140,000

Year to 31 December 2027

Full-year claim - £210,000

Notes

1. SBA will be available for £210,000 each year until the full £7 million has been relieved.

2. The £2 million expenditure identified as P&M integral features will be added to the special rate pool and will attract Full expensing, AIA or WDA at 6% as appropriate.

SUMMARY

Capital allowances allow a tax deduction for the cost of certain capital items spread over the life of the business. The following key points should be noted:

Plant and machinery

- WDA, AIA and FYA are computed for periods of account
- WDA is 14% per annum on a reducing balance basis on the main pool and 6% per annum on the special rate pool.
- A Hybrid rate of main Pool WDA may be necessary where the accounting period straddles 6 April 2026 (1 April for corporation tax).
- AIA is given at 100%.
- The maximum amount qualifying for AIA for a 12 month period is £1,000,000
- FYA may be at 100% or 40% depending on the type of expenditure.
- Not all P&M is pooled – assets with private use are separated
- A short-life asset election may be made to de-pool P&M assets
- Any capital allowances claim is reduced for private use
- A business is not required to claim the full AIA, FYA or WDA
- A balancing adjustment may be required when an asset is sold
- Where the cash basis is used to prepare the accounts, most items of plant and machinery will be deducted from profits when purchased and any disposal proceeds will be included on sale. However, capital allowances will apply to any cars used by the business – the cost of cars is not deductible under the cash basis.

Structures and Buildings Allowance

- Applies to qualifying expenditure incurred on or after 29 October 2018
- SBA is calculated at 3% of the qualifying expenditure per year
- Balancing allowances or charges do not apply on disposal
- SBA is not available when using the Cash basis.

Questions for students

See Appendix 2 for practice questions relating to Chapters 6 and 7. Answers are available online at https://spiramus.com/uk-taxation-for-students-20267-answers.

CHAPTER 8

Sole Trader Business Losses

Introduction

In some years, rather than making a trading profit, a sole trader may incur a trading loss. This chapter looks at how a sole trader may utilise such losses when they arise and obtain tax relief.

Trading losses

There are various ways in which a sole trader may choose to claim tax relief for a trading loss.

A trading loss can be:

- carried forward and offset against future profits from the same trade (section 83)
- offset against net income of the tax year of the trading loss and/or the previous tax year (section 64)
- after a claim against income, offset the remaining loss against chargeable gains (section 71).

Extended forms of trading loss relief are available in specific situations as follows:

- in the first four years of trade (section 72)
- upon cessation of a trade (section 89)
- following the incorporation of a sole trader's business (section 86).

It is usual to refer to the possible use of trading losses by the appropriate section number. Each of the above section numbers refers to the Income Taxes Act 2007 (ITA 2007).

If the relevant conditions are satisfied, the taxpayer may claim a deduction for the trading loss as detailed further below.

Where for a period of account a trading loss arises, the assessable trading profit for the relevant tax year is treated as "nil" (see Example 8.1 below).

Calculation of trading losses

Trading losses are calculated and matched to a tax year broadly following the basis period rules as described in Chapter 6.

Example 8.1

Amina has been trading for many years and her recent results were as follows:

Year to 30 June 2026	Profit £48,500
Year to 30 June 2027	Loss £8,200

Using the Current year basis, calculate Amina's trading profit for 2026/27

Answer

6 April 2026 to 30 June 2026	Profit £48,500 x 86/365 days =	11,427
1 July 2026 to 5 April 2027	Loss £8,200 x 279/365 days =	(6,268)
Assessable profit 2026/27		5,159

Example 8.2

Harry's results were as follows

Year to 31 December 2026 Loss £75,000

Year to 31 December 2027 Profit £18,000

Using the tax year basis, calculate Harry's assessable profits or loss for 2026/27.

Answer

6 April 2026 to 31 December 2026	Loss 75,000 x 270/365 =	(55,479)
1 January 2027 to 5 April 2027	Profit 18,000 x 95/365 =	4,685
Total loss 2026/27	(55,479 + 4685) =	(£50,794)

Trading loss carry forward (section 83)

Any trading loss can be carried forward indefinitely to be offset against future profits from the same trade. The trading loss must be used against future trading profits as soon as possible. This relief is given automatically for any losses not subject to an alternative claim.

Example 8.3

John has been trading for a number of years and prepares his accounts to 31 March each year. He has the following tax adjusted results:

Year ended 31.3.26	trading loss	£10,000
Year ended 31.3.27	trading profit	£3,000
Year ended 31.3.28	trading profit	£36,000

How can John use section 83 relief?

Answer

Tax year	**2025/26**	**2026/27**	**2027/28**
Basis period	*31.3.26*	*31.3.27*	*31.3.28*
Trading profit	0	3,000	36,000
Section 83 loss relief	____	(3,000)	(7,000)
Net trading profit	0	0	29,000

Note

1. It is important to note the layout which should be used (i.e. tax years across the page).
2. Where a trading loss occurs (e.g. in y/e 31.3.26 above), the assessment for the tax year for which this period of account is the basis period (i.e. 2025/26) is "0" and hence "0" appears under "Tax year 2025/26". The trading loss itself of 10,000 for y/e 31.3.26 only appears when it is being utilised against other trading profits (i.e. for tax years 2026/27 and 2027/28).

Trading loss offset against taxable income (ITA 2007 section 64)

A trading loss for a period of account can be offset against the net income of the tax year in which the loss arises and/or the net income of the immediately preceding tax year.

The taxpayer can choose which option to adopt. However, whichever option is chosen, the trading loss must be offset to the maximum possible extent in the tax year of claim against that year's net income (i.e. before personal allowances).

There are effectively four possible options under this section:

- trading loss offset *only* against net income of the tax year of the loss
- trading loss offset *only* against net income of the tax year prior to the tax year of the loss
- trading loss offset against the net income of the tax year of loss *and* then the net income of the prior tax year
- trading loss offset against net income of the prior tax year *and* then the net income of the tax year of the loss.

The taxpayer can choose any of these four options. The loss must be claimed within one year of 31 January following the end of the tax year in which the loss arose.

Remember, **net income** is **total income less reliefs** (see Chapter 2).

Where net income for a tax year exceeds the trading loss then the trading loss should be deducted in order, first from non-savings income, then any balance remaining from savings income and then dividend income for the relevant tax year.

Where a trading loss arises in two succeeding tax years, the trading loss from the earlier tax year must be offset before the later trading loss may be offset.

Example 8.4

Aisha has been trading for several years and prepares her accounts to 31 October each year and has the following results:

Year ended 31.3.25	trading profit £34,000
Year ended 31.3.26	trading loss (£48,000)
Year ended 31.3.27	trading profit £40,000

Aisha also has other income for 2024/25 and 2025/26 of £5,000 and £6,000 respectively.

How should Aisha utilise the loss to 31.3.26?

Answer

	2024/25	2025/26	2026/27
Trading profit/loss	34,000	nil	40,000
Less:			
Section 83 relief	nil	nil	(9,000)
Net trading profit/loss	34,000	nil	31,000
Other income	5,000	6,000	nil
Total income	39,000	6,000	31,000
Less:			
Section 64 relief	(39,000)	nil	nil
	nil	6,000	31,000
Less:			
Personal allowance	wasted	(6,000)	(12,570)
Taxable income	nil	nil	18,430

Notes

1. The trading loss for the year ended 31.3.26 creates a trading loss for the tax year 2025/26. Any of the four options described above may be chosen.
2. It can be seen, however, that to offset any part of the trading loss in the tax year 2025/26 would not be of any benefit as Taxable income for that year is in any event "nil" even without using the trading loss due to the personal allowance. Therefore, under section 64, the only effective option is to offset the 2025/26 trading loss against net income of the prior tax year 2024/25.
3. It should be noted that because of the section 64 loss claim, the personal allowance for 2024/25 is wasted.
4. After this offset 48,000 - 39,000 = 9,000 of trading loss remains unrelieved. This must then be carried forward under section 83 against future *trading profits* (not net income) of future tax years (i.e. in this example 2026/27).

In general, the most tax efficient way to utilise section 64 relief is to offset the trading loss against the prior tax year's net income and if any unused trading loss remains, then claim against the net income of the tax year of the loss. In other words, in most cases, the sooner tax relief can be obtained, the better. However, if the rate of tax charged on other income of the year of loss is higher than the previous year, then a current year claim should be prioritised.

Cap on income tax reliefs

Since 6 April 2013, there has been a restriction on the maximum relief that can be claimed against other income under section 64 or section 72. The loss claim against other income is restricted to the greater of £50,000 and 25% of adjusted total income. There is no cap on the loss that can be claimed against profits of the same trade. Adjusted total income is total income less gross personal pension contributions paid. The cap also applies to allowable loan interest.

Example 8.5

Greg has been trading for a number of years and prepares his accounts to 30 September each year and has the following results:

Year ended 31.03.26	trading profit	£28,000
Year ended 31.03.27	trading loss	(£100,000)

Greg also has rental income for 2025/26 of £60,000.

What is the maximum loss that Greg can claim for 2025/26 under section 64?

Answer

Before the loss claim, Greg's tax position for 2025/26 is as follows:

Trading profits	(to 31.03.26)	28,000
Rental income		60,000
Total Income		88,000

Greg may claim, under section 64, the loss to 31.3.27 to be utilised against the trading profits of the previous year, without restriction. However, the claim against other income is limited to the greater of £50,000 and 25% of adjusted total income. The loss claim against 2025/26 will be:

Trading profits	28,000
Rental Income	60,000

Less s64 loss	(78,000)
Net income	10,000

Notes

1. The maximum loss available against trading profits is the full amount of the trading profits of 28,000, without restriction.

The maximum loss available against other income is restricted to the greater of:

(a) 50,000, and

(b) 25% of adjusted total income (i.e. 88,000 x 25% = 22,000)

Therefore, the claim is limited to 50,000.

The total s64 loss claim will be 78,000 (28,000 + 50,000).

2. The personal allowance would then be deducted from net income to calculate taxable income. As net income is less than the personal allowance, the balance of the personal allowance will be wasted.
3. The balance of the loss, £22,000 (100,000-78,000), could be used in 2026/27 or carried forward.

Trading loss offset against capital gains (section 71)

It may make sense to return to this section after you have studied Capital gains tax in Chapter 13.

This relief is a little unusual as it permits an *income* loss to be offset against a *capital* gain. Normally, income losses may only be offset against income and capital losses only against capital gains.

This loss relief is only available for any tax year after loss relief against other income has been claimed under section 64.

The trading loss for the tax year must first be offset against the net income of the tax year and assuming part of the trading loss remains unrelieved, this surplus may then be offset against the net capital gains of the same tax year.

However, although the trading loss is offset against the current year's net gains, the actual amount of the surplus trading loss available for relief is, in fact, the *lower* of the unrelieved trading loss and net capital gains less capital losses brought forward.

Example 8.6

Lucy has the following income and gains arising for 2026/27:

Trading loss	(£30,000)
Net other income	£20,000
Capital gain	£40,000
Capital loss	£16,000

Unrelieved capital loss brought forward from earlier years £12,500

The capital gains annual exemption for 2026/27 is £3,000.

Calculate for 2026/27:

(a) the section 64 loss relief against net income, and

(b) the additional section 71 loss relief against chargeable gains.

Answer

(a) Income tax computation, 2026/27

Net income	20,000
Less: section 64 loss relief	(20,000)
Taxable income	nil

Therefore, the unrelieved trading loss for 2026/27 is 30,000 less 20,000 = 10,000.

(b) Capital gains computation 2026/27

Current year gain		40,000
Current year capital loss		(16,000)
		24,000
Less: section 71 trading loss relief – *lower* of:		
(i) Unrelieved trading loss after s.64 relief	10,000	
(ii) Net current year gains	24,000	
Less: b/f capital loss	(12,500)	
	11,500	(10,000)
		14,000
Less capital loss b/f claimed		(11,000)
		3,000
Less: annual exemption		(3,000)
Taxable amount		nil

Notes

1. Before section 71 relief could be claimed for the tax year 2026/27, the trading loss must first be relieved under section 64 against net income for 2026/27.
2. As the net income is reduced by the section 64 loss to £0, the personal allowance is wasted.
3. As a surplus trading loss of 10,000 remains after section 64 relief, then section 72 relief can be claimed.
4. The amount of the surplus trading loss of 10,000 which is available to be offset against net current year capital gains (i.e. 24,000) is the *lower* of the surplus trading loss (i.e. 10,000) and net current tax year capital gains (i.e. 24,000) less any capital losses brought forward (i.e. 12,500) i.e. 11,500. In this case, the whole of the surplus trading loss of 10,000 is available for offset against the capital gains for the tax year 2026/27.
5. Having offset the trading loss against net capital gains under section 72, the resulting 14,000 net capital gains remaining can then be reduced by using part of the capital loss brought forward.
6. The amount used under point 5. above is restricted to leave a balance equal to the annual capital gains exemption for 2026/27, i.e. 3,000 (see Chapter 13). The final chargeable gains amount is then "nil".
7. 1,500 of the capital loss brought forward (i.e. 12,500 – 11,000) can then be carried forward for offset against future capital gains.

Trading losses offset in the early years of trade (section 72)

In the early years of a sole trader's business, where trading losses arise, there may be no other income available to claim these against. However, a special loss relief is available for losses arising in the early years of a new trade.

Any trading loss arising in the first four tax years of a trade may be claimed against the net income of the three tax years immediately preceding the tax year of the trading loss, beginning with the earliest and ending with the latest tax year (i.e. a so-called First In First Out (FIFO) basis). The loss must be claimed within one year of 31 January following the end of the tax year in which the loss arose.

Although section 72 only applies in these particular circumstances, a sole trader may still choose to utilise either sections 64, 83 and/or section 71 if preferred. Generally speaking, however, in these circumstances section 72 is likely to give maximum tax relief sooner.

A typical scenario might be where an employee decides to leave employment and set up their own sole trader business. Under section 72, any early tax year trading losses might be carried back and offset against the earlier tax year's net income, which will, of course, include the person's previous employment income. It may then be possible to obtain a tax refund for some or all of those earlier tax years to help with the cash flow of their new business.

Example 8.7

Tim started in business on 1 July 2026 (i.e. 2026/27) and prepares his accounts to 30 June each year. His results are as follows:

Year ended 30 June 2027	Trading loss	£30,000
Year ended 30 June 2028	Trading profit	£15,500

Before setting up his own business, Tim was an employee and received the following salary:

2025/26	£33,000
2024/25	£28,000
2023/24	£21,000

Tim also receives savings income of £500 each tax year.

Show Tim's tax position for all years, if loss relief under section 72 is claimed.

Answer

First, it is necessary to calculate Tim's trading profit/loss for each tax year. This involves using the basis period rules discussed in Chapter 6.

His first tax year is 2026/27 and produces a trading loss as follows:

Year ended 30 June 2027	Trading loss	£30,000 x 279/365 days = (22,932)

The second tax year is 2027/28 and overall, there is a net profit

Year ended 30 June 2027	Trading loss	£30,000 x 86/365 days =	(7,068)
Year ended 30 June 2028	Trading profit	£15,500 x 279/365 days =	11,848
Net Profit			4,780

The usual options are available to offset the loss for 2026/27 against other income of the current or previous year or to carry forward the loss against future profits of the same trade. However, as an early year loss, there is the option to carry back the loss for three years.

	2023/24	2024/25	2025/26	2026/27	2027/28
Trading profit	n/a	n/a	n/a	nil	4,780
Salary	21,000	28,000	33,000	nil	nil
Savings income	500	500	500	500	500
Net income	21,500	28,500	33,500	500	5,280
Less:					
Section 72 relief	(21,500)	(1,432)			
Net income	0	27,068	33,500	500	5,280

Notes

1. For each year the revised Net income would be reduced by the personal allowance available.
2. Under section 72 the loss for 2026/27 is carried back three preceding tax years to 2023/24 and offset against that tax year's net income first and then any remaining loss against 2024/25.
3. Note that the use of the trading loss in 2023/24 results in a loss of the personal allowance for that tax year.
4. The cap of income tax reliefs must be considered in section 72 claims.

How would the above position compare if Tim had instead decided to utilise section 64 and section 83 relief rather than section 72 relief?

	2023/24	2024/25	2025/26	2026/27	2027/28
Trading income	n/a	n/a	n/a	nil	4,780
Less:					
Salary	21,000	28,000	33,000	nil	nil
Other income	500	500	500	500	500
Net income	21,500	28,500	33,500	500	5,280
Less:					
Section 64 relief			(22,932)		
Net income	21,500	28,500	10,568	500	5,280

Notes

1. The trading loss of 2026/27 could be claimed under section 64 against other income for 2025/26 or 2026/27. However, as the income for 2026/27 would be covered by the personal allowance, the loss is fully carried back to 2025/26 in full.

Comparing the net income under each option shows the same overall results. However, full calculations including personal allowances would be required to make a final decision for the optimum loss claim.

Trading losses in the closing year (section 89 terminal loss relief)

Terminal loss relief can arise when a sole trader ceases to trade.

A terminal loss is calculated as the trading loss of the last 12 months of trading.

Under section 89 such a loss may be claimed against any trading profits of the three tax years preceding the tax year of cessation (taking the later tax years first; i.e. a LIFO basis approach). The loss must be claimed within four years from the end of the tax year in which the trade ceased.

The terminal loss is calculated as the trading loss of the last 12 months of trading less any part of which may have been relieved first under section 64. The terminal loss is calculated by adding together the following components:

(i) the actual trading loss from 6 April to the date of cessation; and

(ii) the actual trading loss incurred from a date 12 months before the date of cessation to the following 5 April.

If either (i) or (ii) produces a profit, then it is assumed to be nil for the purpose of calculating the terminal loss.

Example 8.8

Lynn prepares her accounts to 30 June each year. Lynn ceased to trade on 31 May 2026. Her trading profits and losses are as follows:

Year ended 30 June 2024	Trading profit £36,000
Year ended 30 June 2025	Trading profit £22,000
11 month period ended 31 May 2026	Trading loss £44,000.

Show Lynn's position assuming a section 89 terminal loss claim is made.

Answer

The terminal loss is the trading loss for the 12 months 1.6.25 to 31.5.26 (date of cessation).

2026/27 (6.4.26 to 31.5.26)	
Trading loss for this period	
Loss to 31/5/26 44,000 x 56/335 days =	(7,355)
2025/26 (1.6.25 to 5.4.26)	
Trading loss for this period	
Loss to 31/5/26 44,000 x 279/335 days =	(36,645)
Profit to 30/6/25 22,000 x 30/365 days =	1,808
	(34,837)
Therefore, terminal loss	(42,192)

Notes

1. The terminal loss claim is restricted to £42,192 as calculated above.
2. The terminal loss can be carried back against profits of the same trade of 2025/26, 2024/25 and 2023/24 in that order

Trading loss relief following incorporation of a sole trader business (section 86)

It is not unusual for a sole trader after having traded for a while to contemplate converting their business into a limited company. Normally, any unused losses may only be carried forward against profits of the same trade. However, subject to the satisfaction of certain conditions, unrelieved accumulated trading losses arising before the date of incorporation from the sole-trader business may be carried forward to be offset against the first available income of the former sole trader which he or she receives from the company, provided the shares allotted are still held. Available income includes, for example, salary, interest and dividends. This relief will only apply where the business is transferred to and continues to be carried on by a limited company and the whole or main consideration is the allotment of shares to the former sole trader.

The trading losses unrelieved and carried forward are offset first against earned income (i.e. salaries and directors' fees) and then against unearned income (i.e. dividends).

Example 8.9

On the advice of his accountant, Vlad transferred his sole trader business to a limited company, VC Ltd, on 1 July 2024. The consideration for the transfer was an issue of ordinary shares. As of the date of the transfer of the business, Vlad had unrelieved trading losses of £55,000. Vlad's salary from the company is £16,000 per annum and dividends of £5,000 per annum are received in December each year.

Show how Vlad will obtain relief under section 86 for the trading losses from his business.

Answer

	2024/25	**2025/26**	**2026/27**
Employment income	12,000	16,000	16,000
S86 loss relief	(12,000)	(16,000)	(16,000)
Dividends	5,000	5,000	5,000
S86 loss relief	(5,000)	(5,000)	(1,000)
Net income	nil	nil	4,000

Notes

1. The trading loss of 55,000 has been offset in each tax year, commencing with the tax year 2024/25, first against the salary Vlad draws and then against any dividends received.
2. The salary of 12,000 for 2024/25 arises because Vlad only worked for VC Ltd in that tax year for nine months i.e. 1.7.24 to 5.4.25 giving 9/12 x 16,000 = 12,000.
3. The trading loss of 55,000 is exhausted in the tax year 2026/27.
4. There is no loss relief against National Insurance Contributions, so Vlad may have a Class 1 NIC liability for some years on his salary.

SUMMARY

- Utilising trading losses in the most tax efficient manner may require several "what if" calculations to be prepared to review the various options.
- In general, it will be beneficial to claim losses against income that attracts a tax charge at the highest rate and as far as possible, avoids wasting personal allowances.
- Assuming that none of the special circumstances arise (e.g. trade cessation; incorporation; etc.) then, generally speaking, trading losses of a tax year should be offset under section 64 against the prior tax year's net income and any surplus loss remaining unrelieved should then be offset under section 64 against current tax year net income. Any remaining unrelieved trading loss can then be carried forward under section 83 to be offset against future trading profits.

Questions for students

See Appendix 2 for practice questions relating to Chapter 8. Answers are available online at https://spiramus.com/uk-taxation-for-students-20267-answers.

CHAPTER 9

Partnerships

Introduction

This chapter examines how partners in a trading partnership are taxed on their share of profits.

General

The first thing to note is that a partnership is not a separate taxpayer. Whereas a company is a taxpayer, separate from its shareholders, directors and employees, a partnership is not.

Consequently, it is the individual partners, and not the partnership itself, who are taxed.

Basis of assessment

Although a partnership is not a separate taxpayer, an overall partnership tax adjusted trading profit is computed for a period of account adopting the same rules as for a sole trader (see Chapter 6). The default accounting method is also the cash basis with the option to use the traditional accruals method of accounting.

This overall partnership trading profit is then allocated amongst the partners according to the profit sharing ratios laid down in the partnership agreement and each partner is then subject to income tax and NIC on their share of the profits. A partnership tax return is required each tax year to supply this information to HMRC with filing penalties for each partner for late submission.

Each partner is effectively treated as if he or she is, in fact, a sole trader, applying all the normal rules to identify their basis period (see Chapter 6). In addition, all the choices of how relief may be claimed for trading losses (e.g. section 64, section 83 etc.; see Chapter 8) also apply to each partner individually on their share of the loss.

Partnership profit sharing arrangements

Each partner is entitled to a share of the partnership profit or loss for a period of account.

In a simple partnership, each partner will be entitled to a percentage share of the profits (or using partnership share ratios). However, other prior allocations may be made. For example, partners may be entitled to a "salary" before the remaining profits are shared (these amounts are not, however, salaries in the employment income sense; see Chapter 10).

It is also not unusual for a partner to receive interest on any capital which they may have contributed to the partnership. Again, this is a share of the profits and not assessed as savings income.

Therefore, in sharing out any partnership profit for a period of account, any interest paid on capital during that period of account and any "salaries" already paid again during that period must be taken into consideration, before profit shares.

Example 9.1

John, Jackie and James commenced trading as a partnership on 1 June 2026. They share profits in the ratios of 3:2:1. They each contributed capital as follows and each receives interest thereon at 5%:

John	£50,000
Jackie	£45,000
James	£30,000

Each partner is to receive a salary of £25,000 per annum.

The partnership accounts are prepared to 31 May each year and the tax adjusted trading profits for the partnership are as follows:

Year ended 31 May 2027	£125,000
Year ended 31 May 2028	£200,000

Calculate each partner's assessable trading profits for the tax years 2026/27 and 2027/28.

Answer

	John	**Jackie**	**James**	**Total**
Period of account:				
1.6.26 to 31.5.27:				
Salary	25,000	25,000	25,000	75,000
Interest on capital:				
5% of £50,000	2,500			2,500
5% of £45,000		2,250		2,250
5% of £30,000			1,500	1,500
Balance of profit share				
3:2:1	21,875	14,583	7,292	**43,750**
Total	49,375	41,833	33,792	125,000
Period of account:				
1.6.27 to 31.5.28:				
Salary	25,000	25,000	25,000	75,000
Interest on capital:				
5% of £50,000	2,500			2,500
5% of £45,000		2,250		2,250
5% of £30,000			1,500	1,500
Balance of profit share				
3:2:1	59,375	39,583	19,792	**118,750**
Total	86,875	66,833	46,292	200,000

Notes

1. The steps in the calculation for each period of account are as follows:

First, salary and interest on capital are calculated for each partner and then aggregated;

Second, the total balance of profit share (the figure in bold above i.e. **43,750**) is calculated by deducting the total salaries plus total interest on capital from the trading profit for that period of account (i.e. for 1.6.26 to 31.5.27 125,000 – (75,000 + 2,500 + 2,250 + 1,500) = 43,750

Third, this total balancing profit share figure (i.e. 43,750) is then divided according to the profit share ratios (i.e. 3:2:1) to give the amounts *21,875 14,583 and 7,292* for John, Jackie and James respectively.

Finally, salary, interest on capital and profit share are added to find the total share of the profits for each partner, ensuring that the total of this for all of the partners matches the partnership profits for the period.

2. The above steps are then repeated for each subsequent period of account.

It now becomes necessary to work out each partner's individual trading profit assessment for each tax year.

Remember that to do this, the normal sole trader basis period rules apply. Thus:

Partner	**Basis period**	**Assessable profit share**		
John				
2026/27	1/6/26 to 5/4/27	49,375 x 309/365 days =		41,800
2027/28	6/4/27 to 31/5/27	49,375 x 56/365 days =	7,575	
	1/6/27 to 5/4/28	86,875 x 309/365 days =	73,546	
				81,121
Jackie				
2026/27	1/6/26 to 5/4/27	41,833 x 309/365 days =		35,415
2027/28	6/4/27 to 31/5/27	41,833 x 56/365 days =	6,418	
	1/6/27 to 5/4/28	66,833 x 309/365 days =	56,579	
				62,997
James				
2026/27	1/6/26 to 5/4/27	33,792 x 309/365 days =		28,607
2027/28	6/4/27 to 31/5/27	33,792 x 56/365 days =	5,185	
	1/6/27 to 5/4/28	46,292 x 309/365 days =	39,190	
				44,375

Notes

1. As the partnership started to trade on 1 June 2026 then the tax year 2026/27 is the first tax year of trading.
2. Each partner is effectively treated as a sole trader and their assessable profits are computed accordingly.

Changes of profit shares and partnership changes

It may be that partners' salaries, interest on capital and balance of profit shares may change during a period of account. In this case, this needs to be taken into account. Nevertheless, the above approach is still adopted.

Typically, during the lifetime of a partnership, some partners will leave the partnership and new partners will join. Partners who leave are treated as ceasing to trade. Similarly, those joining are treated as commencing to trade.

For the partners who continue to trade both before and after such changes, there are no tax effects upon them; they will simply continue to be assessed on the normal, tax year basis.

Example 9.2

Neil and Kevin have been in partnership since they started trading on 1 April 2026. The partnership accounts are prepared to 31 March each year. On 1 April 2027, Sue joins the partnership. On 30 September 2027, Kevin retires from the partnership, leaving Neil and Sue as partners.

For simplicity, in this case, the profits are always shared equally and there are no salaries or interest on capital paid.

Profits have been calculated under the cash basis as:
Year ended 31 March 2027 £120,000
Year ended 31 March 2028 £180,000

Show the assessments for each partner for the relevant tax years.

Answer

Period of account	**Neil**	**Kevin**	**Sue**	**Total**
Year to 31 March 2027				
Profit share				
1:1	60,000	60,000		120,000
Period of account				
Year to 31 March 2028				
Profit share to 30 September 2027 (Kevin's retirement date)				
1:1:1	30,000	30,000	30,000	90,000
Profit share 31 March 2028				
1:1:1	45,000	______	45,000	90,000
Total for the year	75,000	30,000	75,000	180,000

Name of partner	**Tax year**	**Basis period**	**Assessable profit**
Neil	2026/27	1/4/26 to 31/3/27	60,000
	2027/28	1/4/27 to 31/3/28	75,000
Kevin	2026/27	1/4/26 to 31/3/27	60,000
	2027/28	1/4/27 to 30/9/27	30,000
Sue	2026/27	Not a partner	
	2027/28	1/4/27 to 31/3/28	75,000

Note

1. In this example, as the accounts are prepared in line with the tax year, the calculations are much simpler than for any other accounting date.

Capital allowances

As in the case of the sole trader, capital allowances are treated as a tax-deductible trading expense when using the traditional accounting option.

However, it may be that some assets are owned directly by the partnership, for example, office equipment and furniture (both qualifying as plant and machinery for capital allowance purposes; see Chapter 7) whereas some assets are owned by the individual partners, for example, motor cars.

In such cases, capital allowances are computed on all assets for the relevant period of account of the partnership as normal. Individual partners cannot claim capital allowances on their own behalf.

Example 9.3

John and Anne are in a partnership that owns all the assets except for two cars which they each own individually. The partnership prepares annual accounts using the traditional accruals method, therefore, capital allowances are available.

For the accounting period ended 5 April 2027, the partnership's adjusted trading profit *before* capital allowances is £175,000. John and Anne share profits 3:2 respectively. John's salary is £20,000 p.a. and that of Anne £25,000 p.a.

The main pool partnership assets have a tax written down value as at 5 April 2026 of £100,000.

John's car has a tax written down value at this time of £20,000 and Anne's is £10,000. Both cars have CO_2 emissions of less than 50g/km.

John uses his car 70% for business; Anne uses her car 60% for business.

Calculate John and Anne's profit allocations.

Answer

Capital allowances for the period of account 6/4/26 to 5/4/27.

	General Pool	Private use cars		CA Claimed
		John	Anne	
TWDV 5/4/26	100,000	20,000	10,000	
WDA @ 14%	(14,000)			14,000
WDA @ 14%		(2,800)	(1,400)	
		John 2,800 x 70% =		1,960
		Anne 1,400 x 60% =		840
		Capital allowances claim		16,800
TWDV 5/4/27	86,000	17,200	8,600	

Therefore, partnership adjusted taxable trading profit for the year ended 5.4.27 is:

Trading profit pre CAs	175,000
Less CAs	(16,800)
Trading profit post CAs	158,200

Partnership Profit Allocation for Period of account 6.4.26 to 5.4.27

	John	Anne	Total
Salary	20,000	25,000	45,000
Balance of profit share 3:2	67,920	45,280	113,200
Profit share	87,920	65,280	158,200

Trading losses

Trading losses are allocated to individual partners in the same way that partnership profits are allocated.

Once allocated each partner may then individually utilise any of the loss reliefs available to a sole trader (see Chapter 8).

If, as a result of the profit allocation, some partners have losses and some profits, then the losses must first be reallocated against the profit-making partners.

Limited liability partnerships (LLP)

Such partnerships are a relatively new trading style.

The basic concept is that under such partnerships, each partner's liability to contribute to, for example, third parties' claims against the partnership and partnership losses is limited by agreement. Normally, a partner's exposure to such items is joint and unlimited.

For tax purposes, the partner's taxable profits are as calculated above. However, the one difference is in connection with losses. The amount of any trading loss which may be offset against a partner's other income is limited to the amount of capital the partner has contributed to the partnership.

SUMMARY

- The key issue to note in connection with partnerships is that the partnership is not itself taxed. Instead, the individual partners are taxed on their share of the partnership profit.
- However, to ascertain a partner's share of the partnership profit requires that the partnership's overall taxable profit be computed. This is done in the same manner as for a sole trader. The profits are then divided between the individual partners following the partnership agreement and each partner is then effectively assessed to income tax on their share of the profits following the basis of assessment for sole traders.
- Relief for trading losses is available to each partner as they are for a sole trader.

CHAPTER 10

Employee Taxation

Introduction

This chapter considers the tax aspects associated with employees, including the taxation of non-cash benefits provided by an employer, for example, a company car.

Employment income is taxed under the Income Tax (Earnings and Pensions) Act 2003 (ITEPA 2003).

Employed or self-employed

Identifying whether an individual is an employee (i.e. works for an employer under a contract of employment) or is self-employed (i.e. works for himself/herself in his/her own business) is important as the tax treatments are different in each case. Currently, this question is often in the news in connection with various celebrities and workers within the "gig economy". This is a question of the facts and existing law and not a simple matter of choice.

An employee is taxed under ITEPA 2003, whereas a self-employed individual is taxed under the provisions of ITTOIA 2017 (see Chapter 6).

The basic distinction between the two is that an employee has a contract *of* service whereas a self-employed individual will have a contract *for* services. However, any contract must reflect the actual terms of the engagement.

Although there are no exact rules for determining whether an individual is self-employed or an employee, factors that would be taken into account in previously decided cases include:

- the control over how and when the work is to be done;
- a self-employed worker is expected to provide their equipment;
- a self-employed worker can hire helpers or a substitute when personally unavailable;
- a self-employed worker bears a financial risk and can profit from their good work;
- the degree of management exercised;
- whether work is carried out for only one client/customer;
- the mutual obligation to provide work and perform work;
- method of payment for work done;
- an employee is entitled to holiday and sick pay entitlement.

As indicated above, usually no single factor determines the issue. All of the factors must be reviewed and then a decision can be made based on the overall picture.

Some of the main differences between the self-employed and an employee are:

- a self-employed person is liable to income tax under the self-assessment provisions and may be required to make two payments on account of the tax year's liability and a balancing payment (see Chapter 21), whereas an employee pays income tax on earnings each month (or week) under Pay As You Earn Regulations (PAYE) i.e. self-employed income tax payments are made later;
- the allowable expense rules (i.e. those expenses which are tax deductible) for an employee are more restricted than for the self-employed i.e. more difficult to satisfy; and
- a self-employed person pays Class 4 National Insurance Contributions (NICs) whereas an employee pays Class 1; the latter is usually greater than the former (see Chapter 20).

Personal Service Companies

Many individuals choose to work for their clients using their own limited companies, referred to by HMRC as 'personal service companies' and in recent years there have been many high profile cases considering this area of taxation.

A limited company can be a tax efficient way for an individual to provide their services. The individual may divide the income that they take from their company between salary and dividends, with a resulting saving as NICs are not charged on dividends. By using a limited liability company, individuals are also protected to a certain extent from business risk.

The term 'personal service companies' was introduced in April 2000 under the so-called IR35 legislation. The legislation applies to relevant engagements, where a "worker" provides services to a client through an intermediary, usually a company, where, if the intermediary company did not exist, the individual providing services to a client would be treated as an employee and not as self-employed.

In effect, the personal service company rules treat almost all income from relevant engagements during a tax year as a deemed salary. The deemed payment is subject to both income tax and NICs, removing any benefits of drawing income as a dividend or simply leaving profits in the company. There are detailed rules for these calculations which are beyond the scope of this text.

Employment income

An individual is liable under ITEPA 2003 to income tax on employment income. This may include salary, wages, tips/gratuities and so-called money's worth (i.e. something capable of being converted into money) plus amounts treated as earnings (i.e. benefits in kind as detailed below).

Basis of assessment

Receipt of money earnings

Employment income is generally taxable when received, not when earned even if they do not relate to that tax year. Receipt is considered to occur at the earlier of the following:

- when payment is made of or on account of earnings, or
- when a person becomes entitled to payment.

For directors, receipt can occur earlier:

- at the date when a sum is agreed or credited in the company's accounts or records (e.g. crediting the director's account will constitute receipt);
- the end of a period of account if the amount of the director's income is determined for that period before it ends; or
- the date that the director's income for a period of account is determined, if after the period ends.

Example 10.1

Peter receives an annual bonus based on the results of his employer. Based on his employer's results for the year to 31 March 2026, Peter was entitled to a bonus of £12,500 and this was made available to him on 1 July 2026. For the year to 31 March 2027, Peter is due a bonus of £15,600 and becomes entitled to this on 14 August 2027. How much bonus will be assessable on Peter during the year to 5 April 2027?

Answer

It is irrelevant which period the bonus relates to. Using the rules above, Peter became entitled to the bonus of £12,500 on 1 July 2026 and this will be included in his taxable employment income to 5 April 2027. The bonus of £15,600 will fall to be assessed in the following tax year.

Receipt of non-money earnings

Benefits (other than non-cash vouchers)

Earnings not consisting of money or cash are normally treated as received in the tax year when the benefit is provided. This rule applies to the provision or use of:

- cash vouchers;
- credit tokens;
- living accommodation;
- cars, vans and related benefits;
- loans;
- other benefits in kind;
- use of an asset without transfer; and
- transfer of used assets.

Non-cash vouchers

For non-cash vouchers, receipt occurs:

- in the tax year in which the cost of provision is incurred; or

- if later, the tax year in which the voucher is received by the employee.

Otherwise, receipt occurs when the benefit is provided to the employee.

Vouchers and credit tokens

Non-cash vouchers (i.e. one exchangeable for goods or services but not cash) give a benefit equivalent to the expense incurred by the employer in providing the vouchers (i.e. not on their exchange value).

Cash vouchers (i.e. vouchers which can be exchanged for cash) are treated as pay and therefore are treated as income equal to the cash exchange value.

Credit tokens (e.g. a company credit card) give rise to a benefit equal to the cost to the employer of providing the goods, services etc. obtained using the credit token.

Benefits in kind

In addition to receiving a salary, an employee may also receive benefits in kind or "perks". Benefits in kind refer to items of additional remuneration that are not in the form of cash, such as the use of a company car, an interest-free loan or the provision of private health insurance etc. The employer directly purchases the goods or services and provides them to an employee.

Although these are not rewards in the form of monetary consideration, they are provided in return for work done or services provided by the employee. They are therefore subject to income tax and are added to the salary etc to calculate total employment income.

The legislation sets out how benefits in kind are to be valued for income tax for each tax year (For example, if a company car is provided during three tax years, a benefit in kind will arise for each of the three tax years).

However, not all benefits are subject to income tax – some benefits are exempt from income tax, as detailed later in this chapter.

Approach to use when working out the value of a benefit

When working out the value of a benefit for a tax year, the general approach is usually:

1. Work out the value of the benefit for a whole tax year according to the relevant provision.
2. Reduce the value in Step 1 to the extent that the benefit is not available for any part of the tax year (e.g. because it was provided partway through the tax year).
3. Deduct from the value arrived at in Step 2 any deductible employee contributions towards the benefit (e.g. because the employee may contribute to the cost of the benefit). Any amounts made good must be paid by 6 July following the end of the tax year to be deductible.

Taxable value of benefits in kind

General rule

Where a benefit in kind is provided or given to an employee, the general rule is that the taxable value of the benefit is the cost to the employer, unless a specific statutory rule applies, for example, for company cars.

The cost to the employer will be the marginal or additional cost where "in-house" benefits are provided, such as free flights for staff by an airline.

Example 10.2

ABM Ltd pays private medical insurance premiums for its employee Alan. The cost to the employer is £500. The insurance would cost Alan £650 personally.

Alan's taxable benefit is the cost to his employer of £500.

In other words, Alan's total employment income will be increased by £500.

Assets made available for private use

A taxable benefit also arises when an employee is permitted private use of an asset without ownership being transferred to the employee. In other words, the asset continues to belong to the employer.

In general, the measure of the benefit is the greater of:

- the annual value of the use of the asset; and
- the annual amount paid by the employer as rent or hire charges.

The annual value is calculated as 20% of the asset's market value on the date that it is first provided to the employee.

The benefit is reduced by employee contributions and apportioned where the asset is provided for part of the tax year only.

Example 10.3

Janet is provided by her employer with a television for her personal use. It is provided on 6 July 2026 at which time its market value is £700.

Calculate the benefit to Janet for the tax year to 5 April 2027.

Answer

The annual benefit = 20% x 700 = 140

However, as Janet only had the use of the television from 6 July 2026, the benefit in kind for 2026/27 will be 140 x 9/12 months = 105

These general rules do not apply, however, where a benefit is taxed according to its own specific statutory rule including living accommodation, company cars, vans and beneficial loans.

Transfer of an asset following use

If an asset, other than a car, owned by the employer and previously made available to an employee for use, is subsequently transferred to an employee, the benefit arising from the transfer of the asset from the employer to the employee is the *greater* of:

- the market value of the asset at the date of transfer; and

- the market value of the asset when first made available for the employee's use less the aggregate of the benefits for use already assessed on the employee.

Example 10.4

Ollie has been using a motorbike provided by his employer from 6 April 2024 until 6 October 2026. On 6 October 2026, Ollie was given the motorbike by his employer when its market value was £2,750.

On 6 April 2024, the market value of the asset was £6,000.

Calculate Ollie's benefit for each relevant tax year.

Answer

The use benefit will be as follows:

2024/25	20% x 6,000 =	1,200
2025/26	20% x 6,000 =	1,200
2026/27	20% x 6,000 x 6/12 =	600

On 6 October 2026, Ollie was given a previously used asset.
The benefit of the purchase will be the greater of:

1. 2,750 (i.e. market value of the asset at the date of purchase), and
2. 6,000 – [1,200 + 1,200 + 600] (i.e. market value when first made available less benefit in kind for its use) = 3,000

Therefore, Ollie will be assessed on the benefits as follows:

2024/25		1,200
2025/26		1,200
2026/27	600 + 3,000 =	3,600

Note

If Ollie had been given the motorbike outright on 6 April 2024, the benefit in kind would have been £6,000, being the market value of the asset at that time. You will note that the aggregate of the benefits in kind in the above example is also £6,000.

Living accommodation

The measure of the taxable benefit for the provision of living accommodation depends on whether the accommodation is job-related or not.

Not job-related accommodation

The benefit for the provision of accommodation comprises two parts:
Firstly, the *greater* of:

- the annual value of the accommodation, *and*
- the rent paid by the employer

plus an additional charge where the cost of providing the accommodation exceeds £75,000. The additional charge is:

(Cost of provision - £75,000) x appropriate percentage.

The cost of provision is found by adding the original expenditure incurred by the employer to acquire the property and the cost of any improvements incurred *before* the tax year in question.

The *appropriate percentage* is the official rate of interest applying to beneficial loans for the relevant tax year (currently 3.75% for the tax year 2026/27).

Cost of provision versus market value

"Market value" is substituted for "cost of provision" if the property has been owned by the employer for more than six years *at the date of the employee taking up occupation.* Note, however, that unless the cost of the accommodation was £75,000 or greater, market value cannot apply. Thus, if the original cost of providing the accommodation is less than £75,000, no additional charge can apply even if the market value exceeds this cost.

Improvement expenditure incurred on the property *before the beginning of a tax year* increases the cost or market value as appropriate for that tax year.

Deductions from the additional charge occur for *bona fide* business use of the accommodation and/or for rent paid by the employee that exceeds the benefit under the normal charge (i.e. any rent paid by the employee is first offset against the basic charge and then against the additional charge).

Example 10.5

Dougie was provided with a house on 6 April 2026 which was purchased by his employer, DMP plc, for £550,000 in January 2022. The annual value of the house is £2,000 and Dougie pays rent of £500 a month to the company.

Calculate Dougie's assessable benefit for 2026/27, assuming the official rate of interest is 3.75%.

Answer

Benefit equals:

Annual value	2,000
Additional benefit 3.75% x (550,000 – 75,000)	17,812
	19,812
Less: Employee contribution (i.e. 500 x 12)	(6,000)
	13,812

Note

If the house had in fact been purchased before 6 April 2020, then the market value on 6 April 2026 would be substituted for the cost of the accommodation.

Example 10.6

MBT Ltd purchased a flat in 2006 for £100,000. Expenditure was subsequently incurred by MBT Ltd on property improvements of £60,000 in 2013 and a further £50,000 in December 2025. MBT Ltd made the property available, rent-free, to an employee, Michelle, on 6 April 2026.

The market value of the property was £250,000 on 6 April 2026 and £320,000 on 6 April 2027.

The annual value of the property is £1,200.

Calculate Michelle's assessable benefit for 2026/27, assuming the official rate of interest is 3.75%.

Answer

Annual value		1,200
Additional benefit	3.75% x (250,000 – 75,000)	6,562
		7,762
Less: Contribution by employee		nil
Assessable benefit in kind		7,762

Notes

1. Additional benefit - at the date of the first occupation by Michelle, the flat has been owned by MBT Ltd for more than six years after purchase; therefore, market value is substituted for cost i.e. 250,000 is used to determine the additional benefit.
2. The improvements in December 2026 (i.e. during the tax year 2026/27) will not affect the computation of the benefit for the tax year 2026/27 but will impact the benefit for the tax year 2027/28. For the tax year 2027/28, the additional charge will be based on the market value of 250,000 plus 50,000 i.e. 300,000.

Job-related accommodation

No benefit arises if the occupation of the property is 'job-related' i.e.

- where it is necessary for the employee to reside there to perform his or her duties, e.g. a caretaker; *or*
- where it is customary to occupy it for the better performance of his or her duties; *or*
- if it is provided for the employee's personal security.

The first two exceptions do not apply to directors, other than full-time working directors who do not own more than 5% of the employing company's ordinary share capital.

Ancillary expenses connected with living accommodation

Ancillary expenses of accommodation include:

- heating
- lighting
- cleaning
- repairs and maintenance
- provision of furniture (at 20% of market value – see below)

Telephone costs (i.e. calls and line rental) are *not* regarded as "ancillary expenses", although they are treated as a benefit and taxable.

Where the accommodation is "job-related" the amount of the "ancillary expenses" which are treated as a benefit are normally restricted to 10% of "net earnings" i.e. salary plus benefits (other than ancillary benefits in question) less certain expenses (primarily, pension contributions to the employer's pension scheme and any own car mileage allowance expense claims). Note also that there is no assessment on council tax or rates paid by an employer where the accommodation is job-related.

The 10% restriction does not apply to directors, other than full-time working directors without a material interest.

Example 10.7

Peter's employer PVP Ltd provides him with accommodation which cost £70,000 and has an annual rateable value of £1,000. In addition to providing the accommodation, PVP Ltd also bears the costs of the accommodation during 2026/27 as follows:

Electricity	1,340
Gas	1,200
Cleaning and maintenance	2,500
Telephone	850
Structural repairs	3,000

It has been agreed with the tax authorities that 70% of the telephone call charges relate to business use. The line rental included in the telephone costs is £50.

Calculate the assessable benefit for 2026/27 in respect of the ancillary expenses.

Answer

Benefits are taxable as follows:

Ancillary expenses:	
Electricity	1,340
Gas	1,200
Cleaning and maintenance	2,500
	5,040
Telephone: line rental	50
Call costs	800
Less: business calls	(560)
	5,330

Notes

1. In addition, the accommodation benefit itself will be the annual value of £1,000.
2. Ancillary expenses exclude telephone costs.
3. Line rental cannot be split into business and private elements; therefore, all the line rental cost is taxable.
4. Structural repairs are not taxable as they are the liability of the landlord and not the employee occupying the property.
5. If the accommodation had been job-related and Peter's salary had been £35,000 then the expenses benefit would have been the lower of 5,040 (total ancillary expenses) or 10% of (35,000 +50 +800 -560) = 3,529.

Motor cars

Motor cars remain one of the most popular benefits provided to employees.

Not only is the provision of a car (a so-called company car) a taxable benefit but where any private fuel (i.e. petrol or diesel) is paid for by the employer this gives rise to an additional benefit.

Where a company car is made available for private use by an employee, the annual benefit in kind is calculated as follows:

(List price – capital contribution paid by the employee) x % (based upon CO_2 emissions)

List price includes the original list price of the car (as published by the manufacturer at the time of the car's original registration), delivery charges (excluding road fund licence) and accessories fitted at the time of purchase. This may not be the actual price paid by the employer when purchasing the car, particularly if second-hand (In fact, the car could be leased by the employer).

Capital contribution by the employee applies where the employee contributes to the purchase price of the car. However, this figure is capped with a maximum deduction of £5,000.

% refers to the percentage which is determined according to the CO_2 emissions of the car as follows:

CO_2 Emissions	**2026/27**
Zero emissions	4%
1g/km to 50g/km	
Electric range: 130 miles or more	4%
70 -129 miles	7%
40 -69 miles	10%
30-39 miles	14%
Less than 30 miles	16%
51g/km to 54g/km	17%
55g/km to 59g/km	18%
60g/km to 64g/km	19%
65g/km to 69g/km	20%
70g/km to 74g/km	21%
75g/km to 79g/km	21%

For each complete 5g/km above 75 g/km, the % increases by 1%, but an overall maximum of 37% applies. Note that for electric or hybrid cars with CO_2 emissions below 50 g/km, lower percentages apply based on the electric driving range in miles.

For cars with a diesel engine, the % worked out as above is then increased by 4% (but again, subject to a maximum of 37%). Diesel cars that meet the RDE2 standard will not be subject to this extra charge.

Where any accessory is added after delivery of the car, for the tax year in which they are fitted (and any subsequent tax years) the list price is increased by the cost of such items except that any individual accessory costing up to £100 is ignored.

The benefit in kind calculated as above is regarded as covering not only the use of the car but also various running costs such as road tax, repairs and maintenance, insurance etc. paid for by the employer (other than car fuel which as noted above is taxed as a benefit separately).

If the employee is required to make a payment towards the private use of the car, then this is deducted from the calculated benefit in kind.

If the car is not provided for the full tax year, the car benefit is apportioned on a time basis. In addition, the car must be unavailable for a continuous period of at least 30 days for a reduction to apply, for example, due to a repair.

Example 10.8

Graham is provided with a company car by his employer on 6 April 2026. The car has a CO_2 emission of 148g/km. The car cost Graham's employer £16,750 and has a list price of £25,000. Graham would like to know the likely benefit if the car is petrol and if it is diesel (Not RDE2 standard).

Answer

The base % is 21%

For each complete 5g/km above 75g/km the % increases by 1%

148g/km rounded down to 145 less base 75 = 70 above

70/5 increases the percentage by 14%

The % is therefore 21% + 14% = 35%

The benefit in kind is the list price of £25,000 x 35% = £8,750

If the car has a diesel engine, then the benefit is as above i.e. 35% but plus 4% = 39%. However, the maximum is 37%. Therefore, if the car has a diesel engine the benefit in kind would be increased to £25,000 x 37% = £9,250

Notes

1. The cost of the car is *completely* ignored. The benefit in kind is calculated on the list price of the car.
2. Graham will continue to be assessed to income tax on the benefit in kind for the car in subsequent years where the car remains available to him.

Example 10.9

Julia is provided with a petrol company car by her employer on 6 October 2026. The car has a CO_2 emission of 127 g/km and a list price of £19,000.

Accessories were fitted in December 2026 costing £65, after Julia took delivery, and for £150 in May 2027.

Julia is required to contribute £30 per month towards the running costs of the car.

Calculate Julia's taxable car benefit.

Answer

The base % is 21%

For each complete 5g/km above 75g/km the % increases by 1%

127g/km rounded down to 125 less base 75 = 50 above

50/5 increases the percentage by 10%

The % is therefore 21% + 10% = 31%

The annual benefit in kind is £19,000 x 31% = £5,890. However, the car was only available to Julia for six months of this tax year.

Therefore, the benefit = 6/12 x 5,890 = £2,945. From this, Julia's contribution of £30 per month can be deducted (6 x £30) giving a net taxable benefit for 2026/27 of £2,765 (£2,945 - £180).

Note
The accessory fitted after delivery of £65 in 2026/27 is below the £100 threshold and thus ignored; the accessory fitted in May 2027 of £150 will be taken into account for 2027/28 and later tax years.

Example 10.10
Scott is a director of SBF Ltd. The company provided him with a company car with CO_2 emissions of 48g/km and an electric range of 45 miles throughout 2026/27. The list price of the car was £36,000 and cost the company £25,000.

Scott provided a capital contribution of £6,000. Scott's total mileage for the tax year was 12,500 miles, of which 9,000 miles were on business.

Car tax, repairs and maintenance and car insurance paid by the employer for the tax year 2026/27 amounted to £2,750.

Calculate Scott's car benefit for 2026/27.

Answer
The car benefit percentage is 10% from the table based on the emissions and electric range.

The list price of £36,000 is reduced by £5,000 in respect of the capital contribution (Any additional contribution above £5,000 is ignored).
The annual benefit in kind is (£36,000-£5,000) x 10% = £3,100

Notes
1. The cost of the car to the employer is irrelevant.
2. The deduction for Scott's capital contribution is capped at £5,000.
3. The various expenses of the car are ignored as, other than fuel, such expenses are included in the car benefit.
4. Car mileage is also totally irrelevant.

Pool cars

There is no benefit for an employee provided with the use of a pool car.

A pool car is a car that meets *all* of the following conditions:

- the car is used by more than one employee or director, *and*
- there is no (or merely incidental) private use, *and*
- the car is not kept at or near the home of the employee overnight.

Car fuel benefit

Car fuel benefit arises when any private fuel is provided to an employee with a company car by reason of his or her employment.

The car fuel benefit is based on the same CO_2 emissions used in the calculation of the car benefit itself. The same percentage figure will be used for both calculations (i.e. car benefit and fuel). Again, the maximum percentage is 37%.

To calculate the fuel benefit, the relevant percentage figure will be multiplied by a set figure for the year. For the year 2026/27, the figure is £29,200.

Therefore, if the car has a list price of less than £29,200, the fuel benefit will be higher than the car benefit.

Unlike the general rule for benefits where an employee's contributions reduce the value of any benefit if an employee makes any contribution towards car fuel costs, these contributions do *not* reduce the benefit *unless* the employee reimburses the full cost of all of their private fuel for the year, in which case there is no fuel benefit.

Example 10.11

Stephen is provided with a petrol-fuelled company car throughout the tax year 2026/27. The car has CO_2 emissions of 130g/km.

Stephen's employer pays for all the running expenses of the car including fuel for private purposes.

Stephen pays £20 per month towards the cost of private fuel.

Calculate Stephen's car fuel benefit for the tax year 2026/27.

Answer

% used to calculate the company car tax benefit itself for 2026/27 is:
[[21% + [(130 – 75)/5 x 1%]] = 32%.

The fuel scale charge for 2026/27 will therefore be:
29,200 x 32% = 9,344.

Notes

1. There is no reduction for the £20 contribution as Stephen does not pay for ALL private fuel.
2. As with other benefits, the benefit would be reduced on a time basis if the car is not available for the whole tax year.

Example 10.12

Liz is employed by LSS Ltd. The company provided her with a diesel company car (Not RDE2 standard) with CO_2 emissions of 100 g/km throughout 2026/27.

The list price of the car is £25,000 and cost her employer £18,700. All car fuel is paid for by Liz's employer.

Liz's business mileage for the tax year 2026/27 was 20,000 miles and the running costs of the car for this period (excluding car fuel costs) were £1,650.

Calculate Liz's benefits in kind for the tax year 2026/27.

Answer

Car benefit
Benefit % = [[21% + [100 – 75]/5]] = 26% +4% diesel supplement = 30%
Benefit 30% x 25,000 = 7,500

Fuel benefit
Benefit = 30% x 29,200 = 8,760
Total benefits – 7,500 + 8,460 – 16,260

Note

The cost of the car, the mileage and actual running costs have no impact on the calculation of the taxable benefits.

There is currently no fuel benefit where an employer allows an employee to charge a fully electric car at the employer's cost (Electricity is not "fuel").

Car park space and chauffeurs

The provision of a personal chauffeur creates an additional taxable benefit, but the provision of a car park space at or close to the workplace is exempt.

Car transferred to an employee

If a car is transferred to an employer, a benefit in kind will arise equal to the market value of the car at the date of transfer less any amount paid for the car by the employee. Any amounts previously assessed on the employee as a benefit in kind in respect of the car have no impact on the taxable amount.

Vans

Vans are treated differently and, generally, more favourably than motor cars.

For 2026/27, where a van is provided to an employee, with no restriction on private use, there is an annual benefit in kind of £4,170, regardless of engine capacity and list price. From 6 April 2021, there is no benefit in kind where a zero-emission van is provided.

However, the benefit is nil where the van is made available to the employee primarily for business travel and private use by the employee is prohibited, although ordinary commuting (travel from home to work) and insignificant private mileage are acceptable (for example one or two private trips a year and regular slight detours, for example, to stop at a shop on the way to work).

There is an additional van fuel benefit of £798 for the tax year 2026/27, where private fuel is provided.

Beneficial loans

Interest-free or cheap loans to employees can give rise to a taxable benefit.

Loans that are caught are those where the interest paid by the employee in a tax year is less than that which should have been paid based on the official rate of interest of 3.75%.

However, if throughout a tax year, the total value of all such loans does not exceed £10,000, there is no taxable benefit in kind. If an individual has multiple loans from the same employer, then these must be aggregated.

A loan used for a qualifying purpose that would be eligible for income tax relief is excluded (see Chapter 3).

The measure of the benefit is calculated either using the average method *or* an alternative precise method and is the difference between the interest actually paid and that given using the official rate.

The alternative precise method gives a more accurate figure and may be used if either the employee or the HMRC so request.

Example 10.13

On 6 April 2026, Marion borrowed £10,500 from her employer for a family holiday. Her employer charged interest at the rate of 1% per annum. The loan is still outstanding on 5 April 2027.

Calculate Marion's benefit for the tax year 2026/27 using the average method.

Answer

Average debt = [[Amount outstanding at 6.4.26 + Amount outstanding at 5.4.27]/2]
= [[10,500 + 10,500]/2] = 10,500

Benefit = 10,500 x 3.75%	393
Less the interest paid by Marion £10,500 x 1%	(105)
Taxable benefit	288

Note

In this example, the benefit in kind would be identical under the alternative method. If Marion had borrowed £10,000 only, then there would have been no benefit in kind.

Example 10.14

If Marion repaid £4,000 on 5 December 2026, what would her taxable benefit under the average method be?

Average debt = [[10,500 + [10,500 - 4,000]/2] = 8,500

Benefit = 8,500 x 3.75%	318
Less the interest paid by Marion (see Example 10.15 below)	(91)
Taxable benefit	227

Note

Although the average debt was less than the £10,000 limit, the maximum debt during the tax year was £10,500, therefore, over the limit.

Example 10.15

If Marion repaid £4,000 on 5 December 2026 what would her taxable benefit be under the alternative precise method?

Answer

Under the precise method the benefit would be:

	10,500 x 3.75% x 8/12 (April to November)		262
plus	(10,500-4,000) x 3.75% x 4/12 (December to April)		81
			343
Less: Interest paid			
	10,500 x 1% x 8/12 (April to November)	70	
plus	(10,500-4,000) x 1% x 4/12 (December to April)	21	
			(91)
Taxable benefit			252

In this case, the HMRC would elect to tax Marion on the benefit as calculated under the precise method as this provides a greater taxable amount.

Note

Under the precise method, interest is calculated on the exact amount of loan outstanding. Therefore, in the above example, £10,500 was outstanding from 6.4.26 to 5.12.26 (i.e. eight months) and after Marion's repayment of £4,000, only £6,500 remained outstanding from 6.12.26 to 5.4.27 (i.e. four months).

Example 10.16

Jeff, an employee, borrows £12,000, from his employer, on 6 October 2026, to buy a new kitchen. His employer does not charge interest on the loan. The full amount of the loan is still outstanding on 5 April 2027.

Calculate Jeff's taxable benefit for the tax year 2026/27 using the average method.

Answer

Benefit = [[Amount outstanding at 6.10.26 + Amount outstanding at 5.4.27]/2] x 3.75% x 6/12
= [[12,000 + 12,000]/2] x 3.75% x 6/12 = 225

Note

As the loan is only outstanding for six months i.e. 6 October to 5 April in 2026/27, then interest is calculated only for this period; hence the use of 6/12ths.

Loan written off

Where an employee loan is written off either in whole or in part, the amount written off is taxable.

Exempt benefits

As mentioned above, a number of benefits in kind do not give rise to an income tax charge on the employee. The main exempt benefits include:

- provision of one mobile phone (Payment of an employee's own mobile phone contract would not be exempt);
- free or subsidised canteen meals if available to *all* employees;
- employer contributions to approved pension plans;
- provision of car park space at or near the place of work (or reimbursement to the employee of costs in paying for such a car park place);
- certain gifts and entertainment provided by third parties; non-cash gifts from a third party up to £250 in a tax year are exempt;
- an annual party or function if the cost to the employer per employee does not exceed £150/year (If the cost is more than £150, the full amount is taxable);
- up to £6 per week as payment towards additional household costs incurred by employees who are required to work from home;
- welfare counselling;
- provision of in-house sports and recreational facilities;
- the first £8,000 of removal or relocation expenses (any excess is taxable);
- work-related training;
- workplace nurseries;
- job-related accommodation;
- interest-free or cheap loans not exceeding £10,000 in a tax year;

- trivial benefits that cost less than £50 (£300 limit per tax year for some directors);
- incidental personal expenses when required to stay away from home on business overnight (up to £5 per night in the UK or £10 if overseas);
- provision of vehicle battery charging at a workplace;
- provision of work buses; and
- non-cash long service awards after at least 20 years' service (Gifts valued up to £50 per year can be tax free).

Salary sacrifice (optional remuneration arrangements)

Many employers offer their employees the opportunity to take a reduced salary in exchange for a benefit in kind. Where an employee takes a benefit in kind and forgoes pay, the amount subject to income tax and class 1 NIC will be calculated as the higher of the cash foregone or the current taxable value of the benefit in question.

Example 10.17

Jonathan accepts an offer to take a reduction in his gross pay of £250 per year and in return is provided with a mobile phone with unlimited private use. What is the income tax position?

Answer

This is an example of an optional remuneration agreement. Jonathan will be assessable on the greater of the pay foregone and the taxable value of the benefit in kind received. The taxable benefit in kind in respect of one mobile phone is £nil. Therefore, Jonathan will be assessed on £250 as additional employment income (i.e. exactly the same as before the salary sacrifice).

There are some exceptions to this rule. For example, the above rules would not apply where salary is sacrificed for allowable pension contributions and if salary is sacrificed for an electric car, then the above rules do not apply and the taxable amount would be calculated using the normal car benefit rules.

Lump sum payments on termination or variation of employment

Such payments may be tax free, partially taxable or fully taxable as detailed below.

Where a taxable payment is made in connection with a person leaving an employment it is taxed in the year of *receipt,* not the year of leaving.

Example 10.18

Jill had her contract of employment terminated on 31 December 2025. She received a compensation payment on 30 June 2026.

If the compensation payment is subject to income tax it will be liable in the tax year of receipt i.e. 2026/27 not in the tax year in which Jill's contract was terminated i.e. 2025/26.

It should be noted that any taxable termination payment is assessed as non-savings income but as the highest slice of income, after dividend income.

Tax free payments

Where a lump sum payment is made:

- under an approved pension scheme; and/or
- made on account of injury, accidental death or disability,

it is exempt from income tax.

Taxable payments

Contractual entitlement

Payments to which an employee is contractually entitled (i.e. are provided for in the contract of employment) are taxable in full e.g. terminal bonuses.

Payments in lieu of notice

If an employer makes a payment in lieu of notice (i.e. a payment made by the employer where the employer has not given the employee the required period of notice specified in the contract of employment) then such payment will be fully taxed as earned income whether contractually entitled or not.

Redundancy payments and ex gratia payments

Any statutory redundancy pay and additional voluntary (Ex gratia and non-contractual) payments made by an employer are tax free up to £30,000 with the excess taxable and subject to Class 1A NIC.

Statutory redundancy pay is a payment that is legally required to be made by the employer when an employee is made redundant. HMRC may argue that an *ex gratia* payment made at or near retirement is an unapproved pension payment and would, therefore, be taxable in full.

Other payments

The cost of the provision of counselling and helping an employee to find new employment (or self-employment) is not a taxable benefit.

A departing employee may be paid an amount in return for agreeing to limit his or her future activities, for example, not to compete with an ex-employer and such an amount is fully taxable.

Allowable deductions from employment income

In arriving at the net taxable employment income of an employee, certain deductions may be made.

General rule

The general rule is that an employee may deduct an expense if the expense has been incurred *wholly, exclusively and necessarily in* the performance of their employment duties (ITEPA 2003 section 336).

For example, no deduction is allowed for expenses which have not been incurred *in* the performance of the duties but in order to carry out the duties, e.g. payment of a fee to an employment agency used to find a job, or the costs of normal commuting to work.

The need to meet the wholly, exclusively *and* necessarily test has resulted in few expenses being eligible for deduction, mainly on the grounds that very few expenses are necessarily incurred. By "necessarily" it is inferred that the duties of the employment require that the expenses be incurred; it is not sufficient that the expenses are incurred due to the personal choice of the employee.

By way of example, a bank manager who joined a London club where he could meet clients was not able to deduct the expense from their earnings. The reason was that the expense had not been incurred *necessarily – he could have met the clients anywhere.*

Similarly, the wholly and exclusively part of the test requires that the expense is incurred solely for the purposes of the employment. Therefore, if the expense has been incurred partly for business and partly for private purposes then no part of it will be deductible by the employee. In some situations, however, where it is possible to split an expense into a business and private element, the former will be deductible. This will generally not be possible or is likely to prove very difficult.

Business entertainment expenses are specifically denied as a deductible expense for an employee. In other words, an employee cannot deduct expenses they may decide to incur on business entertaining. However, the more likely situation would be where an employer reimburses the employee for such expenses. In this situation, the reimbursement is taxable on the employee but in this case, the employee is allowed an equal deduction for the expenses incurred (*Remember that the employer is likely to be required to disallow the entertaining expenses incurred in their adjusted profits computation – see Chapter 6*).

Travel expenses

Travel expenses are allowed as a deduction if the employee is required to incur the expenses in the course of their employment and the expenses are necessarily incurred on travelling in the performance of their employment duties.

Travel costs incurred in travelling from home to work are not incurred in the performance of the employee's duties and are therefore not deductible. However, where an employee travels, for example, from one office of their employer to another office, or to visit a customer, such travel expenses are deductible. Travelling sales employees, for example, would be able to deduct their travel expenses as they travel from customer to customer without a fixed workplace.

There are detailed rules regarding costs incurred travelling to a temporary workplace. The general rule is that travel costs to a temporary workplace are deductible. A temporary workplace is one in which an employee attends or intends to attend for no more than 24 months.

If an employee receives a sum to cover travel expenses but chooses not to actually incur a similar liability, then the excess will be taxable.

Example 10.19

Lorna is provided with £150 to purchase a first-class train ticket to attend a business meeting. Lorna only spends £85 on a second-class ticket. What is Lorna's income tax position?

Answer

The expense payment of £150 by Lorna's employer is treated as earnings. From that amount, she can deduct the £85 that she actually incurred and is taxed on a net amount of £65.

Business use of own vehicle– approved mileage allowance payments

A company car is a car made available to an employee by their employer. Any taxable benefit associated with the car is calculated as described above.

However, in some cases, an employee may use their own car for business travel.

If an employee is reimbursed for their business mileage by their employer there will be no tax liability if the reimbursed amounts are no greater than the approved mileage allowances.

The approved mileage allowances are as follows:

- 55p per business mile for the first 10,000 business miles in the tax year;
- 25p per business mile for business mileage above 10,000 business miles.

Where the payment by the employer is *less* than the above allowances the difference may be claimed by the employee as additional tax-deductible expenses against employment income. If the allowances paid by the employer *exceed* these allowances then the excess is taxable on the employee.

Example 10.20

Gareth uses his car in his employment. During the tax year 2026/27, Gareth travelled 22,000 miles of which 12,000 miles were on business.

Gareth's employer pays a flat business mileage allowance of 60p per mile.

Calculate Gareth's tax position for the mileage allowance.

Answer

Employer payment	= 12,000 x 60p	=	7,200
Approved mileage allowance	= 10,000 x 55p + 2,000 x 25p	=	6,000

Gareth will therefore be treated as receiving taxable income of 7,200 - 6,000 = £1,200

Example 10.21

If instead, Gareth's employer had only provided a payment of 10p per mile, what would be his income tax position?

Answer

Of the approved amount calculated above of £6,000, Gareth only received 12,000 x 10p = 1,200.

As he received less than the approved mileage allowance, he will be able to claim a deduction against his employment income of 6,000 - 1,200 = £4,800

Reduced mileage rates of 24p and 20p per mile apply to business use of own motorcycles and bikes respectively.

Professional subscriptions

A deduction is allowed for any approved professional membership fees or subscriptions that an employee pays that relate to the work carried out in their employment. HMRC provide a regularly updated list of professional bodies approved for tax relief (referred to as List 3).

Specifically authorised deductible expenditure

In addition to the above items, certain expenditure if incurred by an employee is specifically authorised as deductible from their taxable employment income. This includes:

- contributions to an approved occupational pension scheme;
- payments to charity under a payroll deduction scheme operated by an employer (Payroll giving scheme);
- certain industry-specific flat-rate expenses, for example, uniform allowances for nurses and police officers.

Reimbursed expenditure

No liability to income tax arises where allowable expenses are reimbursed by the employer to the employee.

An exemption applies for allowances or reimbursement of actual expenses incurred in connection with incidental overnight expenses up to the maximum of £5 per night in the UK (£10 non-UK). If these limits are exceeded, no part of the exemption applies.

Employment income computation – a comprehensive example

Example 10.22

During the tax year 2026/27, Dilip was paid a gross annual salary of £48,500 by ARL plc. Income tax of £8,100 was deducted under PAYE.

On 1 January 2027, Dilip personally paid a professional subscription of £320 to an HMRC approved professional body.

During 2026/27, ARL plc paid private medical insurance of £400 on behalf of Dilip.

In July 2026, ARL plc gave Dilip £100 to take a client to dinner to discuss their business plans. The actual cost of the meal was £120 and Dilip was not reimbursed for the additional cost.

ARL plc provided Dilip with a mobile phone that he could use for private calls; the cost to ARL plc was £30 per month.

Dilip used his private motor car for business purposes. He travelled 6,500 miles in the performance of his duties for ARL plc during 2026/27 for which the company paid him an allowance of 50 pence per mile.

During the tax year, Dilip contributed 4% of his salary to ARL plc's HMRC-registered occupational pension scheme and this was matched by his employer.

What is Dilip's taxable employment income for the year to 5 April 2027?

Answer

	£
Salary	48,500
Professional subscriptions paid	(320)
BIK – Private medical insurance	400
Entertaining	0
BIK – Mobile phone	Exempt
Business mileage	
- received (6,500 @ 50p)	3,250
- allowable (6,500 @ 55p)	(3,575)
Occupational pension (48,500 x 4%)	(1,940)
Occupational pension employer's contribution	Exempt
Assessable employment income	46,315

Notes

1. As the cost of entertaining covers the amount received, there is no assessable amount. However, Dilip is not allowed a deduction for the extra expenditure.

2. One mobile phone is exempt.

3. The PAYE of £8,100 would be deducted from Dilip's income tax liability to find the income tax payable.

SUMMARY

- An individual's employment income can typically comprise salary plus taxable benefits in kind, less any allowable expenses.
- Employment income is taxed as non-savings income.
- Different rules apply to certain benefits. If there is no specific rule, then the general rule of "cost to the employer" is applicable or 20% of the market value for the private use of an asset.
- Specific rules apply to cars, vans, accommodation and loans.
- Some benefits are tax free.
- Expenses may be deducted in arriving at an employee's taxable earnings although in general allowable deductions are limited.

Questions for students

See Appendix 2 for practice questions relating to Chapter 10. Answers are available online at https://spiramus.com/uk-taxation-for-students-20267-answers.

CHAPTER 11

Personal Tax: Overseas Aspects

Introduction

For many years, the concept of UK tax residence was based on case law and guidance notes. However, following some high-profile cases, the statutory residence test was introduced by Finance Act 2013. A UK tax resident individual is, generally, subject to UK income tax and capital gains tax on their worldwide income and gains.

A non-UK resident may still be liable to UK income tax on profits arising from a trade or profession carried on in the UK, and a UK property business. Non-residents are generally exempt from UK capital gains tax except for gains arising on the sale of UK properties.

The statutory residence test

An individual is a resident in the UK for tax purposes if they meet:

- one of the automatic UK tests; or
- the sufficient ties test

for any tax year (6 April to the following 5 April).

There are up to three steps to the statutory residence test.

Step one – if the individual meets any one of the three **automatic overseas tests**, they will be a non-UK resident. Otherwise, go to step two.

Step two – if the individual meets any of the **automatic UK tests,** they will be a UK resident. Otherwise, go to step three.

Step three – if the steps above prove to be inconclusive, then the individual must consider the **sufficient ties test** to determine their UK tax residence status.

When considering the number of days in the UK, an individual will be considered to be in the UK for any day that they remain in the UK at midnight.

Automatic overseas tests

If an individual meets any one of the three automatic overseas tests, they are considered non-resident for the tax year.

The three tests are as follows:

(1) An individual who was a UK resident for one or more of the previous three tax years spends less than 16 days in the UK during a tax year.

(2) An individual who was not a UK resident for any of the previous three tax years spends less than 46 days in the UK during a tax year.

(3) An individual working full-time overseas. In addition, the individual may only work up to 31 days in the UK, for more than three hours, and they must spend less than 91 days in the UK overall (HMRC has provided

comprehensive guidance on the meaning of "working full time" in their RDR3 statutory residence test online notes).

Automatic UK tests

If the individual did not meet any of the above tests, next you must consider the automatic UK tests.

An individual will automatically be considered UK resident for a tax year if:

(1) they are in the UK for 183 days or more during a tax year;

(2) an individual's only home is in the UK. They must stay there for at least 30 days during the tax year and the property must be available for 91 consecutive days or more (or they also have an overseas home but live in that property for less than 30 days in the tax year); or

(3) they work full-time in the UK for any period of 365 days if all or part of that period falls within the tax year.

Sufficient ties test

If an individual did not meet any of the tests detailed above, the sufficient ties tests should be used to determine UK residence status for the tax year.

The number of ties that are needed to be considered a UK resident is determined by the number of days spent in the UK during a tax year.

There are two tables. The first is for individuals who have been UK resident for one or more of the previous three tax years.

Days spent in the UK during the tax year	*UK ties needed*
Up to 15	Automatically non-resident
16 – 45	At least 4 ties
46-90	At least 3 ties
91-120	At least 2 ties
121 -182	At least 1 tie
183 or more	Automatically resident

The second table is for individuals who have not been resident in any of the previous three tax years.

Days spent in the UK during the tax year	*UK ties needed*
Up to 15	Automatically non-resident
16 – 45	Automatically non-resident
46-90	At least 4 ties
91-120	At least 3 ties
121 -182	At least 2 ties
183 or more	Automatically resident

The possible ties referred to above are as follows:

(1) A spouse, civil partner or child under 18 years old is UK resident.

(2) Accommodation is available in the UK for a continuous period of at least 91 days and at least one night is spent there during the tax year.
(3) Working in the UK on at least 40 days during the tax year.
(4) 90 days or more in the UK in either or both of the previous two tax years.

A final fifth test only applies to individuals who have been resident for one or more of the previous three tax years:

(5) The UK is the country in which the individual is present for the greatest number of days during that tax year.

Example 11.1

Bruce is visiting the UK for the first time in his lifetime, for a holiday and will remain in the UK from 1 May 2026 until he leaves on 8 June 2026, a total of 38 days.

Answer

As Bruce was not a UK resident for any of the previous three years and spent less than 46 days in the UK during the tax year, he meets one of the automatic overseas tests and is not a UK tax resident for 2026/27.

Example 11.2

Connie has always been a resident in the UK, spending at least 320 days in the UK every year, until she purchased a property in Spain and moved there to live on 5 April 2026. She keeps her home in the UK where her husband continues to live for the majority of the time. Connie visits her husband, staying in her UK home for 80 days during 2026/27. Connie is retired and does not work. What is Connie's UK tax residence status?

Answer

When looking at the automatic overseas tests, Connie fails as she has previously been resident and is in the UK for more than 16 days during 2026/27.

Next, we need to consider the automatic UK tests. Connie does not meet any of these as she was in the UK for less than 183 days, has an overseas home and is not working during 2026/27.

Therefore, we must consider the sufficient ties tests. As Connie is a "leaver" and was in the UK for 80 days, she will be considered a UK resident if she has three or more ties.

Connie has three ties (out of the five possible ties) as follows:

1. Connie's spouse is a UK resident.
2. Connie has accommodation available in the UK.
3. Connie spent more than 90 days in the UK in each of the previous two tax years.

Therefore, Connie will continue to be treated as a UK tax resident for 2026/27.

Notes

Connie's tax status in Spain will not impact the ruling on her UK tax status. By 2028/29 the third tie above may not be applicable and Connie may no longer be a UK resident.

Alternatively, Connie could reduce the number of days that she spends in the UK to 45, during 2026/27, in which case she would need four ties to be considered a UK resident.

Strictly, an individual is resident or not for the whole tax year. However, a tax year may be split in certain circumstances, for example where:

- an individual comes to the UK for permanent residence or starts to have a home in the UK;
- comes to the UK to work full-time;
- leaves the UK for permanent residence abroad and ceases to have a UK home; or
- leaves the UK to take up full-time employment abroad.

In these "split year" cases, a tax year is apportioned into periods of residence and non-residence.

New UK resident individuals – FIG regime

For over 200 years, non-UK domiciled, UK residents benefited from a special UK tax regime allowing unremitted income and gains to escape UK taxation. These special rules have been abolished from 6 April 2025 and are replaced with a new four-year foreign income and gains (FIG) regime.

The FIG regime is available to individuals during their first four years of UK tax residence after at least ten consecutive years of non-UK residence. Under the FIG regime, non-UK income and gains are fully exempt from UK taxation for the individual's first four years of UK residence. After these four years, all UK residents are taxable on their worldwide income and gains. For the FIG regime, residence will be determined using the statutory residence test. Years of UK residence before 6 April 2025 are included. Therefore, for individuals who have been UK tax residents since the 2021/22 tax year, their first four years of UK residence have passed and they will not be eligible. The FIG regime rules must be claimed on the appropriate self-assessment tax return. If the FIG regime rules are claimed, the individual will not be entitled to the income tax personal allowance and the capital gains tax annual exemption for the year.

As a result of these changes, domicile is no longer considered in UK income tax and capital gains tax issues.

Example 11.3

Nick arrived in the UK on 6 April 2026, having never previously been a UK resident. In addition to his UK income, he continues to hold savings overseas, earning interest and receives rent from several overseas properties.

How will Nick benefit from the FIG regime?

Answer

Normally, as a UK resident, Nick would be subject to UK income tax on his worldwide income. However, as he has not been a UK resident for ten consecutive years, he is eligible to claim the FIG regime rules for his overseas income.

Therefore, for 2026/27, 2027/28, 2028/29 and 2029/30, Nick can claim 100% relief from income tax and capital gains tax for his overseas savings and properties. After these initial four years, he will be taxable on his worldwide income and gains as any other UK resident. However, he will lose entitlement to his personal allowance and CGT annual exemption for the years covered by the FIG exemption.

Double tax relief

An individual may be a tax resident in more than one country and, therefore, may be taxed twice on the same income. The UK has entered into bilateral double tax treaties with many countries, which typically exempt such income from taxation in one of the countries, as specified in the individual treaty.

Otherwise, relief will be provided for overseas tax suffered against an individual's UK income tax liability. Such double tax relief (DTR) may be available either unilaterally (i.e. under the UK's domestic tax laws) or under a double tax treaty.

Any overseas income liable to UK tax is included "gross" (i.e. before foreign taxes are deducted).

In ascertaining the extent of any DTR, the credit for any foreign tax will be the lower of:

- the foreign tax paid on the foreign income; and
- the UK tax on that foreign income.

Example 11.4

John, a UK resident individual, received a salary of £25,000 for the tax year 2026/27.

In addition, during that tax year, John received overseas rental income of £1,950 after foreign tax of £1,050 had been deducted and interest on a foreign bank account of £8,000 after local foreign tax of £1,500 had been deducted.

Calculate John's income tax liability for 2026/27.

Answer

John is entitled to DTR on the two sources of overseas income.

First, it is necessary to calculate John's income tax liability on *all* income (i.e. his UK and foreign sources) before determining the amount of DTR.

	Non-Savings	Savings	Dividends
Employee income	25,000		
Overseas income:			
Rental income (Gross)	3,000		
Bank interest (Gross)		9,500	
Less:			
Personal allowance	(12,570)		
Taxable income	15,430	9,500	Nil

	Taxable income	Rate of tax	Tax liability
NSI	15,430	20%	3,086
SI	1,000	0%	0
	8,500	20%	1,700
	24,930		4,786

Therefore, income tax liability before DTR = 4,786

This amount is reduced by any foreign tax credit i.e. foreign tax paid on overseas income.

UK income tax charged on the foreign rental income = 3000 x 20%		= 600
Foreign tax paid on rental income		= 1,050
Therefore, DTR is the lower of the two figures i.e. 600.		
This procedure is now repeated for the foreign bank interest		
The UK income tax charged on the foreign bank income		= 1,700
Foreign tax paid on bank income		= 1,500
Therefore, DTR is the lower of the two figures i.e. 1,500		
Therefore:		
Income tax liability (pre-DTR)		= 4,786
Less:		
DTR on rental income	600	
DTR on bank income	1,500	
Total DTR		(2,100)
Net UK income tax liability		2,686

In the case of the foreign rental income, the UK income tax liability was less than the foreign tax paid on that income.

SUMMARY

- An individual's UK tax residence status for each tax year is determined by the statutory residence tests.
- UK resident individuals are liable to UK income tax on their worldwide income and gains.
- New UK tax residents may be able to benefit from an exemption from overseas income and capital gains for their first four years in the UK, under the FIG regime.
- Where tax is also paid overseas, Double tax relief (DTR) is available to reduce the UK income tax liability on the relevant overseas income but such DTR cannot exceed the UK income tax liability on that particular source of non-UK income.

CHAPTER 12

Pension Contributions

Introduction

In this chapter, we will consider income tax relief for payments by individuals into pension schemes and the limits on contributions attracting relief.

Most businesses no longer offer defined benefit schemes to their employees and instead contribute to defined contribution schemes. However, for the ease of clarity in this text, occupational schemes refers to defined benefit schemes.

Occupational pensions or defined benefit schemes

An occupational pension or defined benefit scheme is established by an employer to provide its employees with a pension on retirement. Most occupational pension schemes are approved by registering with HMRC. The approval means that several tax advantages are available to both employers and employees. Unless a scheme is registered with HMRC these tax advantages are not available.

Under this type of scheme, the amount of pension payable on retirement to an employee is linked to the employee's remuneration before retirement, together with the employee's length of service. Therefore, these schemes are often referred to as final salary schemes. In this text, these schemes are referred to as occupational pension schemes, although some occupational schemes could, in real life, be defined contribution schemes.

A typical occupational pension scheme will require the employee to make contributions to the pension fund out of their salary whilst working for the employer. The employer will deduct each month (or week) this contribution from the employee's gross salary before the calculation of income tax under PAYE, therefore immediately giving income tax relief on the contributions (In income tax computations, show the gross salary and deduct the employee's occupational pension contributions - See Chapter 10). An employer may also contribute to this fund on behalf of its employees.

Example 12.1

Ali is employed by DEF Limited. He received a salary of £55,000 and taxable benefits in kind of £6,600. Ali contributes 4% of his salary to his employer's occupational pension scheme and this contribution is matched by his employer.

What is Ali's taxable employment income?

Answer

Salary	55,000
Less Ali's occupational pension contributions (4%)	(2,200)
Add Taxable benefits in kind	6,600
Taxable employment income	59,400

Notes

The employer's pension contributions are not taxable or deductible but will be included when calculating pension savings for the annual allowance.

For the employer, any pension contributions made on behalf of employees are tax deductible in computing trading profits. There is also no upper limit on employer contributions, although in certain circumstances relief may be spread over a number of years.

For the employee, the contributions made on their behalf by their employer are not taxable as benefits for income tax purposes (see Chapter 10). As mentioned above, an employee's contributions to an occupational pension scheme are deducted in arriving at taxable employment income. There is no relief for NIC purposes.

At retirement, pensions are taxable even when payable under an approved scheme. However, an employee may commute a part of their pension entitlement into a tax-free cash lump sum. After any such commutation, the remaining pension payable will be reduced.

Personal pensions or defined contribution schemes (Money purchase schemes)

Personal pension schemes, sometimes referred to as defined contribution schemes, were originally primarily for those who are self-employed. In addition, some employees, whether or not a member of an occupational pension scheme, may now also take out a personal pension. As mentioned above, employers may establish defined contribution schemes on behalf of their employees.

The benefits on retirement from Personal pension schemes are wholly dependent upon the amount of the contributions and the tax-free investment growth within the pension fund and not on the employee's final salary. However, there are defined limits on the contributions that may be paid.

At retirement (or at any time from age 55, increasing to 57 from 6 April 2028), several options are available, for example, drawing 25% of the fund as a tax-free lump sum and purchasing a pension (referred to as an annuity) with the balance. This annuity is taxable and there is a limit on the maximum tax-free lump sum.

As with occupational pension schemes, there are tax benefits available for personal pension schemes assuming the scheme is approved by HMRC (see below).

Unlike occupational schemes, where an employee contributes to a personal pension it is unusual for an employer to also contribute. However, where the employer does contribute, a tax deduction in computing the employer's trading profits will normally be given. The employer's contribution will not be treated as a taxable benefit on the part of the employee.

Contributions by an individual are made net of basic rate tax (i.e. net of 20%). In other words, on making the contribution the individual deducts income tax at source at the rate of 20%. The pension fund itself may then claim back from HMRC the tax deducted which is then added to the individual's fund.

However, the individual is entitled to tax relief at their highest rate of tax i.e. 40% or 45%. Where, for example, an individual is liable to income tax at 40% the extra 20% of tax relief (i.e. 40% less 20% at source) is obtained by extending their basic and higher rate bands by the gross allowable personal pension contributions (see Chapter 4).

Example 12.2

Sandra makes a net pension contribution of £8,000 in 2026/27 to a personal pension scheme. On making the payment Sandra deducted income tax at the basic rate of 20% from the gross payment. Therefore, we must "gross up" the net contribution to determine the gross amount:

Net 8,000 x 100/80= 10,000 gross

If Sandra is a higher or additional rate taxpayer (i.e. she pays tax at the 40% or 45% rate) then she will be entitled to further tax relief which will be obtained by extending the basic rate and higher rate bands by her gross contribution of £10,000. Therefore, Sandra's basic rate band will be extended from £37,700 to £47,700, with a similar extension to the higher rate band (See Chapter 4).

Pension contribution limits

Income tax relief will be available on pension contributions paid by UK resident individuals aged under 75, subject to the following limits.

There are two limits to the pension contributions that may be relieved in any tax year. First, a limit on the amount that qualifies for income tax relief and secondly, a check to see if the annual allowance has been exceeded.

The limit on pension contributions that qualify for income tax relief is an amount equal to the greater of £3,600 gross and the individual's relevant UK earnings for the tax year. Relevant UK earnings include employment income, self-employed profits and partnership trading profits. Where an individual has low or no UK relevant earnings, their maximum limit is £3,600 (£2,880 net) per year. Non-taxpayers may also make use of this lower limit to obtain basic rate tax relief on pension contributions.

However, pension savings over the annual allowance, currently £60,000 per year (subject to a restriction for individuals with adjusted income above £260,000) will give rise to an annual allowance charge. For this calculation, pension savings include all tax allowable pension contributions of the individual as well as any employer contributions.

Where an individual does not fully use their annual allowance, any balance is carried forward for up to three years and may be utilised after the current year's annual allowance on the basis of the earliest year first ("FIFO"). This unused amount may only be carried forward where the individual was a member of a pension scheme for the earlier year. (Until 5 April 2023, the annual allowance was £40,000)

Example 12.3

Iwan has taxable profits from his self-employment for 2026/27 of £135,000. Iwan first joined a personal pension scheme in 2025/26 when he contributed £25,000.

What is the maximum amount of pension contributions that Iwan can obtain income tax relief on for 2026/27 and how much could be paid without exceeding his available annual allowance?

Answer

Iwan's maximum limit for tax relief on pensions for 2026/27 is £135,000, equal to his relevant earnings. However, if contributions exceed his annual allowance plus any unused allowances brought forward, he will be subject to an annual allowance charge.

Annual allowance for 2026/27			60,000
Unused annual allowance brought forward:			
2023/24	Not available as not a member of a pension scheme		
2024/25	Not available as not a member of a pension scheme		
2025/26	Annual allowance	60,000	
	Used	(25,000)	
	Balance to carry forward		35,000
Maximum annual allowance for 2026/27			95,000

Iwan may, therefore, make pension contributions of £95,000 gross (£76,000 net) during 2026/27 without incurring an annual allowance charge.

Basic rate tax relief is obtained by paying the contributions net and any higher rate relief will be obtained by extending his basic rate band by the gross amount of his contributions (See chapter 4).

Where an individual's adjusted income exceeds £260,000, the annual allowance is reduced. The reduction is £1 for every £2 above £260,000 subject to a minimum allowance of £10,000. Adjusted income is calculated as total income plus any occupational pension contributions paid personally and by their employer. This restriction will only apply where an individual has threshold income above £200,000. The threshold income is net income less any personal pension contributions. This threshold test ensures that a one-off increase in employer contributions does not lead to the individual coming into the charge.

Annual allowance charge

Where pension savings (or "Pension Inputs") exceed the annual allowance, an annual allowance charge will apply. The individual will receive income tax relief as normal on their full contributions up to the relevant earnings but the pension savings over the annual allowance will be charged to income tax as the highest slice of the income. This charge does not form part of the calculation of the individual's taxable income, it just gives rise to this charge. Therefore, for example, it is not included when calculating adjusted net income to establish the personal allowance.

Example 12.4

Lana's income for 2026/27 is as follows:

Employment	160,000
Self-employment	45,000
Bank interest	11,000
Dividends	8,000

During the year Lana paid net personal pension contributions of £36,000. In addition, she pays 10% of her employment income into an occupational pension and this is matched by her employer. Lana has unused Annual allowances brought forward from previous years of £7,200.

Calculate Lana's income tax liability for 2026/27 including any annual allowance charge.

Answer

Lana's rate bands will be extended by her GROSS personal pension contributions:

Net £36,000 x 100/80 = £45,000 (See chapter 4). Her basic rate band is therefore increased from 37,700 to 82,700 and her higher rate band from 125,140 to 170,140.

	Non-Savings	**Savings**	**Dividends**	**Total**
Employment	160,000			
Less				
Occupational pension contribs.	(16,000)			
Self-Employment	45,000			
Bank interest		11,000		
Dividends			8,000	
Totals	189,000	11,000	8,000	
Less: PA	-			
Taxable income	189,000	11,000	8,000	208,800

Non-savings	£
82,700 @ 20%	16,540
87,440 @ 40%	34,976
18,860 @ 45%	8,487
Savings	
11,000 @ 45%	4,950
Dividends	
500 @ 0%	-
7,500 @ 39.35%	2,951
Annual allowance charge (See below)	

9,800 @ 45%	4,410	
Income tax liability	72,314	

Annual allowance for 2026/27	60,000
Add: Unused brought forward	7,200
Less: Total pension savings for 2026/27	
Gross personal pension contributions	(45,000)
Occupational pension contributions	
Employee	(16,000)
Employer	(16,000)
Excess pension savings	9,800

Notes

Lana's personal allowance is reduced to nil as her adjusted net income exceeds £125,140.

The income tax liability is calculated as normal, giving income tax relief as appropriate for both the personal pension contributions and the employee's occupational pension contributions.

The total pension savings are then compared with the annual allowance for 2026/27 and the unused annual allowance brought forward to find the excess. This is then taxed at the highest marginal rate, in this case after the dividends. As the basic and higher rate bands have been used in full, this is taxed at the additional rate of 45%.

Money purchase annual allowance

Where an individual has started to flexibly draw down on their personal pension fund, the money purchase annual allowance limits the maximum personal pension contributions that can qualify for tax relief to £10,000 per tax year. This restriction will not apply where the full pension fund has been drawn as a tax free lump sum (up to 25% of the fund) plus a lifetime annuity. Also, the limit does not apply to occupational pension scheme contributions.

Lifetime allowance

In addition to the annual limits, an overall lifetime allowance was introduced. However, this charge is abolished from 6 April 2023.

SUMMARY

- Pensions, whether state, occupational or personal, are taxable on the recipient as non-savings income.
- Contributions to occupational or personal pension funds attract income tax relief for individuals. How income tax relief is given, however, differs.
- Tax relief for contributions to an occupational pension scheme is obtained by the employee deducting the contributions from his or her salary.
- In the case of personal pension contributions tax relief is obtained by way of a basic rate deduction from contributions plus an extension of the basic and higher rate bands.
- When making contributions, individuals must be aware of the limits for income tax relief and the annual allowance charge.

Questions for students

See Appendix 2 for practice questions relating to Chapter 12. Answers are available online at https://spiramus.com/uk-taxation-for-students-20267-answers.

CHAPTER 13

Capital Gains Tax: General Principles

Introduction

This chapter introduces capital gains tax and considers how an individual's capital gains and losses are calculated and the rates of capital gains tax. We will then consider some of the reliefs that may enable a capital gains tax liability to be reduced or avoided.

Basic principles

Capital gains tax (CGT) is a tax on the profit made on the disposal of *capital* assets, for example, shares, properties and antiques. If the sale is in the course of a trade, then it would be subject to income tax as trading income. For example, the one-off sale of a painting by an individual may give rise to a capital gain but the sale of the same painting by an art dealer is likely to be trading income. The badges of trade (Chapter 6 Appendix) would be used to consider if a transaction is taxable as trading income or subject to CGT.

Only *individuals* are liable to capital gains tax. Companies are not liable to capital gains tax although they are liable to corporation tax on capital gains (see Chapter 17). Partnerships are not chargeable – any gain is divided between the individual partners.

However, not all capital assets are liable to capital gains tax when disposed of (see below).

Technically speaking, a liability to capital gains tax arises when a chargeable person (e.g. an individual) makes a chargeable disposal (e.g. a sale) of a chargeable asset (e.g. a painting).

At its simplest, a capital gain on the sale of a capital asset is computed as follows:

Sale proceeds	£35,000
Less:	
Cost of asset	£15,000
Capital gain	£20,000

As will be seen below, the actual computation can be a little more complicated.

For example, the "Cost of asset" may include elements of expenditure other than simply the original cost of the asset.

In any tax year, capital gains from the sales of assets are aggregated and any capital losses are offset giving, for any individual, either a net capital gain or net capital loss (note that how losses are offset can be very important).

The annual exemption

Every individual is entitled to an annual CGT exemption, which is £3,000 for the tax year to 5 April 2027.

This represents the value of gains that an individual can make in the tax year free of CGT. It is the last item to be deducted when calculating an individual's capital gains for a tax year. It cannot be carried forward or backwards if unused and it cannot be surrendered to any other individual (for example, a husband cannot surrender any unused portion to his wife or vice versa). It is not available to companies and special rules apply to trusts.

Chargeable assets

All assets are liable to CGT unless they are exempt.

Examples of capital or more correctly chargeable assets, include:

- paintings
- jewellery
- listed and unlisted shares
- goodwill of a business
- plant and machinery
- land and buildings and leases
- cryptocurrency.

Exempt capital assets include:

- National Savings certificates and premium bonds
- motor vehicles suitable for private use (but not personalised number plates)
- most government securities
- decorations awarded for valour, unless acquired through purchase
- life assurance policies when held by the original beneficial owner
- investments held within Individual Savings Accounts (ISAs)
- foreign currency for the individual's private use
- pension rights
- prizes and betting winnings
- tangible movable property with a life of 50 years or less (wasting chattels) except items of plant and machinery subject to capital allowance claims.
- a house occupied exclusively throughout the period of ownership as a main residence.

Any disposals to a charity are also exempt.

Chargeable disposal

A charge to CGT can arise whenever there is a disposal. Usually, this follows the sale of an asset but other types of chargeable disposal include:

- the gift of an asset
- the loss or destruction of an asset;

- the creation of one asset out of another e.g. the grant of a lease out of a freehold;
- the receipt of compensation (e.g. insurance proceeds; other than for personal injury or wrongs).

Disposal proceeds are usually the amount received less any incidental costs of sale, for example, auctioneer fees. In the case of a gift to anyone, or a sale at undervalue, the sale proceeds are replaced by the market value at the time of the disposal. This market value will be treated as the cost for the person acquiring the asset.

Connected persons

An individual is connected with:

- their spouse or civil partner;
- their relatives (in this case meaning brothers, sisters, ancestors (i.e. parents) and lineal descendants (i.e., children, grandchildren etc.));
- the relatives of their spouse or civil partner; and
- the spouses/civil partners of their relatives and to their spouse/civil partner's relatives.

Transactions between connected persons are treated as if any gift or sale is, in fact, a sale at the market value of the asset at the appropriate date. The actual price paid, if any, is irrelevant.

Also, any capital loss arising on a connected person transaction can only be offset against capital gains of the same or future tax years on disposals to the same person.

Inter-spouse transfers

Spouses and civil partners are treated as two separate persons for CGT (as they are for income tax purposes) and each is therefore entitled to their own annual exemption.

Losses of one spouse/civil partner cannot be offset against the gains of the other.

However, disposals between spouses or civil partners living together do not give rise to chargeable gains or allowable losses. At the date of the transfer, the asset is assumed to have been transferred at its cost. This will then give neither a gain nor a loss to the transferor.

The cost of the asset to the recipient is the same as the cost to the donor.

On a subsequent sale of the asset, the calculation would follow the normal rules.

Example 13.1

Colin purchased an asset in April 2010 for £13,000. He transferred it to his wife Mary on 16 July 2018 when it had a market value of £18,000. Mary then sold it on 1 June 2026 for £30,000. Mary made no other disposals during 2026/27.

Show the CGT position for Colin and Mary.

Answer

When Colin transferred the asset to Mary no chargeable gain arose. Mary is assumed to have acquired the asset at no gain/no loss to Colin and her cost will, therefore, be £13,000. On the sale in 2026/27, Mary's CGT position would be as follows:

	£
Disposal proceeds	30,000
Less: Cost	(13,000)
Gain	17,000
Less:	
Annual exemption	(3,000)
Taxable gains	14,000

Notes

If Colin and Mary were not married, Colin would have been treated as disposing of the asset on 16 July 2018 at its market value of £18,000 giving rise to a capital gain of £5,000 (£18,000 - £13,000). Mary would be treated as acquiring the asset at market value and therefore her gain on the sale on 1 June 2026 would have been £12,000 (£30,000 - £18,000). The total gain remains at £17,000 - £5,000 for Colin and £12,000 for Mary.

From 6 April 2023, couples that have separated can still claim no gain/no loss treatment for up to three years after they cease to live together, or longer as part of a formal divorce agreement.

The timing of a disposal

This is normally the *date of an unconditional contract* for the disposal *not* the date of receipt of the proceeds. This is usually when legal ownership of the asset changes.

A gift is made on the date when ownership of the asset changes hands.

An asset lost is disposed of at the time of loss, but, if compensation is received (e.g. from an insurance company) the date of disposal is normally the date of receipt of the compensation.

Allowable expenditure

This comprises three elements:

- *cost*
    - o the price paid or
    - o market value when an item is received as a gift or
    - o probate value at date of death if inherited.
- ***the incidental costs of acquisition and disposal***
  i.e. fees for professional services; advertising costs.

- ***enhancement costs so long as they are reflected in the nature of the asset at the date of disposal***
  i.e. an extension to a property.

Legal costs of defending the title to an asset would also be included as part of the cost of the asset.

It is *not* possible to deduct expenditure which is:

- deductible from trading income as a trading expense; *or*
- interest on a loan taken out to acquire the asset; *or*
- recoverable from a third party.

Example 13.2

Helen bought an asset in May 2024 for a cost of £15,000 plus incidental costs of acquisition of £500. She sold the asset two years later for £17,500 and incurred further costs on disposal of £250.

Calculate Helen's capital gain.

Answer

Gross sale proceeds	17,500
Less: Incidental costs of disposal	(250)
Net sale proceeds	17,250
Less:	
Cost of asset	(15,000)
Incidental costs of acquisition	(500)
Capital gain	1,750

Example 13.3

Grant inherited an asset in July 2021 on the death of his Aunt. The Aunt had purchased the asset in 1998 for a cost of £6,000 and the probate value on her death was £20,000. Grant sold the asset in 2026 for £34,000 and incurred further costs on disposal of £500.

Calculate Grant's capital gain.

Answer

Gross sale proceeds	34,000
Less: Incidental costs of disposal	(500)
Net sale proceeds	33,500
Less:	
Cost of asset – Probate value	(20,000)
Capital gain	12,500

Notes

Grant paid nothing for the asset. As he inherited it on his Aunt's death, his cost is treated as the probate value of £20,000. The original cost to his Aunt is ignored.

If an asset was acquired on or before 31 March 1982, then the cost is replaced by the value of the asset at 31 March 1982.

Part disposals

There may be occasions where a disposal is made of only part of the original asset that was acquired. For example, an antique table and chairs could be acquired as a set at auction and at a later date, only the table is sold. More commonly this section may apply where a parcel of land is acquired, part is retained and part sold, for example, a 10-hectare field is acquired as pasture and subsequently two hectares are sold to a developer. These rules do not apply to shares.

In these circumstances, the cost of the part sold must be established. The cost of the part disposed of is determined by the formula A/A+B, where A represents the gross consideration for the disposal and B the market value of the remaining property.

Example 13.4

Ian bought a 10-hectare field in April 2005 for a total cost of £30,000. He sold two hectares to a developer in May 2026 for £25,000. As at May 2026, the remaining eight hectares have a market value of £40,000.

Calculate Ian's capital gain.

Answer

First, establish the "cost" of the part sold using A/A+B

A = the consideration for the disposal i.e. £25,000

B = the market value of the remaining property i.e. £40,000

Cost of land sold: Total cost £30,000 x (25,000/(25,000+40,000)) = 11,538

(The balance of the cost (£18,462) relates to the eight hectares retained)

Gain on disposal of 2 hectares May 2026

Sale proceeds	25,000
Cost (as calculated)	(11,538)
Gain	13,462

For small part disposals of land, the individual may elect to deduct the sale proceeds from the cost, so that no gain arises until a subsequent sale. For these purposes, small means that the proceeds of the part disposal do not exceed £20,000 and the consideration does not exceed 20% of the market value of the whole piece of land as it comprised immediately before the disposal.

Chattels

As noted above, chattels (tangible moveable property – something that you can touch, move and legally own) that are wasting assets (with a life expectancy of 50 years or less) are usually exempt from capital gains tax. This would include, for example, boats, clocks and animals. Gains on the sale of plant and machinery items that have been included in a capital allowances claim are not exempt (any losses will not be allowable for CGT purposes).

Any gain (or loss) arising on the sale of a non-wasting chattel, for example, antique furniture, jewellery or paintings, is exempt where both the disposal proceeds and cost do not exceed £6,000.

If the proceeds exceed £6,000 but the cost is £6,000 or less, any gain arising is restricted to 5/3 of the gross consideration less £6,000. Effectively, the assessable gain will be the lower of this amount and the gain calculated under normal rules.

Finally, as the gains can be exempt or restricted, there is also a restriction on any losses arising. If a non-wasting chattel is acquired for more than £6,000 and the sale proceeds are £6,000 or less, the sale proceeds are deemed to be £6,000, therefore reducing any allowable loss.

These rules are summarised in the following table:

<table>
<tr><th></th><th></th><th colspan="2">Proceeds</th></tr>
<tr><th></th><th></th><th>Up to £6,000</th><th>Over £6,000</th></tr>
<tr><td rowspan="2">Cost</td><td>Up to £6,000</td><td>Exempt</td><td>Restrict gain to
5/3 x (Gross proceeds - £6,000)</td></tr>
<tr><td>Over £6,000</td><td>Loss arises.
Treat sale proceeds as £6,000</td><td>Normal gain</td></tr>
</table>

Example 13.5

Donald sells four individual paintings that are not part of a set during 2026/27.

The first painting cost £2,500 and was sold for £5,800. As the cost and proceeds are both less than £6,000, the gain is exempt.

The second painting cost £3,000 and was sold for £9,000. The gain is calculated as £6,000 (£9,000-£3,000). However, the gain is restricted to 5/3 x the gross proceeds less £6,000. This is £5,000 (5/3 x (9,000-6,000)). The gain is therefore reduced to £5,000.

The third painting cost £7,000 and was sold for £10,000. As both of these amounts are above £6,000 there is no adjustment and the gain is £3,000.

The final painting was purchased for £7,000 and was sold for £5,000. As the painting cost more than £6,000 but was sold for less than this amount, then the loss is restricted by treating the sale proceeds as £6,000. This gives an allowable loss of £1,000 (£6,000-£7,000).

Private or main residence relief

For most individuals, the largest or perhaps only capital gain that they will make in their lifetime is on the sale of their main residence. Fortunately, if the property was occupied by the owner throughout their period of ownership as their main residence, the gain is fully exempt from CGT. The exemption can include gardens or grounds, usually up to 0.5 hectares.

If this is not the case, the gain is apportioned on a time basis between periods of occupation as a main residence and other periods. The proportion of the gain apportioned to occupation as a main residence is exempt from CGT and the balance is chargeable.

However, the rules are even more generous and some periods of absence are deemed to be periods of occupation, further reducing the chargeable gain.

First, the last nine months of ownership are treated as a period of occupation, whether so occupied or not, provided that the property has actually been the owner's main residence at some time. (This was introduced, for example, to avoid a CGT liability when an individual acquires a new private residence but has a delay selling their old home).

Example 13.6

Sandra bought her house on 1 June 2016 for £70,000. She lived in the house until 30 December 2023 when she moved in to live with her parents. Sandra's house remained unoccupied until it was sold on 31 May 2026 for £160,000.

Calculate Sandra's capital gain.

Answer

Sale proceeds May 2026	160,000
Less: Cost June 2016	(70,000)
Gain	90,000
Main residence relief (100/120)	(75,000)
Taxable gain	15,000

Notes

The house was owned for 120 months. Sandra occupied the house as her main residence for 91 months. In addition, the last nine months of ownership are treated as a period of deemed occupation. Therefore, 100 months of the gain are exempt. The exempt gain is calculated as 90,000 x 100/120 months.

In addition, certain other periods of absence will be treated as occupied. However, these rules require that the property is occupied as the owner's main residence *both* before *and* after the period of absence. The periods that may be deemed to be periods of occupation are:

1. any period or periods of absence, for any reason, up to three years in total;
2. any period or periods up to four years in total where the owner was required to live elsewhere for reasons of work in the UK; and
3. any period where the owner works overseas.

These periods may be aggregated to cover a longer period.

Example 13.7

Lindsey bought a house in Birmingham in January 2013 for £105,000 and lived there as her main residence until June 2016. She decided to go travelling with a friend and remained outside the UK until she returned to her house at the end of December 2018. After living in the house for 15 months, Lindsey was seconded to work in Glasgow and lived there for five years, returning to her house in April 2025. After living in the house for eight months, Lindsey moved to live with a friend and the house was eventually sold for £240,000 in December 2026.

What is her chargeable gain?

Answer	£	
Sale proceeds	240,000	
Less: Cost	(105,000)	
Gain	135,000	
Main residence relief 158/168 months	(126,964)	*See below*
Chargeable gain	8,036	

Main residence relief calculation:

From January 2013 to June 2016	Actual occupation	42 months
July 2016 to December 2018	Absent	30 months
January 2019 to March 2020	Actual occupation	15 months
April 2020 to March 2025	Absent (Work in the UK)	60 months
April 2025 to November 2025	Actual occupation	8 months
December 2025 to December 2026	Absent	13 months
Total period of ownership		168 months

Lindsey had a total of 103 months (30+60+13) out of 168 months of total ownership when she was absent from the property but we must consider whether any of these months can be treated as occupied.

First, the last nine months of ownership are always treated as a period of occupation and this rule will, therefore, cover 9 months of the 13 month period of absence from December 2025 to December 2026.

Then we must look at the other periods of absence. The 30 month period commencing July 2016 was both preceded and followed by a period of actual occupation, therefore this can be treated as a period of occupation using up 30 months of the three-year limit, under condition 1) above.

The period of 60 months commencing April 2020 was again both preceded and followed by a period of actual occupation. As Lindsey was absent due to working elsewhere in the UK, four years or 48 months of this period can be treated as occupied under condition 2). However, in addition, the remaining six months of the three years for any reason may also be used, giving 54 months in total treated as occupied.

Therefore, Lindsey had 65 months of actual occupation (42+15+8) plus 93 months of deemed occupation (9+30+54) giving a total of 158 months treated as a main residence. Therefore, there are only 10 months during which Lindsey is not treated as occupying the house. Lindsey will therefore only be taxable on 10/168th of the gain.

If there is a delay in occupying a main residence following acquisition due to construction, redecoration or alteration, or the delay of the sale of a previous main residence, then provided that the period does not exceed 24 months, it will be treated as a period of occupation as a main residence.

An individual may only have one main residence. A taxpayer has two years from the date of first having two residences to elect for one of them to be treated as their main residence, otherwise, the question will be determined by HMRC based on the facts of each case. Such an election may then be altered at a subsequent date. A married couple may only have one main residence between them.

If part of a residence is used exclusively for business purposes, this proportion of the gain will not be eligible for main residence relief.

An additional relief arises when part of a main residence is let. The relief only applies to periods when the owner also continues to occupy part of the property as his or her main residence. The gain that is chargeable due to the period of letting is reduced by the lower of £40,000, the amount of main residence relief or the gain attributable to the period of letting.

Example 13.8

Rosie sold her main residence for a gain of £200,000 in May 2026. Throughout her 12 years of ownership, 25% of the property was let out, whilst Rosie remained in occupation.

The gain not covered by main residence relief is £200,000 x 25% = £50,000

However, letting relief will be available. This will be limited to the lower of

1) £40,000; 2) £150,000; or 3) £50,000.

The taxable gain will £50,000 - £40,000 = £10,000

Calculating the capital gains tax liability

Capital gains are effectively taxed as though they are the highest part of an individual's income (see Chapter 2).

In other words, *income tax* is charged on non-savings, savings and then dividend income as normal (see Chapter 2) and then any capital gains are treated as on top of these categories and taxed appropriately.

Any capital gains falling into the basic rate band are charged at 18%. Any gains that exceed the basic rate band are charged at 24%.

Personal allowances and other income tax reliefs *cannot* be deducted from capital gains. However, any extension to rate bands due to charitable donations under gift aid or personal pension contributions will be available.

Example 13.9

In the tax year 2026/27, David made capital gains of £14,500 before the annual exemption. His taxable income for the tax year is £42,500. Calculate David's CGT liability.

Answer

Capital gains	14,500
Less:	
Annual exemption	(3,000)
Taxable gains	11,500

As David's taxable income (42,500) exceeds the 37,700 basic rate band limit all of the taxable gains are taxed at the higher rate of 24%.

The CGT is therefore 11,500 x 24% = £2,760

Note that if David's basic rate band was increased for gift aid or personal pension contributions, then this extended rate band would also apply to capital gains.

Example 13.10

Heather makes a capital gain, after the annual exemption, of £14,600 in 2026/27.

Her taxable income (all non-savings) for the tax year 2026/27 is £28,000.

Calculate Heather's CGT liability.

Answer

Basic rate band 37,700 less taxable income 28,000 = balance available 9,700

		Rate	**Tax**
		%	£
	9,700	18	1,746
	4,900 (gain: 14,600 – 9,700)	24	1,176
Total capital gains tax payable			2,922

Note that part (£9,700) of Heather's capital gain uses the balance of the basic rate band and is taxed at 18% with the balance of the gain (£4,900) then being taxed at 24%.

Using capital losses

On any sale of a capital asset a capital loss, as opposed to a capital gain, may arise. This would, of course, occur if the sale proceeds were less than the original cost.

Example 13.11

Hugh bought an asset for a cost of £10,000 and sold it for sale proceeds of £8,000. What is his capital gain/loss?

Answer

£8,000 - £10,000 = £2,000 capital loss.

Current year capital losses

Capital losses must be offset against other capital gains of the same tax year, before utilising the annual exemption, which may therefore be wasted.

Carried forward capital losses

Where in a tax year, the total capital losses exceed the total capital gains, the excess capital losses can be carried forward to the succeeding tax years but never carried back (except in the year of death (see below)).

Surplus capital losses in any tax year may only be carried forward for offset against any net capital gains of future tax years. Net capital gains for a tax year refers to capital gains less capital losses for that year. Thus, *current* year capital losses must be offset against *current* year capital gains *before* any capital losses brought forward may be used.

Any capital losses brought forward are deducted before the annual exemption. However, losses brought forward are only required to reduce the gains to an amount equal to the annual exemption. Therefore, the annual exemption need not be wasted.

Example 13.12

Alka has the following gains and losses:

	2024/25	2025/26	2026/27
Gains	2,000	7,000	6,500
Losses	9,000	5,000	1,000

Calculate Alka's capital gains/loss position for each of the above tax years.

Answer

	2024/25	2025/26	2026/27
Gains	2,000	7,000	6,500
Losses	(9,000)	(5,000)	(1,000)
Current Net gains/losses	(7,000)	2,000	5,500
Less:			
Capital loss b/f	0	0 (note 1)	(2,500) (note 2)
Net gains/losses	(7,000)	2,000	3,000
Annual exemption	Wasted	(2,000)	(3,000)
Assessable gains	0	0	0

Notes

1. The capital loss brought forward from 2024/25 is £7,000. However, none of this is used in 2025/26 as the current year's net gains are less than the annual exemption of £3,000 for 2025/26 (£2,000 of the annual exemption is used and the balance is wasted). Therefore, the £7,000 loss is carried forward to 2026/27.
2. It is only necessary to utilise capital losses brought forward to leave chargeable gains equal to the annual exemption of £3,000. Therefore only £2,500 losses are utilised in 2026/27, leaving a balance of £4,500 (7,000 - 2,500) to carry forward against future gains.

Optimal usage of capital losses and annual exemption

There is little choice in how capital losses can be utilised. Losses arising in the year must be offset against current year gains, even if as a result the annual exemption is wasted.

Year of death

Death does not give rise to a disposal of assets for CGT.

In the year of death any capital losses arising in that year, on disposals made before death, may be *carried back to the three tax years* preceding the tax year of death on a LIFO basis and offset against gains assessable in those years.

However, any losses in the year of death must be first offset against gains of that year to the fullest extent.

The losses carried back are relieved against the most recent tax year first but the losses so relieved must be such as to leave in charge sufficient gains equal to the annual exemption for that tax year and similarly for earlier tax years.

The cost of any assets inherited on the death of an individual is treated as the market value at the date of death (the probate value).

Date of payment of CGT

Normally CGT is payable on the 31 January following the tax year in which the gain arose with any income tax/NIC balancing payment. There are no interim payments on account as is the case for income tax (see Chapter 21).

However, for residential property sales, the gain must be reported and the CGT paid within 60 days of completion of the sale. As the individual's overall tax position for the year may not be known at the time, an estimate may be required taking into account any losses already crystallised during the year, any losses brought forward and the annual exemption.

SUMMARY

- Only individuals are liable to capital gains tax. Companies are liable to corporation tax on chargeable gains.
- A capital gain arises when a chargeable person makes a chargeable disposal of a chargeable asset.
- Certain assets are exempt from capital gains tax.
- Individuals are entitled to an annual capital gains tax exemption of £3,000 for 2026/27.
- The rate of capital gains tax is determined by the individual's taxable income. Gains sit on top of income to determine the appropriate rate band. Any gains falling within the basic rate band are taxed at 18% and 24% once the basic rate band has been fully utilised. If the rate bands have been extended (see Chapter 4), then these extended rate bands apply.
- Current year capital losses are offset against current year capital gains before any brought forward unused capital losses and the annual exemption.
- Usually, capital gains tax is due for payment in one lump sum on 31 January following the tax year in which the gains arose. However, on

gains relating to the sale of residential property, the capital gains tax liability is payable within 60 days of completion.

CHAPTER 14

Capital Gains Tax: Shares and Securities

Introduction

This chapter looks at the capital gains tax position on the sale of shares and securities by individuals.

Government stocks and corporate bonds

Government stocks (Gilts) and most commercial bonds i.e. company loan notes (qualifying corporate bonds (QCB)) etc. are *exempt* from capital gains tax when they are held by individuals.

Shares

There is no equivalent exemption from CGT in respect of share disposals by individuals. Disposals of shares, therefore, give rise to either capital gains and/or capital losses.

The main problem when working out the capital gain/loss which may arise on a share sale is identifying which shares in a particular company of those acquired at various different times have been sold.

Example 14.1

Joan has purchased the following ordinary shares in ABC plc:
100 shares on 1 March 2006 for £4,000
50 shares on 3 August 2008 for £1,400
300 shares on 6 October 2012 for £6,250
On 19 September 2026, Joan sold 380 shares.
The question is which of the shares has Joan sold?

Matching rules: for individuals

The tax legislation lays down the following so-called *matching rules* i.e. on any sale of shares of the *same class in the same company* the shares sold are to be matched as follows:

1. with shares acquired *on the same day*, then
2. with shares acquired *within 30 days after* the disposal on a FIFO basis, then
3. with shares acquired *before the date of disposal – the share pool.*

Same day

Any shares which have been acquired on the same day as any sales are assumed to have been sold first (even if the purchase takes place later in the day after the sale).

Following 30 days

This may seem strange and this rule was introduced to counter a practice known as "bed and breakfasting" used, for example, to trigger a loss, then reacquiring the same shares. Thus, any shares which have been acquired within 30 days after the date of any sale are assumed to have been sold next.

Share Pool

Any pool can only contain shares of the same class in the same company (e.g. ordinary 50p shares in ABC plc; or ordinary 25p shares in XYZ plc). In effect, all acquisitions in the pool are combined to establish an average price per share.

Computational procedure

To work out the capital gain/loss on a share sale a number of separate calculations may be necessary. In some circumstances, where the entire shareholding is sold and there are no purchases in the next 30 days, this may be a simple case of deducting the cost of all the shares purchased from the sale proceeds.

However, when only part of the shareholding is sold, then the shares sold must be identified or matched with specific purchases.

The basic approach is to work through the matching rules, matching shares sold with purchases.

STEP 1

Match shares sold with shares acquired on the same day.

Calculate capital gain/loss on these matched shares.

If the number of shares sold exceeds the shares acquired on the same day, then continue to STEP 2 (if this is not the case no further computation is necessary).

STEP 2

Match the shares sold not already matched under STEP 1 with shares acquired in the next 30 days.

Calculate capital gain/loss on these matched shares.

If the number of shares sold exceeds the shares matched under STEPS 1 and 2 then continue to STEP 3.

STEP 3

Match the shares sold not already matched under STEPS 1 and 2 with the shares in the share pool.

Calculate capital gain/loss on these matched shares.

STEP 4

Aggregate the net gains and losses from STEPS 1 to 3 to produce one single capital gain or loss.

Example 14.1 continued from above

As there are no same day or next 30-day acquisitions, the shares sold will be matched with the share pool – effectively an average cost approach.

100+50+300 = 450 shares held before the sale

Total cost 4,000+1,400+6,250 = 11,650

Cost of 380 shares sold: 11,650 x 380/450 = £9,838

Example 14.2

On 1 March 2027, Mehwish sold 3,000 shares in XYZ Ltd for £21,000, after deducting any incidental costs of disposal. Mehwish purchased shares in XYZ Ltd as follows:

	Shares	**Cost**
17 September 2019	2,000	£5,000
3 January 2022	1,500	£2,000
1 March 2027	400	£2,750
25 March 2027	300	£1,900

Calculate Mehvish's capital gain/loss position for the tax year 2026/27.

Answer

STEP 1 [same day]

Of the shares sold on 1 March 2027, 400 are matched with the shares acquired on this date.

	£
Sale proceeds [400/3,000 x £21,000]	2,800
Less: Cost	(2,750)
Gain	50

STEP 2 [next 30 days]

Of the shares sold on 1 March 2027, 300 are matched with shares purchased in the following 30 days after this date, on 25 March 2027.

Sale proceeds [300/3,000 x £21,000]	2,100
Less: Cost	(1,900)
Gain	200

STEP 3

The remaining 2,300 (3,000 – 400 – 300) shares are identified or matched against the pool. For this, the share pool must be established.

	Date	Number of shares	Cost £
Purchase	17/9/19	2,000	5,000
Purchase	3/1/22	1,500	2,000
		3,500	7,000

Therefore, before the sale, there are 3,500 shares in the pool at a total cost of £7,000. The cost of the shares sold from the pool is based on the average share price and can be calculated by using 2,300/3,500 x £7,000 = £4,600. It is important, for future disposals to record this "cost" used to calculate the gain and the number of shares and cost remaining in the pool.

	Date	Number of shares	Cost £
Pool balances from above		3,500	7,000
Sale	1/3/27	(2,300)	(4,600)
Balance		1,200	2,400

It is now possible to calculate the gain on the shares sold from the pool

Sale proceeds [2,300/3,000 x £21,000]	16,100

Less: Cost	(4,600)
Gain	11,500

STEP 4
Calculate the total gain arising on the sale

From STEP 1	400 shares sold	gain	50
From STEP 2	300 shares sold	gain	200
From STEP 3	2,300 shares sold	gain	11,500
Total	3,000	Total gain	11,750

In calculating the actual capital gains tax liability, the gain of £11,750 would be aggregated with any other gains or losses arising in the tax year before the annual exemption and any available losses are deducted to leave the net taxable amount.

Example 14.3
Joe sold 1,000 shares in JSP plc, on 31 January 2027 for £20,000. He bought 1,500 shares on 30 April 2018 for £18,000; 500 shares for £7,000 on 31 May 2020; and 200 shares for £3,600 on 10 February 2026.

Calculate Joe's chargeable gain.

Answer
Same day matching
No shares were bought on the sale date of 31 January 2026.

Following 30 days matching
200 shares were bought in this period on 10 February 2026. Therefore, 200 shares sold are matched with the shares bought in this period.

	£
Sale proceeds [(200/1,000) x £20,000]	4,000
Less: Cost	(3,600)
Gain	400

Share Pool
The remaining 800 shares are identified or matched against the share pool.

	Date	Number of shares	Cost £
Purchase	30/4/18	1,500	18,000
Purchase	31/5/20	500	7,000
		2,000	25,000
Sale	31/1/27	(800)	(10,000)
Balance		1,200	15,000

Sale proceeds [(800/1,000) x £20,000]	16,000
Less: Cost	(10,000)
Gain	6,000

Joe's total chargeable gains = 400+6,000 = £6,400

Scrip and rights issues

Effect of bonus and/or rights issues

The effect of each type of issue is to increase the number of shares held and, in the case of a rights issue, the total cost of the shareholding.

Before matching shares sold with shares purchased, if either a bonus and/or a rights issue occurs prior to any sale of shares, it is first necessary to adjust for the bonus/rights issue. Only after these adjustments are made can the shares sold be matched and the cost identified.

Bonus issues

Bonus or scrip issues are free issues of shares. The shareholder receiving the bonus shares does not pay anything for them.

For tax purposes, the bonus shares are assumed to have been acquired on the same date as the original shares in respect of which they have been issued.

Rights issue

A rights issue is an issue of shares to an existing shareholder but unlike a bonus issue, the shares have to be paid for.

For matching purposes, the rights shares are deemed to be a new acquisition.

Example 14.4

Greta bought 1,500 ordinary shares in UTB plc for £4,000 on 7 February 2017.
On 30 March 2019, a bonus issue of ordinary shares was made of 1 for 2.
Thus, Greta will have acquired an extra 1,500/2 = 750 ordinary shares.
These extra 750 shares will be deemed to have been acquired on 7 February 2017 for no cost.
Assuming, no share disposals, Greta's share pool will be:

	Date	Number of shares	Cost £
Purchase	7/2/17	1,500	4,000
Bonus issue 1:2	30/3/19	750	0
		2,250	4,000

Example 14.5

Ivan bought 1,500 ordinary shares in MKT plc for £5,000 on 12 June 2018.
On 15 May 2025, a rights issue of ordinary shares was offered of 1 for 5 at a cost of £2.50 per share.
Ivan accepted the rights issue and acquired an extra 1,500/5 = 300 ordinary shares.
These extra 300 shares will be treated as acquired on 15 May 2025 for £750 (300 x £2.50).
Ivan's share pool for MKT plc will be:

	Date	Number of shares	Cost £
Purchase	12/6/18	1,500	5,000
Rights issue 1:5	15/5/25	300	750
		1,800	5,750

Take-overs

A take-over occurs when one company acquires the shares of another company. For example, the shareholder in, say, Company A swaps their shares for shares in Company B. Company B is the acquiring company and Company A is the target company or company being acquired.

Take-over bids can be:

- share for share, *or*
- cash for share, *or*
- a mixture of the two.

An entirely share-for-share bid (i.e. with no cash involved, sometimes referred to as paper for paper) is *not* a disposal for CGT purposes provided that as a result of the bid the acquiring company controls either:

- more than 25% of the ordinary share capital of the target company, *or*
- more than 50% of the voting power of the target company.

Share for share

The new shares received in the acquiring company will "step into the shoes" of those originally held in the target company and will take their costs and dates of acquisition and do not give rise to a CGT disposal on the takeover.

Cash for shares

If only cash is received (i.e. no shares are issued) there is a CGT disposal of the old holding in the normal manner with a resulting capital gain or loss.

Share plus cash for shares

Where there is a hybrid take-over, i.e. the consideration for the old shares is a mixture of cash and new shares, the cost of the original shareholding must be split between the cash and value of the shares received and as cash has been received a capital gain will arise.

The allocation of the cost of the original shareholding is done on a pro-rata basis according to the market values of the new shares immediately following the successful acquisition, effectively following the part disposal rules (A/A+B).

The consideration taken in new shares will "step into the shoes" of those shares originally held.

If the cash received on a takeover is "small" then there will be no immediate liability to CGT and the cash received reduces the cost of the new shares etc. received. It will be "small" where it does not exceed either 5% of the total value of the consideration received as a result of the take-over or £3,000.

Example 14.6

Oldco plc was acquired by Newco plc in July 2026. Newco plc offered the shareholders of Oldco plc two ordinary shares and £3.00 cash for every one ordinary share held in Oldco plc.

Trevor owned 2,100 ordinary shares in Oldco plc purchased in March 2007 for £6,000.

The market value of the shares in Newco plc on the day after the takeover was £4 per share.

Calculate Trevor's capital gain on this sale.

Answer

The take-over was made by way of an issue of shares and cash. Therefore, the receipt of cash will give rise to disposal for CGT. The receipt of Newco plc shares will not create an immediate CGT disposal and part of the original cost of Oldco plc shares will be attributed to these new shares.

First, it is necessary to work out the value of the total consideration received by Trevor:

Two ordinary Newco plc shares plus £3.00 cash for every one ordinary share held in Oldco plc.

Trevor held 2,100 Oldco plc shares. Therefore, he will receive:

4,200 Newco ordinary shares valued at	16,800	(4,200 x £4 per share)
Cash	6,300	(2,100 x £3 per share)
Total disposal consideration	23,100	

Second, it is necessary to allocate part of the original shareholding cost to the cash received

The original cost of shares in Oldco plc was £6,000.

Using (A/A+B) allocate (6,300/23,100) x 6,000 = £1,636 to the cash proceeds.

Therefore £1,636 of the cost relates to the cash and the balance is the cost of the Newco plc shares received.

Third, calculate capital gain on the cash received

Sale proceeds 2,100 x £3	6,300
Less:	
Cost	(1,636)
Gain	4,664

Finally, calculate the cost of the Newco Plc shares to carry forward

The original cost of Oldco shares	6,000
Cost of cash as calculated	(1,636)
Cost of Newco shares	4,364

If a takeover includes the issue of securities that meet the conditions to be treated as a qualifying corporate bond ("QCB"), then the gain attributable to the receipt of the QCB is calculated and crystallises when the QCB is disposed of.

SUMMARY

It is important when calculating a CGT liability on a sale of shares to:

- First, identify shares purchased in each of the categories (i.e. same day; next 30 days; share pool).
- Second, adjust the shares purchased in each of these categories for any bonus and/or rights issues.
- Third, match the shares sold with shares purchased in each of these categories until all shares sold have been matched, the cost identified and the gains or losses calculated.
- Fourth, aggregate the resulting gains and losses into a single result.

CHAPTER 15

Capital Gains Tax: Business Reliefs

Introduction

This chapter examines the main CGT reliefs available to an individual involving businesses and business assets. Some of these reliefs are also available to companies.

Replacement of business assets or rollover relief (also available to limited companies)

This relief allows taxpayers, both individuals and limited companies, to replace business assets used in their trade/business without giving rise to a chargeable gain on the sale of the "old" business assets at the date of sale (i.e. new business assets are purchased to replace old business assets). Several conditions must be satisfied.

By election, on the sale of a qualifying business asset, where *all* of the proceeds from the sale are reinvested in another qualifying business asset (or assets), any gain on the sale of the first asset is not taxed immediately but is *deferred* until the replacement asset is itself sold. (It is possible for a further rollover to be made and so on so that the gains are deferred for successive replacements).

This deferral is achieved by simply deducting the gain made on the sale of the old asset from the base cost of the replacement asset.

If all the sale proceeds from the sale of the old asset are not fully reinvested, then only a partial roll-over arises (i.e. part of the gain is taxed immediately with part being deferred).

Conditions for rollover relief to apply

The general conditions for rollover relief are:

- both 'old' and 'new' assets must be used wholly for trade purposes, *and*
- both assets must be within the *qualifying classes of assets* but need not belong to the same class, *and*
- the 'new' asset must be acquired within *one year before to three years after* the date of disposal of the 'old' asset.

The words 'old' and 'new' relate to the asset's position in relation to the business. In other words, the asset may be bought as a second-hand asset from someone else but is still categorised as new for the business which is buying it.

Qualifying assets

The qualifying assets for roll-over relief include:

- land and buildings occupied and used for trading purposes;
- fixed (i.e. immovable) plant and machinery;

- goodwill (not for companies);
- ships, aeroplanes and hovercraft;
- milk quotas; and
- satellites, space stations and spacecraft.

Example 15.1

David sold a building used in his trade, for £140,000 in March 2015, which he had bought for £100,000 in July 2003.

In September 2015 he bought a qualifying replacement asset, for £200,000 and claimed rollover relief.

In June 2026 he sold the replacement asset for £220,000 without any further reinvestment.

Calculate David's CGT position (pre-annual exemption).

Answer

Original asset sale 2014/15

Sale proceeds	140,000
Less:	
Cost	(100,000)
Gain	40,000
Roll-over relief	(40,000)
Taxable gain	Nil

Full rollover relief is available as the full sale proceeds have been reinvested into the replacement asset.

The gain of £40,000 is rolled over against the cost of the replacement asset i.e. deducted from it:

Cost of replacement asset	200,000
Less:	
Rolled-over gain	(40,000)
New base cost	160,000

Sale of new asset June 2026

Sale proceeds	220,000
Less	
New base cost	(160,000)
Gain	60,000

Notes

1. There is no capital gain taxed in 2014/15 but a capital gain is assessed in 2026/27. The rollover relief does not reduce the total gain but defers tax on the original sale until the later sale.
2. If the proceeds from the sale of the new asset are reinvested into new qualifying assets within the permitted time limit, then a further rollover may be claimed.

For individuals, the claim must be made for rollover relief within four years from the end of the tax year in which the disposal occurs or the replacement asset is acquired, whichever is later.

Only partial reinvestment

Where the disposal proceeds of the old asset are *not* fully reinvested the surplus cash retained reduces the gain allowed to be rolled over (and in fact if the surplus cash retained is greater than the gain there will be no rollover at all). In effect, a partial rollover occurs whilst at the same time a CGT liability arises as illustrated in the following example.

Example 15.2

Ethel sold a qualifying business asset for £130,000 making a gain of £45,000 in May 2024. She reinvested £105,000 in a qualifying replacement business asset in August 2026 (within three years after the disposal).

Show Ethel's CGT position (pre-annual exemption).

Answer

The gain on sale of the old asset which is capable of rollover is £45,000.

However, £25,000 (130,000 - 105,000) of the sale proceeds from the sale of the old asset have not been reinvested in any new assets.

The amount which was not reinvested of £25,000 will be taxable as a gain on Ethel immediately, i.e. in the tax year 2024/25.

Only the difference between the original gain and the gain immediately taxed is rolled over.

The gain eligible for rollover is, therefore:

Total gain	45,000	
Rolled-over gain	(20,000)	
Taxed now	25,000	(Proceeds £130,000 less reinvested amount £105,000)

The rolled-over gain is simply the difference between the total gain and the gain taxed now (i.e. the proceeds not reinvested).

Thus, £20,000 will reduce the base cost of the replacement asset to £85,000 (i.e. 105,000 - 20,000).

Notes

The chargeable gain is the lower of the proceeds not reinvested and the full gain. Calculate this first and the rollover relief is the difference between this and the original gain.

If the sale proceeds reinvested had been, say, £85,000 (i.e. 45,000 not reinvested) or less, then the whole gain of £45,000 would have been immediately chargeable with no part being eligible for roll-over:

Total gain	45,000	
Rolled over gain	(0)	
Taxed now	45,000	(Proceeds £130,000 less reinvested amount £85,000)

Non-business use

Where the asset being replaced has not been used entirely for business purposes during the period of ownership the roll-over relief is scaled down.

This can be achieved by assuming the asset is, in fact, two assets one of which was used entirely for business purposes and one asset which was not.

Two separate CGT calculations are then performed normally assuming that the costs and proceeds are pro-rated in the same manner. Alternatively, a single computation may be carried out reducing pro rata according to the amount of business and non-business use.

Example 15.3

Rayhan purchased a factory in July 2011 for a cost of £500,000. 15% of it was let out as Rayhan did not need it for his trade. In May 2026 the factory was sold for £800,000 and a replacement factory was bought for £900,000.

Calculate Rayhan's CGT position (pre-annual exemption).

Answer

Original asset

Sale proceeds	800,000
Less	
Cost	(500,000)
Gain	300,000
Taxable element of gain = 15% x 300,000 =	45,000
Thus, 85% of 300,000 is eligible for roll-over =	255,000
Base cost of new asset 900,000 – 255,000 =	645,000

Depreciating assets

Rollover relief is modified where the new asset purchased is a "depreciating asset". A depreciating asset for this purpose is an asset with an expected life of 50 years or less at the time of acquisition (or will become so in the next 10 years).

Unlike rollover relief, the held-over gain on the sale of the old asset does not reduce the cost of the new asset. This gain is simply "held over" or deferred until the earliest of one of the following three occurrences and then at that time is charged as a gain:

- the sale of the 'new' depreciating asset, *or*
- the cessation of its use in the business, *or*
- the 10 year anniversary of the acquisition of the depreciating asset.

Leases of 60 years or less and fixed plant and machinery are examples of depreciating assets.

Example 15.4

Maggie bought a factory in June 2010 for £250,000. She then sold it for £600,000 in January 2015. In August 2017 she acquired a 40-year lease on a new factory for £750,000 and subsequently sold it in May 2026 for £1,250,000.

Show Maggie's CGT position.

Answer

The reinvestment of the proceeds from the sale of the factory in 2017 was into a depreciating asset (i.e. a short lease). Only *hold-over* relief is available.

Gain on sale of factory = 600,000 – 250,000 = £350,000

This gain is held over until the earliest of the events mentioned above which in this case is the sale of the replacement factory lease in May 2026.

The gain of £350,000 is now taxable in 2026/27 (not 2014/15 when the factory was sold).

In addition, any gain on the assignment (sale) of the lease will also be taxable.

Note

If Maggie did not dispose of the lease in March 2026 and continued to trade, the deferred gain would be taxable in August 2027, the 10-year anniversary of the acquisition of the replacement asset.

Gift relief ("holdover relief")

As mentioned in Chapter 13, the gift of an asset is treated as a disposal made at the market value at the date of the gift. In other words, even though no sale proceeds are received, for CGT purposes a disposal is deemed to have been made at current market value and therefore a gain or loss will arise. (Remember that this is not a problem for married couples and civil partners where assets are transferred for no gain/no loss).

However, a capital gain deemed to have been made on a gift can be deferred by way of gift relief provided:

- the donor (the person making the gift) and donee (the person receiving the gift) jointly elect within four years from the end of the tax year in which the disposal is made, *and*
- the donee is resident in the UK, *and*
- the asset is a qualifying asset.

Qualifying assets

These are:

- business assets; and
- transfers of assets subject to an immediate charge to inheritance tax (namely lifetime transfers of assets to a trust – see Chapter 24).

Transfers of business assets are transfers of:

- business assets used by the donor in his or her business *or* used by his or her personal trading company;
- shares or securities held in the donor's personal trading company; and
- shares or securities in an unquoted trading company.

A *personal company* is one in which the donor controls at least 5% of the voting rights and can be either quoted or unquoted.

Shares in an unquoted company include shares listed on the Alternative Investment Market (AIM).

Note that, unlike the position for roll-over and hold-over relief discussed above for replacement of business assets, in the case of gift relief there is no restriction on the type of assets that qualify other than that they must be used in the business.

Thus, it can be seen that gift relief would not apply, for example, to a gift by a mother to her daughter of a piece of family jewellery or a painting as neither is used in a business.

Effect of gift relief

There are two effects on the donor and donee claiming gift relief:

- the donor will be treated as making neither gain nor loss on the gift, *and*
- the donee will be treated as taking the asset at its market value – the deemed disposal proceeds – but this market value will be reduced by the amount of the gain deferred on the part of the donor.

Example 15.5

Gerald gave a business asset to his son Jim in May 2026 when its market value was £50,000. Gerald originally bought the asset in January 2000 for £22,000. Gerald and Jim make a joint gift relief claim.

What is the CGT position of both Gerald and Jim?

Answer

Gerald	£	
Deemed sale proceeds	50,000	(Actual proceeds £Nil)
Less:		
Cost	(22,000)	
Gain	28,000	
Less:		
Gift relief	(28,000)	
Chargeable gain	nil	
Jim		
Market value of the asset acquired	50,000	
Less:		
Gift relief	(28,000)	
Base cost of asset	22,000	

Note

You will note that, in effect, Gerald's original cost becomes Jim's cost.

Not a pure gift – sale at undervalue

Gift relief also applies where the "gift" is, in fact, a sale but at less than market value to a connected person.

However, in such cases, only part of the gain can be subject to gift relief with part of the gain becoming immediately chargeable.

The part of the gain which is chargeable immediately is the excess of the proceeds received by the donor over the donor's original cost. The balance of the gain can then be deferred i.e. subject to gift relief.

Example 15.6

Sally purchased shares in an unquoted trading company for £50,000 in December 2019. She then sold them to her son Ben for £80,000 in July 2026 when their market value was £175,000. Sally and Ben intend to claim gift relief on the transaction.

What is the CGT position for Sally and Ben?

Answer

Sally	**£**
Deemed sale proceeds (Market value)	175,000
Less:	
Cost	(50,000)
Gain	125,000
Less:	
Gift relief (See Note 3)	(95,000)
Chargeable gain (See Note 3)	30,000
Ben	
Market value of shares acquired	175,000
Less:	
Gift relief	(95,000)
Base cost of shares	80,000

Notes

1. Market value replaces actual sale proceeds as it is a sale to a connected person.
2. If Sally had simply gifted the shares to Ben gift relief of £125,000 would have been available.
3. However, as Ben paid Sally £80,000 then Sally is immediately chargeable on the actual gain arising of £30,000 (i.e. 80,000 – 50,000). Only £95,000 (i.e. the difference between the full gain and the gain taxed now (125,000 – 30,000)) is available for gift relief.

Assets not used wholly for business purposes

Business assets other than shares

It may be that during an individual's ownership of an asset, it qualifies as a business asset for part of the time and as a non-business asset for the rest of the period.

This may occur because the asset was itself used only partly for business purposes throughout its period of ownership or alternatively the asset was used wholly for business purposes but only for a part of its period of ownership.

For individual trading assets (e.g. land and buildings; plant and machinery; goodwill) the overall gain is simply pro-rated accordingly.

Example 15.7

Lionel owns a factory that he purchased in May 2018 for £100,000. In June 2026 Lionel gave the asset to his daughter, Jo, when its market value was £300,000 and a joint gift relief election was made. 80% of the factory has been used in Lionel's business with the remaining 20% being let out to a third party (i.e. this part is not used in Lionel's business).

Show Lionel and Jo's CGT position.

Answer

Of Lionel's gain of £200,000 (i.e. 300,000 - 100,000), 20% of it (i.e. £40,000) is chargeable immediately (the gain attributable to the part let).

The balancing 80% (i.e. 160,000) is eligible for gift relief.

Jo will, therefore, receive the asset at its market value of 300,000 less gift relief of 160,000 giving a base cost of £140,000.

Shares

In the case of a gift of shares, the above rule is applied differently.

Where a gift of shares in a personal trading company is made and not all of the company's assets are business assets then part of the gain on the sale of the shares is not eligible for gift relief.

Only the gain on the shares attributable to any underlying *chargeable* **business** *assets* as opposed to *chargeable assets* of the company qualifies for gift relief calculated as follows:

$$\text{Gain on the gift of shares} \times \frac{\text{Market value of chargeable } \textit{business} \text{ assets}}{\text{Market value of company's } \textit{chargeable} \text{ assets}}$$

An example of chargeable assets of a company that are not chargeable *business* assets would be investments held by the company, for example where the company used its surplus cash to invest in shares of another company. These are investments and therefore not business assets (i.e. they are not used in the company's business).

Transfer of a business to a company (Incorporation relief)

It is not unusual for a sole trader to decide to convert their business to a limited company. This gives rise to a disposal of the assets transferred at market value. Subject to satisfying certain conditions so-called incorporation relief may be available when a person transfers their sole trader business to a company (incorporates) as a going concern for shares in the company.

Incorporation relief permits the transfer to take place without any capital gains tax liability arising on the deemed disposal of the chargeable business assets which would otherwise occur. The capital gain which would arise is rolled over against the cost of the shares issued to the sole trader in exchange for the acquisition of their sole trader business. For the relief to apply, the business and all of its assets, other than cash must be transferred and the relief must be claimed on the individual's tax return.

Example 15.8

Alisha transferred her business to a limited company and in exchange received 1,000 ordinary £1 shares in her new limited company. The business was valued at £90,000 on incorporation. It was agreed that the chargeable gain on the transfer of Alisha's business was £27,000. However, Alisha does not have a capital gains tax liability. Instead, the gain of £27,000 is deducted from the cost of her shares, £90,000, leaving a base cost of £63,000 on any future share disposal.

For complete roll-over relief to apply all of the consideration for the business transferred must be in shares of the acquiring company. If a part of the consideration is in cash, a partial rollover may apply and a CGT liability will immediately arise on the cash element received. In this latter case, the amount of gain eligible for roll-over relief is given by:

$$\text{Capital gain} \times \frac{\text{Value of shares received}}{\text{Total consideration received}}$$

Example 15.9

Clare a sole trader who set up her business in 2021 has decided to transfer her entire business to a limited company CPT Ltd on 31 December 2026 in exchange for an issue of ordinary shares. The assets and liabilities as at 31 December 2026 are as follows:

	Cost	Market Value
	£	£
Assets		
Cash	4,000	4,000
Freehold property	14,000	30,000
Fixtures and fittings	10,000	2,000
Trading stock	2,000	1,200
Goodwill	nil	3,000
Debtors	nil	1,000
TOTAL	**30,000**	**41,200**
Liabilities		
Trade creditors	nil	1,200
Net assets	**30,000**	**40,000**

What is Clare's CGT position for the tax year 2026/27 and what difference would it make if Clare received her consideration as shares worth £25,000 and cash of £15,000 (i.e. a total consideration of £40,000 the sole trader's net worth)?

Answer

Chargeable gains on the transfer of chargeable assets are as follows:

Freehold property:	30,000 – (14,000)	=	16,000
Goodwill:	3,000 – (nil)	=	3,000
Total gain			19,000

(Note that the only other chargeable asset for CGT purposes are the fixtures and fittings, which are sold at less than cost, giving rise to an appropriate balancing allowance/charge obtained for capital allowance purposes, but no capital gain/loss).

Gain eligible for roll-over relief = 19,000 as all consideration in the form of shares.

Base cost of new shares = 40,000 – 19,000 = £21,000

Had the consideration been shares plus cash, then of the £19,000 of gain above only:

[25,000/40,000] x 19,000 = £11,875 of gain can be rolled over against the cost of the shares of £25,000, leaving a cost of £13,125.

The balance of the gain, £7,125 (i.e. 19,000 – 11,875) is taxable immediately.

Business asset disposal relief (previously known as "entrepreneurs' relief")

This relief was introduced by Finance Act 2008 to provide individuals disposing of a business interest some element of CGT relief to replace some of the benefits lost previously by the removal of retirement relief and business asset taper relief.

Although it is referred to as a "relief", it does not reduce the amount of the chargeable gain. Its effect is to reduce the rate of CGT charged on qualifying gains to 18% (the reduced rate was 14% until 5 April 2026).

There is a lifetime limit on the total value of gains that can qualify for Business asset disposal relief. This limit is currently £1,000,000 (£10,000,000 for disposals before 11 March 2020).

The relief may be available to an individual on:

(a) a disposal of the whole or part of a business;

(b) a disposal of one or more assets in use, at the time at which a business ceases to be carried on; or

(c) a disposal of shares in or securities of a personal trading company.

In all cases, for the relief to be available, the business or shares must have been owned by the individual for at least 24 months before the date of disposal, or cessation of the business in respect of (b) above.

Disposal of whole or part of a business

The disposal must be of the whole business or a clearly identifiable part, for example, a separate branch in its entirety. Therefore, it will not apply to the sale of individual business assets, where the business continues unchanged. Relief is not available for non-business assets. Relief may also not be available where goodwill is sold to a related close company.

Disposal of one or more assets in use, at the time at which a business ceases

The disposal must take place within three years after the date of cessation. In this case, the relief is available on the disposal of individual business assets. Again, relief is not available for non-business assets.

Disposal of shares in a company

Throughout the 24-month period prior to disposal, the individual must be an officer or employee of the company, the company's main activities must be trading and the shares must be in the individual's personal company. For this relief "personal company" means a company in which the individual holds at least 5% of the ordinary share capital, at least 5% of the voting rights and at least 5% of the distributable profits and net assets of the company. Therefore, for example, if a husband and wife each hold 4% of the ordinary shares of a trading company, neither would qualify for business asset disposal relief. The shares may be quoted.

Example 15.10

In which of the following three scenarios will business asset disposal relief be available?

Lisa owns and runs two restaurants in neighbouring cities. She closes one of the restaurants and makes a capital gain on the disposal of the property.

Neil has traded for over 10 years and ceases to trade on 7 June 2024. On 1 November 2025, Neil acquired new business premises which he traded from until the cessation of his trade. This property was sold at a gain on 12 December 2026.

Mel owned 6% of the ordinary shares in her employer, a trading company, and had worked for this company for five years when she decided to sell her entire shareholding. She continues to work for the same employer after the sale.

Answer

Lisa will not be entitled to business asset disposal relief as she has disposed of a business asset and not the whole or part of her business. If she had sold the restaurant as a going concern, then she would have sold part of her business and may have been eligible for business asset disposal relief.

Neil will be entitled to business asset disposal relief as the sale occurred within three years of the cessation of trading. The 2-year qualifying period prior to cessation relates to the time that Neil has been trading and not the period of ownership of each individual asset.

Mel will be entitled to business asset disposal relief assuming that the shares entitled her to 5% of the voting rights and at least 5% of the distributable profits and net assets of the company. She was an employee of the company for more than two years before the date of the sale and there is no requirement for her to leave the company or retire.

As mentioned above, there is a lifetime limit on business asset disposal relief (and entrepreneurs' relief for earlier years) of £1 million.

Example 15.11

Lee, a higher rate taxpayer, has owned and run his own business for the last seven years. There are no non-business assets. He sells the entire business in October 2026 for £600,000. The allowable costs are £140,000.

Therefore, Lee has made a taxable gain of £460,000, assuming that Lee has already used his annual exemption.

He can claim business asset disposal relief and, as a result, the rate of CGT will be 18% rather than the normal higher rate of 24%.

After the sale, Lee starts up another business, which he sells after five years at a gain of £700,000, again comprised entirely of business assets. Lee's lifetime limit for business asset disposal relief is £1,000,000. £460,000 was claimed on the earlier disposal. Therefore, relief of £540,000 is available on the later disposal, with the balance chargeable at the normal CGT higher rate.

Where there are both gains and losses during a tax year on assets qualifying for business asset disposal relief, these must be netted off. Otherwise, CGT losses and the annual exemption can be claimed against qualifying and non-qualifying gains in the most advantageous manner to the taxpayer. In determining the rate of tax applicable where there are qualifying and non-qualifying gains, the qualifying gains are taxed first. This will have no impact on the rate of tax applied to these gains but may increase the rate of tax on the non-qualifying gains.

Business asset disposal relief must be claimed by the first anniversary of 31 January following the end of the tax year of disposal (For 2026/27 by 31 January 2029).

Investors' relief

This relief is very similar to business asset disposal relief.

Investors' relief also reduces the rate of CGT for qualifying gains to 18%, and there is a lifetime limit to qualifying gains totalling £1,000,000 (The limit was £10,000,000 for disposal up to 30 October 2024). Broadly, the relief applies to gains on the disposal of ordinary shares subscribed for in cash on or after 17 March 2016 in unlisted trading companies or groups that have been held by the individual for at least three years. The individual must not have been an officer or employee of the company during the period from acquisition to the date of disposal of the shares (There are some limited exceptions to this rule, for instance, in respect of unpaid directors).

Investors' relief must be claimed by the first anniversary of 31 January following the end of the tax year in which the disposal was made.

SUMMARY

- The CGT liability which arises on a sale of qualifying business assets may be rolled over where a replacement qualifying business asset is purchased. If the purchased asset is a depreciating asset (e.g. a lease) then hold-over relief applies. The replacement asset must be acquired during the period commencing one year before the disposal to three years after.
- The relief is only available where the various conditions are satisfied. The failure to reinvest all of the sale proceeds will give rise to an immediate taxable gain on part of the overall gain.
- Gift relief (holdover relief):
    - applies to shares in trading companies and business assets, not all assets;
    - also applies to gifts that are immediately chargeable to inheritance tax;
    - applies not just to gifts but also to sales at below market value; and
    - gift relief needs the consent of both the donor and the donee.

- Incorporation relief can be used to roll over the capital gain that would otherwise arise on the transfer of a business and its assets from a sole trader business to a limited company in exchange for shares.
- Business asset disposal relief is a valuable relief available on the sale of a business or by an employee of shares in a personal trading company, potentially reducing the rate of CGT from 24% to 18%. Failure to meet all of the qualifying conditions will result in the denial of the relief. The relief is available on gains up to the lifetime limit of £1,000,000. Business asset disposal relief must be claimed. This relief was known as entrepreneur's relief up to 11 March 2020.
- Investors' relief works similarly to business asset disposal relief on certain unlisted share disposals.

Questions for students

See Appendix 2 for practice questions relating to Chapters 13 to 15. Answers are available online at https://spiramus.com/uk-taxation-for-students-20267-answers.

CHAPTER 16

Corporation Tax: General Principles

Introduction

We will now start to consider the UK taxation rules for companies. Companies are not liable to income tax or capital gains tax. Companies pay corporation tax on all income, including trading profits and capital gains. Other bodies such as clubs and associations may also be subject to corporation tax. For all limited companies, profits are calculated using the traditional accruals method and applying UK GAAP – the cash basis cannot be used.

Liability to corporation tax

A company's liability to corporation tax depends on its residence. A company that is resident in the UK is liable to corporation tax (CT) on its worldwide profits. Non-resident companies may still be subject to UK tax on profits attributable to a permanent establishment in the UK.

Dividend income from other companies is ***not*** subject to corporation tax but may impact the CT rate and due dates for payment. (Dividends are paid out of after-tax profits, so the paying company has already paid CT on that profit!).

Company residence

The basic rule: place of incorporation

If a company is incorporated in the UK, it is UK resident.

Place of central management and control

If a company is not incorporated in the UK, it may still be UK resident if it is controlled and managed in the UK. In most cases, the control and management of a company are exercised where its board of directors meet and take strategic decisions in relation to the company.

Taxable total profits (TTP)

For each accounting period, not tax year as applies to individuals, it is necessary to calculate a company's Taxable total profits (TTP), which may require separate computations of each income source and capital gains. Corporation tax is charged on the TTP of an accounting period, usually, the period that the annual financial statements or accounts are prepared for.

TTP is equal to the aggregate of the income and chargeable gains made by a company in the accounting period less certain deductions, including losses and qualifying charitable donations.

In computing the TTP for an accounting period the following pro-forma should be used:

Adjusted trading profit	x
Property business profit	x
Non-trading Loan relationship profits	x
(Deduct if a deficit)	
Chargeable gains	x
Total profits	x
Less: Loss claims against TTP	(x)
	x
Less: Qualifying charitable donations	(x)
Taxable Total Profits (TTP)	**X**

Chapters 17 and 18 explain the detailed rules for chargeable gains and losses respectively.

Qualifying charitable donations

A company may obtain a deduction from its TTP for payments to a qualifying charity.

Such payments are made gross (i.e. tax at source is not deducted from the payment; remember an individual makes a gift aid payment net of basic rate income tax). Qualifying charitable donations (QCD) are deductible from TTP after any losses are offset against TTP. Therefore, a claim for losses can result in relief for QCD being lost or wasted.

Only QCDs which are actually paid in an accounting period are deductible.

Dividends

Companies are not subject to CT on the receipt of dividends and do not obtain tax relief for dividends paid.

Each other item included in the calculation of TTP is explained further later in this chapter.

Example 16.1

The adjusted income and gains of BCL Ltd of the accounting period for the year to 30 June 2026 have been calculated as follows:

Adjusted trading profits	275,100
Rental profits	14,200
Dividends received	5,000
Capital gains	94,400
Non-trading loan interest paid	10,500

BCL Ltd paid qualifying charitable donations of £6,000 during the year.

Calculate the TTP of BCL Ltd for the year ended 30 June 2026.

Answer

Adjusted trading profits	275,100
Rental profits	14,200
Capital gains	94,400
Non-trading loan interest paid	(10,500)
Total profits	373,200
Less: Qualifying charitable donations	(6,000)
TTP	367,200

Notes

Dividends received are not included in TTP but will be used to calculate Augmented profits which are used to check the applicable tax rate.

Rates of corporation tax and financial years

Rates of corporation tax are determined not for income tax years but for *financial years* (FY). For example, the financial year 2026 (FY2026) refers to the period 1 April 2026 to 31 March 2027.

For many years, there was a single rate of Corporation tax but this changed from 1 April 2023. For FY2025 and FY2026, there are two rates of Corporation tax:

Main rate	25%
Small profits rate	19%

The Small profits rate applies where augmented profits do not exceed £50,000 (the lower limit). Where augmented profits are above £50,000 up to £250,000 (the upper limit) marginal relief applies. The Marginal relief fraction is 3/200 and Marginal Relief is calculated as:

$$\frac{3}{200}\ x\ (250{,}000 - Augmented\ profits)\ x\ \left(\frac{Taxable\ Total\ Profits}{Augmented\ profits}\right)$$

Augmented profits are calculated as TTP plus non-group dividends received.

Example 16.2

SCO Ltd has TTP of £30,000 for its accounting period for the year to 31 March 2027. The company also received non-group dividends of £10,000 during the year.

Calculate the Corporation tax liability to 31 March 2027.

Answer

First, calculate augmented profits to check against the limits

TTP + Non-group dividends = 30,000+ 10,000 = £40,000

As this is below the Small profits limit of £50,000, Corporation tax will be charged at the Small profits rate of 19%.

CT payable TTP @ 19% = 30,000 @ 19% = £5,700

Notes

It should be noted that Augmented profits are only used to check the applicable tax rate and the CT liability is calculated on TTP only.

Example 16.3

MRC Limited has TTP of £140,000 for the year to 31 March 2027 and did not receive any dividends.

Calculate the Corporation tax liability to 31 March 2027.

Answer

First, calculate augmented profits to check against the limits

TTP + Non-group dividends = 140,000 + 0 = £140,000

As this is above the Small profits limit of £50,000, and below the marginal relief limit of £250,000, Corporation tax will be charged at 25% but this will be reduced by Marginal relief.

CT @ Main rate 140,000 @ 25% = 35,000

Marginal relief

3/200 x (250,000 – 140,000) x (140,000/140,000) = (1,650)

CT payable 33,350

Notes

It should be noted that Augmented profits are only used to check the applicable tax rate and the CT liability is calculated on TTP only.

This equates to an effective rate of CT of 26.5% on profits above the Small profits rate:

50,000 @ 19% = 9,500

90,000 @ 26.5% = 23,850

Total 33,350

If the company did not receive any dividends, TTP and Augmented profits will be equal and therefore the final part of the marginal relief calculation could be omitted.

Example 16.4

XMR Limited has TTP of £160,000 for the year to 31 March 2027 and received dividends of £15,000.

Calculate the Corporation tax liability to 31 March 2027.

Answer

First, calculate augmented profits to check against the limits

TTP + Non-group dividends = 160,000 + 15,000 = £175,000

As this is above the Small profits limit of £50,000, and below the marginal relief limit of £250,000, Corporation tax will be charged at 25% but this will be reduced by Marginal relief.

CT @ Main rate 160,000 @ 25% = 40,000

Marginal relief

3/200 x (250,000 – 175,000) x (160,000/175,000) = (1,029)

CT payable 38,971

Notes

It should be noted that Augmented profits are only used to check the applicable tax rate and the CT liability is calculated on TTP only.

Example 16.5

MRC Ltd has TTP of £2,500,000 for its accounting period for the year to 31 March 2027. The company also received non-group dividends of £75,000 during the year. Calculate the Corporation tax liability to 31 March 2027.

Answer

First, calculate augmented profits to check against the limits

TTP + No-group dividends = 2,500,000 + 75,000 = £2,575,000

As this is above the upper limit of £250,000, Corporation tax will be charged at 25%.

CT payable = 2,500,000 @ 25% = £625,000

Notes

It should be noted that Augmented profits are only used to check the applicable tax rate and the CT liability is calculated on TTP only.

For the financial year 2022 (FY2022), there was a single rate of corporation tax of 19%.

If a company's accounting period straddles more than one financial year, the amount of the profits arising in the accounting period must be apportioned between the financial years in which the accounting period falls to determine the corporation tax liability.

Two separate computations are then carried out and then aggregated to get the company's overall corporation tax liability.

Example 16.6

KRO Ltd has TTP of £600,000 for its 12 month accounting period to 30 June 2023.

Calculate the company's corporation tax liability.

Answer

Part of the accounting period falls within FY2022 and part within FY2023.

Apportion TTP on a time basis TTP into the two financial years covered by the accounting period.

FY 2022

TTP for the 9 months to 31 March 2023 falls within FY 2022

TTP £600,000 x 9/12 = 450,000 x 19% = £85,500

FY 2023

TTP for the 3 months to 30 June 2023 falls within FY 2023

TTP £600,000 x 3/12 = 150,000 x 25% = £37,500

The Marginal relief limit for this 3 month period would be 250,000 x 3/12 = 62,500, therefore, the Main rate of CT applies.

Aggregate the figures to get the corporation tax liability for the whole 12 month accounting period i.e. 1 July 2022 to 30 June 2023.

Corporation Tax = 85,500 + 37,500 = £123,000

Associated Companies

Where a company has one or more associated companies, the Small profits limit and Marginal relief limits are divided by one plus the number of associated companies. Two companies are associated if one controls the other or both are controlled by the same person (and their associates, including spouse, parents, children, siblings and business partners). Non-trading holding companies and dormant companies are ignored but non-resident companies can be included. Control generally means being able to exercise more than 50% of the share capital or voting power *at any time* during the accounting period. Where there is no substantial commercial interdependence between companies it may not be necessary to include a company controlled by an associate.

Example 16.7

ACE Ltd has a TTP of £42,000 for its 12-month accounting period to 31 March 2027. The company also received dividends of £5,000.

100% of the share capital is held by Anne. Anne also owns 60% of the shares in another trading company BAC Ltd and 100% of the shares in a dormant company DCA Ltd.

Calculate the corporation tax liability of ACE Ltd to 31 March 2027.

Answer

ACE Ltd and BAC Ltd are associated as both are controlled by Anne. DCA Ltd is ignored as it is dormant.

The small profits limit and marginal relief limits are divided between the two associated companies.

Small profits limit: 50,000/2 = 25,000

Marginal relief limit: 250,000/2 = 125,000

ACE Ltd: Augmented profits TTP + Dividends received = 42,000+ 5,000 = 47,000

As the Augmented profits of ACE Ltd exceed £25,000 but are below £125,000, marginal relief will apply.

CT @ Main rate 42,000 @ 25% =	10,500
Marginal relief	
3/200 x (125,000 – 47,000) x (42,000/47,000) =	(1,045)
CT payable	9,455

Example 16.8

Ben owns 100% of the shares of BBF Ltd, a trading company. BBF Ltd owns 60% of the shares of one trading subsidiary, BAL Ltd. On 1 March 2026, Ben set up a new non-resident trading company NCO Ltd and again he owns all of the shares.

Finally, Lou, Ben's wife, owns 100% of the shares of LHR Ltd and this company is not interdependent on any of Ben's companies.

All of the companies prepare their accounts to 31 March 2027.

How many associated companies does BBF Ltd have for the year to 31 March 2027?

Answer

BBF Ltd, NCO Ltd and BAL Ltd are all associated for the year to 31 March 2027.

NCO Ltd is controlled by Ben and even though it is non-resident, it is still considered associated. Although it was only incorporated on 1 March 2027, the rules apply where companies are associated at any time during an accounting period.

BBF Ltd owns 60% of BAL Ltd, therefore indirectly Ben also controls this company.

As Lou's company is not interdependent on Ben's companies, it is not considered associated.

Chargeable accounting period

A company's period of account is any period for which a company may prepare its financial statements. This may be for 12 months, less than or more than 12 months. As noted above, however, corporation tax is levied on TTP for an *accounting period.*

An accounting period for corporation tax, however, cannot be longer than 12 months.

A chargeable accounting period *starts*:

- when a company starts to trade; *or*
- otherwise becomes liable to corporation tax; *or*
- immediately after the previous accounting period ends.

A chargeable accounting period *ends* on the earliest of the following:

- 12 months after its start;
- the end of the company's period of account;
- the date that a company ceases to be resident in the UK;
- the date that a company ceases to be liable to corporation tax; *or*
- commencement of the company's winding up.

Short accounting period

Where a company's period of account is for less than 12 months, this period of account is also the company's accounting period.

Corporation tax is computed as above.

Example 16.9

EFD Ltd has TTP of £200,000 for the nine month accounting period from 1 April 2026 to 31 December 2026.

Answer

The whole of the accounting period falls within FY2026

The upper limit is restricted to £250,000 x 9/12 months = 187,500

Therefore, all of the profits are assessed at the Main rate of 25%

Corporation tax liability 200,000 @ 25% = £50,000

Long period of account

If a company's financial statements are prepared for a period of more than 12 months, this complete period cannot be an accounting period because an accounting period for corporation tax purposes cannot be longer than 12 months.

In such cases, the period of account must be split into two separate accounting periods, one for the first 12 months and one for the balance of the period. Two calculations of TTP are then necessary, producing two separate corporate tax liabilities, one for each accounting period, which are *not* aggregated.

In these cases, before any calculations can be carried out it is necessary to split the individual items of income and gains (e.g. rental income; interest income; etc.) comprising the company's profit for the whole period of account between the two accounting periods created. This split is carried out using the following rules:

- trading profits *before* capital allowances are time apportioned;
- capital allowances must be calculated separately for each accounting period (first 12 months, then a short period for the balance);
- property business profits are time apportioned;
- other income is allocated to the accounting period to which it relates (i.e. accruals basis);
- chargeable gains/losses are allocated to the accounting period in which the gains arise based on the date of disposal;
- allocate qualifying charitable donations to the accounting period in which paid; and
- dividends are allocated to the accounting period in which received (only necessary for determining Augmented profits).

Example 16.10

JSC Ltd has the following results for the 16 months to 31 December 2026:

Trading profit before capital allowances	320,000
Property business profit	160,000
Bank interest received and accrued to 31 December 2026	8,000
Capital gain made on 21 August 2026	89,000
UK dividend received 12 September 2026	36,000

Tax written down value of plant and machinery in the main pool as at 1 September 2025 was £100,000. There are no purchases or sales of plant and machinery during the period of account.

Calculate the TTP for the two accounting periods and the corporation tax liability for each accounting period.

Answer

The period of account from 1 September 2025 to 31 December 2026 is divided into an accounting period of 1 September 2025 to 31 August 2026 (the first 12 months) and an accounting period of 1 September 2026 to 31 December 2026.

	1.9.25 to 31.8.26 *(12 months)*	**1.9.26 to 31.12.26** *(4 months)*
Trading profit		
320,000 x 12/16	240,000	
320,000 x 4/16		80,000
Capital allowances (see below)	(16,330)	(3,904)

Property business profit			
160,000 x 12/16	120,000		
160,000 x 4/16			40,000
Interest income			
8,000 x 12/16	6,000		
8,000 x 4/16			2,000
Capital Gain 21 August 2026	89,000		
TTP	**438,670**		**118,096**
Capital allowances			
1.9.25 to 31.8.26 (12 months)			
TWDV as at 1.9.25		100,000	
WDA (16.33%)		(16,330)	
1.9.26 to 31.12.26 (4 months)			
TWDV as at 1.9.26		83,670	
WDA (14% x 4/12)		(3,904)	
TWDV as at 31.12.26		79,766	

1.9.25 to 31.8.26

Corporation tax liability =

FY2025	438,670 x 7/12 x 25%	=	63,972
FY2026	438,670 x 5/12 x 25%	=	45,695
			109,667

1.9.26 to 31.12.26 (upper limit £250,00 x 4/12 = 62,500)

Corporation tax liability =

FY2026	118,096 x 25%	=	29,524

Notes

1. Capital allowances are calculated for the first 12 month period and then for the shorter four-month period. Any additions and disposals would be allocated by date.
2. The hybrid rate of WDA is calculated as: (18% x 212/365) + (14% x 153/365)=16.33%
3. There are separate tax liabilities for the two different accounting periods and these are not added together; they are also payable by different dates; see Chapter 22.

Trading profits

Companies are taxed on their trading profit for an accounting period calculated using the traditional accruals basis and the normal rules regarding the deductibility of expenses apply (see Chapter 6). A calculation of the adjusted profits will be required.

However, unlike sole traders:

- cash basis cannot be used;
- capital items are not deductible – capital allowances may be due;
- there is no disallowance for any private proportion of any expenses (i.e. the full amount of the expense is deductible; this is because, in the case of companies, any private part of an expense (e.g. private fuel costs of a

company car) may be taxed as income of the relevant employee as a benefit in kind; see Chapter 10); and

- there is no restriction for the private element of any asset on which capital allowances may be claimed (see Chapter 7).

Capital allowances

Capital allowances can reduce trading profits and are claimed for accounting periods by reference to acquisitions and disposals in that accounting period.

All allowances are in principle calculated as for sole traders (see Chapter 7) using the same rates except for full expensing as noted below. As companies cannot have private use of assets, there will never be a need to separate assets with private use from the pools.

Groups of companies (see Chapter 19) are only entitled to share one AIA.

Period of account exceeds 12 months

As an accounting period cannot exceed 12 months for corporation tax purposes, writing down allowances can never exceed 18%/6% of the relevant tax written down values/costs (compare this with that of the sole trader where a 15 month period of account may produce writing down allowances of 18% x 15/12; see Chapter 6 and 7).

Where the period of account is over 12 months, two separate capital allowance computations are necessary for each of the two accounting periods which are created (see Example 16.5 above).

Period of account less than 12 months

Where the accounting period is *less* than 12 months, writing down allowances are reduced proportionately. In addition, the AIA limit will also be time apportioned.

Capital allowances: full expensing

The full expensing provisions allow a deduction of 100% for qualifying main pool expenditure. For special rate pool items, a deduction of 50% of the qualifying expenditure is available with the remaining 50% added to the special rate pool from the start of the next accounting period. These enhanced rates do not have a financial limit but are only available on *new, unused* and not second-hand items purchased excluding cars and items available for leasing. Alternatively, where applicable, capital allowances may be claimed as normal utilising the annual investment allowance and writing down allowance as explained in Chapter 7.

Example 16.11

NNM Limited prepares its accounts to 31 December annually and acquires new main pool plant and machinery on 1 August 2026 for £2m. What are the capital allowance options available to NNM Limited?

Answer

Assuming that no other capital expenditure has been incurred, NNM Limited could claim 100% AIA on £1,000,000 and WDA at a hybrid rate of 14.99% on the balance giving total capital allowances of £1,149,900.

Alternatively, full expensing could be claimed providing a deduction of £2,000,000 @ 100% = £2,000,000.

However, a combination would be the best route. Assuming that no other capital expenditure has been incurred, NNM Limited could claim 100% AIA on £1,000,000 and full expensing on the balance of £1,000,000 to give a total claim of £2,000,000.

Example 16.12

Assume the facts are as in example 16.6 above except that the expenditure falls into the special rate pool. What are the capital allowance options available to NNM Limited?

Answer

Assuming that no other capital expenditure has been incurred, NNM Limited could claim 100% AIA on £1,000,000 and WDA at 6% on the balance, giving total capital allowances of £1,060,000.

Alternatively, full expensing could be claimed providing a deduction of £2,000,000 @ 50% = £1,000,000. In addition, £1,000,000 would be added to the special rate pool balance at the start of the next accounting period.

Again, a combination would be the best route. NNM Limited could claim 100% AIA on £1,000,000 and full expensing @ 50% on the balance of £1,000,000 to give a total claim of £1,500,000. The remaining £500,000 would be added to the special rate pool at the start of the next accounting period.

Example 16.13

PDQ Limited has been trading for several years and prepares accounts to 31 December each year. During the year to 31 December 2016, PDQ Limited purchased a new, unused machine, a piece of P&M falling into the main pool, at a cost of £1,300,000. As at 31 December 2025, the TWDV on the pools are as follows:

Main pool	£40,000
Special rate pool	£8,000

Calculate the capital allowances to which PDQ Limited is entitled to for the accounting period to 31 December 2026.

Answer

Hybrid rate of Main pool WDA:

1 January 2026 to 5 April 2026	18% x 95/365 days	=	4.685
6 April 2026 to 31 December 2026	14% x 270/365 days	=	10.356
Hybrid rate (rounded up to 2 decimals)		=	15.05%

		Main Pool	**Special Pool**	**Allowances or Claim**
TWDV brought forward		40,000	8,000	
Additions qualifying for AIA				
Main pool	1,300,000			

AIA (Maximum)	(1,000,000)			1,000,000
Balance	300,000			
Full expensing	(300,000)			300,000
Balance	0			
WDA @ 15.05%		(6,020)		6,020
WDA @ 6%			(480)	480
				CA Claimed 1,306,500
TWDV carried forward		33,980	7,520	

Notes

1. As the expenditure qualifying for AIA exceeds £1,000,000, the AIA claim is limited to £1,000,000. Full expensing is claimed on the balance of expenditure.
2. Note the template used for calculating capital allowances involving AIA.
3. Compare this to example 7.3 for a sole trader.

As can be seen by the examples above in some cases a claim for AIA may be more beneficial.

Where full expensing is claimed a balancing charge will arise on disposal. Where the 100% allowance has been claimed, the balancing charge will be 100% of the disposal value. Where the 50% allowance has been claimed, 50% of the disposal value will be assessed as a balancing charge and the balance will be deducted from the special rate pool balance. If the full expensing claim has been limited to a proportion of the cost with the balance falling into the pool, then a similar apportionment of the proceeds would be required.

Example 16.14

TFS Limited purchased several new lorries for £250,000 during the accounting period to 31 March 2026 and claimed full expensing, reducing its trading profits by £250,000 @ 100% = £250,000.

All of the lorries were sold during the following accounting period for £200,000. What is the balancing adjustment?

Answer

A balancing charge will arise of £200,000 @ 100% = £200,000 and will be added to the trading profits.

It should be noted that if Annual Investment Allowance had been claimed, subject to the annual limit, 100% relief would be available in the year of purchase but on disposal the proceeds would be deducted from the pool, potentially reducing the balancing charge. Therefore, for main pool expenditure, the maximum AIA should be always utilised before any claim for full expensing.

Property business profit

Property business profits are determined in a very similar way as for individuals (see Chapter 5); however, the accruals basis always applies (e.g. dates of receipt of rent are irrelevant). It is, however, assessed for an accounting period (not a year of assessment as for individuals).

Property business profit comprises:

- rents; and
- premiums received on the grant of a short lease (i.e. a lease of 50 years or shorter)

In computing the amount of property business profit the normal rules relating to the calculation of trading profits also apply (see Chapters 5 and 6), e.g.:

- expenses must have been wholly and exclusively incurred for the purposes of the property business;
- capital expenditure is disallowed; and
- general provision for bad debts disallowed etc.

Property business profits from more than one property are aggregated producing a single assessable property business profit figure.

One important point to note is that where a company pays interest on a loan to purchase or improve investment property such interest is *not* allowed as an expense in computing the property business profit (as is the case for individuals; see Chapter 5). The interest is, in fact, deductible against any interest income of the company under the non-trade loan relationship rules. This may give rise to net interest income or loss (see below). In addition, there is no restriction on finance costs paid by a company in respect of residential property as applies to individuals.

Premiums received for grant of a short lease

The rules detailed in Chapter 5 regarding the receipt or payment of a short lease premium also apply to companies. A short lease is one of 50 years or less.

A premium is in effect treated as if it was additional rent in the accounting period in which the lease is granted. However, only part of the premium is chargeable to tax as property business income:

Amount of premium chargeable as property business income =
Premium – [2% x Premium x (duration of the lease in complete years – 1)]

Example 16.15

MNT Ltd received a premium of £10,000 on 1 June 2026 when it let out a property under a 10 year lease to a trading company, PQM Ltd. In addition, a monthly rent of £5,000 is payable on the first day of each month.

Calculate MNT Ltd's property business profit to be included as part of its profit for the accounting period 1 April 2026 to 31 March 2027 and the allowable amounts to be deducted in PQM Ltd's accounting period for the year to 31 December 2026.

Answer

MNT Ltd to 31 March 2027

Both the rent (on an accruals basis) and a proportion of the premium (in the accounting period of granting of the lease) are taxable.

Taxable element of premium = 10,000 – [2% x 10,000 x (10 – 1)] = 8,200

Rents accrued from 1.6.26 to 31.3.27 = £5,000 x 10 months = 50,000

Therefore:
Property business profit = £8,200 + £50,000 = £58,200

PQM Ltd to 31 December 2026

The rent due under the lease should be included in the financial statements of PQM Ltd on an accruals basis.

Rents accrued 1.6.26 to 31.12.26= £5,000 x 7 months = 35,000

PQM Ltd will also be entitled to deduct from its trading profits a proportion of the lease premium. This is calculated as the amount of the lease premium taxable as income on the grantor of the lease spread over the life of the lease.

The amount taxable on the lessor (MN Ltd) is £8,200 as calculated above.

For PQM Ltd the annual deduction is 8,200/ 10 years = £820.

However, as the lease was only in place for seven months in the accounting period to 31.12.26, the deduction will be £820 x 7/12 months = £478.

PQM Ltd would be entitled to a deduction of £820 during the accounting period to 31.12.27 and subsequent years until the full £8,200 is relieved.

Interest income and expenses

Non-trade loan relationships

Non-trade interest income and interest expenses are dealt with under the non-trade loan relationship provisions.

Interest income or loan relationship credits primarily consists of interest income from bank and building society deposits and on loans to other companies. *Interest expenses or loan relationship debits* include the interest payable on a non-trade borrowing such as loans incurred to buy property for renting out (i.e. for a property business) or investments, and any associated costs. The write off of a non-trade loan may also be a loan relationship debit.

Non-trade interest income/expense items are not received/paid as part of the company's trade. Such income and expenses are taxed on an accruals basis and are aggregated to produce a net interest income/expense figure.

Excess of interest income over interest expense

The net amount is included as interest income in the calculation of TTP.

Excess of interest expense over interest income

Where the aggregate interest expense exceeds the aggregate interest income the excess or deficit may be relieved by:

- setting against TTP of the same accounting period (*after* trading losses brought forward but *before* a trading loss of the same or future periods and *before* qualifying charitable donations);
- surrendered as group relief (See Chapter 19);
- carried back and set against surpluses on non-trading relationships for the previous year; or
- carried forward and set against future non-trading profits (this is the default option if other methods of relief are not claimed).

Trade loan relationships

Trade loan relationships refer to the position where the interest payable or receivable is paid/received as part of the company's trade, for example, interest paid on a bank loan to buy new equipment for use in the company's trade. In such cases interest payable is allowed as a trading expense and trading interest receivable is treated as trading income (normally any interest income will not be treated as trading income but income as part of a non-trading relationship; see above).

Comprehensive example

The following provides a comprehensive example of the calculation of adjusted trading profit and TTP for a limited company.

Example 16.16

BRG Limited's accounts for the year ended 31 March 2027 show profits before tax of £656,870.

Included in this amount is rent receivable of 48,000 from letting an investment property.

The expenses deducted when calculating the profit include the following items:
Depreciation of 63,420 has been charged.

Legal expenses have been included of 12,000 in respect of the purchase of new business premises. Accountancy fees of 7,800 were included for the preparation of the annual accounts.

The following items were included under the heading Entertaining:

Meals with customers	860
Christmas gifts of wine for suppliers	600
Staff party	970

Motor expenses include lease fees in respect of two motor cars:

Car 1 CO_2 rating 166 g/km leasing fees	8,000
Car 2 CO_2 rating 48 g/km leasing fees	5,000

Donations were made as follows:

Donation to local charity	100
Donation to national charity	2,000
Political donation	400

The company paid private golf club membership fees for the director of 900.

Capital allowances have been calculated as 288,028.

What is the adjusted trading profit, TTP and corporation tax liability of BRG Limited to 31 March 2027?

Answer

Profit per accounts		656,870
Less: Rents received		(48,000)
Add:		
Depreciation	63,420	
Legals:		
Property purchase (capital)	12,000	

Accountancy	0	
Entertaining:		
Meals for customers	860	
Christmas wine	600	
Staff Party	0	
Car lease restriction		
8,000 x 15%	1,200	
Charitable donations		
Local charity	0	
National charity	2,000	
Political donation	400	
Golf club membership	0	
		80,480
		689,350
Less: Capital allowances		(288,028)
Adjusted trading profits		401,322

Total taxable profits to 31 March 2027

Adjusted trading profit	401,322
Rental income	48,000
Less	
Qualifying charitable donations	-2,000
TTP	447,322

Corporation tax payable to 31 March 2027

TTP £447,322 @ 25% = £111,830

Notes

1. Rent received is not trading income. It is deducted when calculating the adjusted trading profit but must be included in the calculation of TTP.
2. See Chapter 6 for detailed rules of adjustments to trading profits. Where items of expenses are allowable, such as Accountancy no adjustment is required. Some exam conventions require this to be shown as an adjustment of "0" as included in this example.
3. Donations to the national charity are added back as not allowable in the calculation of adjusted trading profit but are deducted as qualifying charitable donations in the calculation of TTP.
4. The golf club subscription is effectively part of the managing director's remuneration. It is, therefore, an allowable part of the company's employment costs but will create a benefit in kind assessable on the individual.

Close companies

Some special tax rules apply to a close company, principally to prevent the shareholders from gaining an unfair tax advantage. A close company is defined as one that is controlled by its directors or five or fewer shareholders. For this purpose, a simple majority of shares will achieve control.

If a close company provides a benefit in kind to a shareholder, who is not an employee or director of the company, then the taxable value of the benefit in kind is effectively taxed as dividend income of the individual.

When a close company makes a loan to a shareholder, there is also a tax charge on the company calculated as 33.75% of the loan, unless the loan is repaid within nine months of the company's accounting period. When the loan is eventually repaid to the company, the tax charge will also be refundable.

Research and development expenditure

To encourage spending on research and development (R&D) by companies, additional relief from corporation tax is given for qualifying expenditure. A merged scheme applies to all companies from 1 April 2024. Research and Development expenditure credit (RDEC) can be claimed by trading companies within the charge to UK Corporation Tax.

To qualify for RDEC a project must seek to make an advance in science or technology relating to the company's trade - either an existing one or a new one to be started based on the results of the R&D. The project may research or develop a new process, product or service or improve on an existing one.

From the date that work starts until the date that the advance is developed or discovered (or the project is stopped) the following costs qualify for relief:

- Employee costs for staff working directly on the R&D project including employers Class 1 NIC and pension fund contributions. For subcontracted staff, only 65% of the relevant payments may be claimed.
- Computer software bought for R&D.
- Data licence costs and cloud computing costs.
- Consumable items used in the R&D including materials and utility costs, such as fuel power and water.

Costs that cannot be claimed include the production and distribution of goods and services, the cost of land, the cost of patents and trademarks, rent or rates.

Under the scheme relief for qualifying expenditure is given as a 20% credit against the Corporation tax liability for the accounting period. However, the credit is deemed to be trading income and is liable to corporation tax. In some circumstances, subject to restrictions, the RDEC may create a tax credit that is repayable to the company.

Example 16.17

RAD plc incurred the following expenditure researching a qualifying project during the year ended 31 March 2027:

Direct R&D staff costs	24,000
Direct administrative support for the R&D department	3,000
Market research	7,000
Heat and light in the R&D department	2,000

Rent and rates for R&D offices/workshops	6,000
New software	5,000
Subcontracted R&D staff	12,000

Calculate the expenditure qualifying for RDEC.

Answer

Direct R&D staff costs	24,000
Administrative support for the R&D department	3,000
Market research – not qualifying	
Heat and light in the R&D department	2,000
Rent and rates for R&D offices/workshops – not qualifying	
New software	5,000
Specialist equipment for R&D project - capital	
Subcontracted R&D staff £12,000 x 65% =	7,800
Total qualifying expenditure	41,800

Example 16.18

For the year ended 31 March 2027, ATL Plc has a turnover of £10,500,000, tax allowable expenses of £5,400,000, capital allowances of £2,010,000 and qualifying R&D expenditure of £1,500,000.

Calculate the corporation tax liability of ATL PLC to 31 March 2026.

Answer

Turnover		10,500,000		
Allowable expenses		-5,400,000		
Capital allowances		-2,010,000		
R&D expenditure		-1,500,000		
Taxable R&D tax credit		300,000		
TTP		1,890,000		
Corporation tax	1,890,000 @ 25%		=	472,500
R&D expenditure credit	1,500,000 @ 20%		=	-300,000
Net CT liability				172,500

Notes

If RDEC was not available the TTP would be £1,590,000 giving a CT liability @ 25% of £397,500. The RDEC reduces the CT liability by £225,000, an effective additional tax relief of 15% (1,500,000 @ 15% = 225,000).

SUMMARY

- Corporation tax is calculated on a company's Taxable Total Profits (TTP) for an accounting period and not by reference to tax years.
- Where financial statements are prepared for a period exceeding 12 months, there are two accounting periods: the first 12 months and the balance of the period with trading profits etc. apportioned or recalculated as appropriate.

- The rate of corporation tax is determined by the Financial Year. The profits of an accounting period may fall into more than one Financial Year.
- From 1 April 2023, there are two rates of Corporation tax and Marginal relief.
- Company tax adjusted trading profits must be established by adding back any disallowable expenses to the accounting profits before tax and deducting any non-trading income and capital gains. However, no adjustments are required for private use.
- Capital allowances can be claimed to reduce the trading profits, including full expensing.
- Non-trade interest received and paid is aggregated to establish the net non-trade loan relationship result.
- Qualifying charitable donations can be deducted when calculating TTP, however, deductions must be made in strict order, which in some circumstances can deny relief for QCD.
- Companies pay corporation tax on capital gains (see Chapter 17).
- Companies may claim additional tax relief for qualifying R&D costs.

CHAPTER 17

Chargeable Gains for Companies

Introduction

This chapter looks at the taxation of capital gains made by companies. Companies are not liable to capital gains tax. As detailed in Chapter 16, companies are liable to corporation tax on their total profits *and* gains, known as taxable total profits (TTP).

Differences from CGT for individuals

Many of the rules applicable to individuals for calculating capital gains also apply to companies.

However, companies:

- do *not* pay capital gains tax but corporation tax on chargeable gains for an accounting period;
- are *not* entitled to an annual exemption;
- are not entitled to business asset disposal relief, gift relief or main residence relief, but rollover relief is available to companies;
- are entitled to indexation allowance (but frozen at 31 December 2017);
- have different rules for the identification of shares disposed of;
- for pre-31 March 1982 assets, the gain is the lower of the gain calculated using the original cost and the gain using the 31 March 1982 value;
- on the sale of certain business assets, roll-over relief may be claimed as for sole traders (see Chapter 15).

Indexation allowance

Indexation allowance is an attempt to allow for inflation (i.e. the time value of money). Indexation allowance is deducted when calculating gains arising to a company, with certain restrictions as detailed below.

The indexation allowance is computed by multiplying the allowable cost of an asset by an indexation factor. The resulting indexation allowance is then deducted, reducing the capital gain on that asset.

The indexation factor is calculated by reference to the change in the Retail Prices Index (RPI):

$$\frac{\text{RPI for the month of disposal (see below) - RPI for the month of acquisition}}{\text{RPI for the month of acquisition}}$$

Indexation allowance is limited to the increase in RPI since March 1982. For earlier acquisitions use March 1982 as the month of acquisition when calculating indexation allowance.

Under Finance Act 2018, indexation allowance has been frozen for disposals after 31 December 2017. Indexation allowance is still given but is only calculated up to 31 December 2017 – for disposals after December 2017, use December 2017 as the month of disposal to calculate indexation allowance. Therefore, indexation allowance cannot apply to assets acquired after 31 December 2017.

The index factor is rounded to three decimal places except when applied to a share pool. In many exam questions, the indexation factor is provided.

Indexation allowance can only reduce any capital gain to nil. Therefore, indexation allowance cannot turn a capital gain into a capital loss or increase a capital loss.

No indexation allowance is available on incidental *disposal* costs. Such costs are simply deducted from gross sale proceeds.

Example 17.1

JKP Ltd sells an asset in December 2026 for £26,000 before selling costs of £400. JKP Ltd acquired the asset in May 2012 for £10,000.

The RPI for May 2012 is 242.4 and for December 2017 is 278.1.

Calculate JKP Ltd's capital gain.

Answer

Gross sale proceeds	26,000	
Less:		
Incidental costs of disposal	(400)	
Net sale proceeds	25,600	
Less: Cost of the asset	(10,000)	
Unindexed capital gain	15,600	
Less: Indexation allowance	(1,470)	(See below)
Indexed capital gain	14,130	

Indexation allowance

The increase in RPI is calculated as:

(RPI for December 2017- RPI for May 2012)/RPI for May 2012

The RPI for May 2012 is 242.4 and for December 2017 is 278.1

(278.1-242.4)/242.4 = 0.147277 rounded to three decimal places = 0.147

Indexation allowance is cost x increase in RPI

Indexation allowance = 10,000 x 0.147 = £1,470

Example 17.2

LMP Ltd sells an asset in June 2026 for £30,000 before selling costs of £1,000. LMP Ltd acquired the asset in March 2008 for £15,000.

In addition, further capital expenditure of £5,000 was incurred in June 2010, enhancing the value of the asset.

Indexation allowance must be calculated separately for the initial cost from March 2008 and from June 2010 for the enhancement expenditure.

The Indexation factor for the period March 2008 to December 2017 is calculated at 0.311 and for the period June 2010 to December 2017 is 0.241

Calculate LMP Ltd's capital gain.

Answer

Gross sale proceeds		30,000
Less: Incidental costs of disposal		(1,000)
Net sale proceeds		29,000
Less:		
Cost of asset	15,000	
Enhancement expenditure	5,000	
		(20,000)
Unindexed capital gain		9,000
Less:		
Indexation allowance		
15,000 x 0.311	4,665	
5,000 x 0.241	1,205	
Total indexation allowance		(5,870)
Indexed capital gain		3,130

Notes

1. A calculation of indexation allowance is required separately for each individual item of cost (e.g. original purchase cost and enhancement expenditure).
2. The indexation factors are provided and do not need to be calculated in this example.
3. If the indexation allowance was £3,130 or more, then the gain would be reduced to Nil. Any excess indexation allowance cannot create a loss.
4. Indexation allowance is only calculated to 31 December 2017.

As can be seen, the indexation allowance simply reduces the amount of the unindexed capital gain, it cannot create or increase a loss.

Example 17.3

WXT Limited sold an asset in May 2026 for £26,000 having acquired it in January 2015 for £24,500.

The RPI for January 2015 is 255.4 and for December 2017 is 278.1.

Calculate WXT Ltd's capital gain.

Answer

Gross sale proceeds		26,000
Less:		
Cost of asset		(24,500)
Unindexed capital gain		1,500
Less:		
Indexation allowance (Maximum)	2,180	
Indexation allowance (Restricted)		(1,500)
Indexed gain		0

Notes

Indexation allowance cannot create or increase a loss. The full indexation allowance would create an overall loss. Therefore, indexation allowance is restricted to £1,500, giving an indexed gain of £Nil.

Indexation allowance

The increase in RPI is calculated as:

(RPI for December 2017 - RPI for January 2015)/RPI for January 2015

(278.1-255.4)/255.4 = 0.08888 rounded to three decimal places = 0.089

Indexation allowance is cost x increase in RPI

Indexation allowance = 24,500 x 0.089 = £2,180

Share identification and indexation for share pools

Where share disposals are made by companies rather than individuals, the matching rules are slightly different.

Shares in a single company sold by a company are matched as follows:

1. First, with acquisitions on the same day
2. Then, with acquisitions within the nine days preceding the date of disposal on a first-in, first-out basis
3. Finally, with shares in the pool.

Companies are entitled to indexation allowance up to the date of a share sale or 31 December 2017, if earlier.

Therefore, it will be necessary to calculate the indexed cost of the share pool at the date of any share disposals. It may be necessary to calculate the indexation allowance on a "rolling basis".

In calculating the pool cost it is necessary to index the pool cost (without rounding to three decimal places when working out any indexation factors) between successive events (i.e. subsequent purchases and sales) to find the indexed cost before the disposal. The indexed cost of any shares disposed of can then be calculated and deducted from the pool.

Example 17.4

JSD Ltd acquired 1,000 shares in ABC plc in October 2000 for £3,000. In August 2005 a further 2,000 shares in ABC plc were acquired for £7,000 and in October 2010 a further 1,500 shares in ABC plc were acquired for £4,000.

JSD Ltd then sold 3,000 shares in ABC plc on 11 May 2026 for £15,600.

JSD Ltd prepares its accounts to 31 March each year.

RPI was as follows:

October 2000	171.6
August 2005	192.6
October 2010	225.8
December 2017	278.1

What is JSD Ltd's chargeable gain for its accounting period ended 31 March 2026?

Answer

No shares in ABC plc were purchased either on the same day of the sale (i.e. 11 May 2026) or in the nine days prior to it.

Therefore, any matching is with shares forming part of the share pool. Before any matching can be done the indexed value of the pool as at the date of the share sale must be calculated. The indexation allowance("IA") must be calculated between each event, creating a "rolling" indexed cost.

ABC plc shareholding	Number of shares	Cost	Indexed cost
		£	£
October 2000	1,000	3,000	3,000
IA 10/2000 to 8/2005 £3,000 x (192.6-171.6)/171.6 =			367
			3,367
August 2005	2,000	7,000	7,000
	3,000	10,000	10,367
IA 8/2005 to 10/2010 £10,367 x (225.8-192.6)/192.6 =			1,787
			12,154
October 2010	1,500	4,000	4,000
	4,500	14,000	16,154
IA 10/2010 to 12/2017 £16,154 x (278.1-225.8)/225.8 =			3,741
			19,895

Therefore, in May 2026, before the sale, 4,500 shares were held with a cost of £14,000 and an indexed cost of £19,895 (the difference between these two amounts being the cumulative indexation allowance)

May 2026 sale	(3,000)	(9,333)	(13,263)
Pool balances	1,500	4,667	6,632

The gain can now be calculated:

May 2026 3,000 shares sold proceeds	15,600
Less: Cost	(9,333)
Indexation allowance (Note 3)	(3,930)
Gain	2,337

Notes

1. The pool is indexed to each successive event (i.e. each subsequent purchase and sale) in turn until the pool value as at the date of any sale is known. Indexation factors are not restricted to three decimal places.
2. The cost of the shares sold in May 2026 is calculated as 14,000 x 3,000/4500 and a similar apportionment is used for the indexed cost.
3. The indexation allowance on the sale is the difference between the indexed cost of £13,263 and the cost of £9,333. In this case, there seems little point in showing these amounts separately, but this calculation can be useful when ensuring that indexation allowance does not create or increase any loss.
4. A similar share pool calculation will be required for each shareholding.

Scrip and rights issues

The comments made in connection with bonus and rights issues for individuals in Chapter 14 apply equally to companies, subject to the fact that indexation allowance will apply to the cost of rights issues.

Capital losses

A capital loss must be offset against any chargeable gains of the same accounting period and any unrelieved amount of loss may then be carried forward for offset against future chargeable gains.

Capital gains reliefs applying to companies only

Substantial shareholdings exemption

From April 2002, a chargeable gain made by a company on the disposal of the whole or any part of a qualifying substantial shareholding in another trading company is exempt from corporation tax.

A qualifying substantial shareholding is an ordinary shareholding of 10% or more. The shareholding must give a beneficial entitlement of at least 10% of profits available for distribution to shareholders *and* assets available for distribution on a winding up. In addition, the disposing company must have held the qualifying shareholding for a continuous period of at least 12 months during the six years preceding the disposal. This allows part disposals to continue to qualify for relief for five years after the shareholding has fallen below 10%.

The 12 months rule can also be met where the shares are in a new company, where that company received assets from another 75% group company and the assets transferred were used by another group trading company for the 12 months before the transfer. F(2)A2017 has also extended the relief to certain holdings of less than 10% provided it cost at least £20 million.

Similarly, capital losses on such shareholdings are not allowable.

Where the substantial shareholdings exemption applies, it is automatic and does not require an election.

Replacement of business assets or Roll-over relief

Chargeable gains roll-over relief is not available for companies concerning the sale and purchase of intellectual property (e.g. goodwill, patents, etc. (Asset classes 4 to 7A detailed in TCGA1992 section 155)).

Chargeable gains roll-over relief continues to be available for other chargeable assets as for individuals, as described in Chapter 15.

SUMMARY

- A company's capital gains are included in TTP for an accounting period and are subject to corporation tax.
- Companies are not entitled to an annual CGT exemption, but gains may be reduced by indexation allowance.
- Indexation allowance reduces the gain by the increase in the RPI between acquisition and disposal. Indexation allowance cannot increase or create a loss. Indexation allowance is frozen at 31 December 2017.

- Share identification or matching rules for companies are different to the rules for individuals.
- Companies can take advantage of the relief for replacement business assets and the substantial shareholding exemption.

CHAPTER 18

Company Losses

Introduction

This chapter examines how a company may claim corporation tax relief for any losses incurred.

The following chapter will look at how a company's trading loss may be used by other companies in the same *group* as the loss-making company.

Types of loss

An ongoing company may incur various losses for an accounting period including:

- a trading loss
- a property business loss
- net interest loss (or loan relationship deficit)
- a capital loss.

Trading losses

A company making a trading loss for an accounting period has three options:

1. Claim CTA2010 section 37 to offset the loss against total profits for the same accounting period (current year claim).
2. Once a claim has been made against current year profits, a further claim, under section 37, can be made to offset the loss against total profits for the 12 month period preceding the loss-making period (previous year claim).
3. Carry forward trading losses arising on or after 1 April 2017 against a specified amount of total profits for future accounting periods (CTA2010 section 45A).

A trading loss is computed in the same way as a trading profit for any accounting period. Capital allowances increase any loss claim and it is possible to claim less than the maximum capital allowances available to reduce an excessive unusable loss. Several "what if" calculations may be required to establish the optimal loss claim, reflecting the tax rates across different years and the possible loss of relief for QCD.

Claim against total profits of the current year (CTA2010 section 37)

Under section 37, a company may make a claim for the trading loss to be set against total profits of the same accounting period. The loss reduces profits before the deduction of qualifying charitable donations (QCD) as noted in the example below.

The loss must be relieved to the maximum amount possible – the claim will be for the lower of the available loss or the total profits of the year of claim, which may deny relief for QCD.

Loss claims under section 37 must be made within two years after the end of the loss-making accounting period.

Example 18.1

LMC Ltd has the following results for the year to 31 March 2027:

	£
Trading loss	(118,000)
Chargeable gains	40,000
Net interest income	15,000
Qualifying charitable donations	(2,000)

How much section 37 loss relief can be claimed against profits to 31 March 2027?

Answer

	£
Trading profit	0
Chargeable gains	40,000
Net interest income	15,000
Total profits	55,000
S37 Current year loss claim	(55,000)
	0
Qualifying charitable donations	Wasted
TTP	0

Notes

1. Trading profit to 31.3.27 is £Nil. (Do not include the loss in the computation at this point).
2. Losses must be claimed to the full extent of profits and gains.
3. Loss relief is given before relief for qualifying charitable donations (QCD). For the year to 31.3.27, this means that relief for QCD is lost or wasted.
4. A loss memo is a useful way of tracking losses arising and utilisation:

Loss year ended 31 March 2027	118,000
Current year claim	(55,000)
Balance of loss	63,000

Claim against total profits of the previous year (CTA2010 section 37)

After the loss has been claimed against the total profits of the accounting period of the loss, a further optional claim may be made to carry back any remaining trading loss to the previous 12 months. (Compare this to the position for sole traders under the equivalent section 64; see Chapter 8). There is, however, no requirement to carry back any unrelieved loss – this claim is optional.

The loss must be relieved to the maximum amount possible – the claim will be for the lower of the available loss or the total profits. It is not possible, for example, under section 37 to carry back to the previous 12 months only part of the unrelieved loss; the maximum possible relievable loss must be carried back.

Loss claims under section 37 must be made within two years after the end of the loss-making accounting period.

Example 18.2

Following on from example 18.1 above, LMC Ltd has the following results for the year to 31 March 2026:

	£
Trading profit	44,000
Chargeable gains	6,000
Net interest income	9,000
Qualifying charitable donations	(1,500)

How much of the balance of loss may be claimed under section 37 against profits to 31 March 2026?

Answer

	£
Trading profit	44,000
Chargeable gains	6,000
Net interest income	9,000
Total profits	59,000
S37 Previous year loss claim (Carry back claim)	(59,000)
	0
Qualifying charitable donations	Wasted
TTP	0

Notes

1. Losses must be claimed to the full extent of profits and gains.
2. Loss relief is given before relief for qualifying charitable donations (QCD). For the year to 31.3.26, this means that relief for QCD is lost or wasted.
3. The loss claim is optional but cannot be made unless a current year claim has been made.
4. The loss memo can be updated:

Loss year ended 31 March 2027	118,000
Current year claim	(55,000)
	63,000
Previous year claim	(59,000)
Balance of loss	4,000

Accounting periods of different lengths

It may be that a company's accounting year end changes. This would then mean that the length of the accounting period will vary.

For example, a company may make its accounts up to 31 December each year. Following the preparation of the accounts to say 31 December 2026 the company may then decide to change to a 31 March year end. Accounts will then be prepared to 31 March 2027 and 31 March each year thereafter. The accounting period to 31 March 2027 will thus be only three months long.

In such a case, care is needed in offsetting any trading losses carried back, as detailed in the following example.

Example 18.3

JK Ltd has the following results:

	Year ended 31.12.25	3 months to 31.3.26	Year ended 31.3.27
Trading profit	80,000	150,000	(750,000)
Chargeable gains	20,000	40,000	30,000
Net interest income	25,000	15,000	40,000
QCD	12,000	3,000	15,000

Show how section 37 losses can be claimed.

Answer

The loss strategy set out above requires that the trading loss for the accounting period ended 31.3.27 should be used first against current income and gains; then against those of the previous 12 months.

In this case, the previous 12 months are the period 1.4.25 to 31.3.26. This period includes nine months of the accounting period ended 31.12.25 (i.e. 1.4.25 to 31.12.25) and the three months from 1.1.26 to 31.3.25.

Finally, if any surplus loss remains it will be carried forward to the accounting period ending 31.3.26.

	Year ended 31.12.25	3 months to 31.3.26	Year ended 31.3.27
Trading profit	80,000	150,000	nil
Less:			
Chargeable gains	20,000	40,000	30,000
Net interest income	25,000	15,000	40,000
Total profit	125,000	205,000	70,000
Less:			
Section 37 loss current year			(70,000)
Section 37 loss	(93,750)	(205,000)	
Less:			
QCD	(12,000)	(Wasted)	(Wasted)
TTP	19,250	nil	nil

Notes

1. The trading loss of £750,000 is first used, under section 37, against "total profit" to 31.3.27 of £70,000 leaving £680,000 loss remaining.
2. The surplus can then be carried back and offset against "total profit" of £205,000 for the three months to 31.03.26. However, under section 37, the £680,000 loss can be carried back 12 months. £205,000 of it has been carried back three months.
3. The balance (i.e. £680,000 less £205,000) can still be carried back a further nine months covering the period 1.4.25 to 31.12.25. The profits available for offset for these nine months are 9/12 x 125,000 = 93,750. The remaining profits arose up to 31.3.25 and are therefore not inside the 12 month carryback period.
4. Of the trading loss of £750,000, some £368,750 has been used under section 37 leaving £381,250 for future carry forward.

5. The QCD for the accounting periods ended 31.3.26 and 31.3.27 are unrelieved. They cannot be carried back or forward for relief.

Carry forward against total profits (CTA2010 section 45A)

Section 45A provides relief for losses carried forward. Trading losses arising on or after 1 April 2017 may be carried forward and claimed against total profits of future accounting periods

A claim under section 45A may specify the amount of the loss to be claimed and, for example, may be restricted to avoid wasting relief for QCD. If any loss remains, then this will continue to be carried forward. A claim must be made within two years of the end of the accounting period of relief.

There are three conditions that must be met for section 45A losses to be set off against total profits:

1. the company must continue to carry on the trade in all subsequent accounting periods up to and including the one in which the losses are offset;
2. the trade must not have become small or negligible in the loss-making period; and
3. the trade must be carried on commercially in both the loss-making period and period of set-off.

Example 18.4

Following on from Example 18.2 above, LMC Ltd has the following results for the year to 31 March 2028:

	£
Trading profit	18,000
Chargeable gains	0
Net interest income	6,000
Qualifying charitable donations	(1,000)

How much of the balance of loss may be claimed under section 45A against profits to 31 March 2028?

Answer

	£
Trading profit	18,000
Chargeable gains	0
Net interest income	6,000
Total profits	24,000
S45A Loss brought forward	(4,000)
	20,000
Qualifying charitable donations paid	(1,000)
TTP	19,000

Notes

1. Loss relief is given before relief for qualifying charitable donations (QCD). For the year to 31.3.28, this leaves sufficient profits so that relief for QCD is not lost. However, the

loss claim may be for a specified amount. Therefore, it is possible to avoid the loss of relief for QCD.

2. The loss memo can be updated:

Loss year ended 31 March 2027	118,000	
Current year claim (APE 31.3.27)	(55,000)	*(Example 18.1)*
	63,000	
Previous year claim (APE 31.3.26)	(59,000)	*(Example 18.2)*
	4,000	
Carry forward claim (APE 31.3.28)	(4,000)	
Balance of loss	0	

The loss has now been claimed in full.

Restriction on carried forward loss claims

For carry forward loss claims after 1 April 2017, there is a cap on the losses that may be relieved.

Generally, the loss restriction only limits the amount of losses that can be claimed by carrying forward where profits are above £5 million. The restriction limits the carry forward loss claim to £5 million referred to as the deductions allowance, plus 50% of profits above £5 million. If the accounting period is less than 12 months then the £5 million limit is time apportioned. It is also shared by group companies.

Example 18.5

FGH Ltd has total profits for the year to 30 June 2026 of £12 million and post-1 April 2017 losses brought forward of £20 million. What is the maximum claim under section 45A?

Answer

The section 45A loss claim will be restricted to £5 million plus 50% of the remaining profits of £7m, giving a maximum of £8.5m profits to be relieved by carried-forward losses. The result of this is that FGH Ltd will pay corporation tax on the remaining profits of £3.5m.

The remaining loss will be available to carry forward to future accounting periods, with any claim limited as above.

Terminal loss relief (CTA2010 section 39)

Where a company ceases to trade, a loss may arise, which can no longer be carried forward. Terminal loss relief is available for the trading loss for the last 12 months of trading.

A company must first claim relief under section 37 against total profits of the loss making accounting period. The remaining loss arising in the last 12 months of trading, or terminal loss, may then be carried back (under CTA2010 section 39) against income and gains (before QCD) of the three previous years, giving relief against later years first (LIFO basis).

Example 18.6

YZ Ltd has the following results:

	Year ended 31.12.25	Year ended 31.12.26	3 months to 31.3.27
Trading profit	50,000	50,000	(250,000)
Chargeable gains	50,000	40,000	30,000
Net interest income	25,000	15,000	40,000
Qualifying charitable donations	12,000	3,000	15,000

YZ Ltd ceased to trade on 31 March 2027.

Show how the trading loss to 31 March 2027 may be used.

Answer

	Year ended 31.12.25	Year ended 31.12.26	3 months to 31.3.27
Trading profit	50,000	50,000	nil
Chargeable gains	50,000	40,000	30,000
Net interest income	25,000	15,000	40,000
Total profit	125,000	105,000	70,000
Less:			
Section 37 loss			(70,000)
Section 39 losses	(75,000)	(105,000)	
Less:			
QCD	(12,000)	(nil)	(nil)
TTP	38,000	nil	nil

Notes

1. Under section 37, £70,000 of the trading loss for the three months ended 31.3.27 has been offset against other profits to 31.03.27. This leaves £180,000 losses to be relieved.
2. The terminal loss is for the last 12 months (i.e. 1.4.26 to 31.3.27 and is the aggregate of the trading losses for the periods 1.4.26 to 31.12.26 and 1.1.27 to 31.3.27. For the period 1.4.26 to 31.12.26 a trading profit, not a trading loss arose. For the purpose of calculating the terminal loss, this is ignored.
3. £105,000 of the Terminal loss is claimed against the year to 31.12.26 to reduce total profits to £Nil. The remainder of the loss, £75,000 is claimed against total profits to 31.12.25.

Property business losses

A property business loss for an accounting period must be set off against non-property business income and chargeable gains (Total profits) of the same accounting period before QCD. The relief is given before relief for any trading losses and must be for the lower of the available loss or the total profit – a partial claim is not allowed. This current year claim is automatic and a formal claim is not required.

Any unrelieved property business loss may be carried forward and claimed against total profits of future accounting periods before QCD. However, the amount of the claim for brought forward losses may be limited to any specified amount to prevent wasting relief for QCD. Alternatively, any unrelieved property business loss may be surrendered as group relief (see Chapter 19).

Non-trading loan relationship debits

As mentioned in Chapter 16 where the aggregate non-trading loan relationship debits (broadly non-trading loan interest) exceeds the aggregate non-trading-interest income the loss arising may be relieved by:

- claiming against total profits of the same accounting period (*before* the trading losses, property business losses and *before* qualifying charitable donations);
- carried back and set against surpluses on non-trading loan relationships of the previous year; or
- carried forward and set against future total profits;
- surrendered as group relief (see Chapter 19).

Relief is not automatic and may be claimed for a specified amount.

Capital losses

As mentioned in Chapter 17, a capital loss must be offset against any chargeable gains of the same accounting period and any unrelieved amount of loss is then carried forward for offset against future chargeable gains. The limit of brought forward losses that may be relieved is subject to the same restriction on carried forward trading loss claims detailed above.

Capital losses may not be carried back to earlier accounting periods.

Loss strategy

Losses should be used in the most tax efficient manner available. Usually, this will mean using the loss as soon as possible but care should be taken to avoid wasting tax relief for QCD.

In addition, losses should be utilised against profits subject to the highest rate of corporation tax and the most efficient strategy may be to maximise claims against post-1 April 2023 profits where the higher main rate of 25% applies.

SUMMARY

- Since April 2017, the rules for companies to claim loss relief have generally become more flexible. However, for some larger companies, there will be a limit on the amount of loss relief that may be claimed.
- A company may make a current year claim for relief for trading losses against other income and gains of the loss-making accounting period. After this, the company may optionally claim relief against profits of the previous 12 months.
- Alternatively, subject to meeting the qualifying conditions, a claim may be made for loss relief of a specified amount in subsequent accounting

periods. This carry forward claim is limited to the deductions limit, usually £5 million plus 50% of the profits above £5 million.

- Property losses and excess non-trade loan relationship deficits can be relieved in-year or carried forward.
- Additional relief is available for losses in the final year of trading under the terminal loss rules.
- Capital losses must first be offset against in-year capital gains and are then carried forward against future capital gains.
- Alternative loss claims should be reviewed to maximise the benefit of the relief.

CHAPTER 19

Groups of Companies

Introduction

Chapters 16 to 18 examined the corporation tax position of a single company.

This chapter looks at the position where there is more than one company and together the companies form a *group* for corporation tax purposes. Each company in a group is charged to CT separately. However, there are several advantages for group companies.

Definition of group

There are *two* definitions of a group for corporation tax purposes. The definition depends upon whether the objective is to ascertain whether group relief is available for losses or whether the capital gains advantages apply.

Group relief

The term group relief refers to the ability of one company in a group, as defined below, (referred to as the *surrendering* company) to give or surrender a trading loss to another company in the same group (referred to as the *claimant* company).

Both the surrendering and claimant companies must be within the charge to UK corporation tax (i.e. be resident in the UK or trading in the UK through a permanent establishment). However, an overseas company can be used to link UK based companies, for example, where an overseas parent company has two wholly owned UK subsidiaries, a group relief claim would be possible between the UK companies.

In addition to group relief for trading losses, a company can also surrender net non-trade loan relationship debits, excess QCD and property business losses of an accounting period to another group company.

For group relief purposes two companies are members of the same group if one of the companies is a 75% subsidiary of the other *or* both companies are 75% subsidiaries of a third company.

A company is a *75% subsidiary* of another company if:

- 75% or more of its ordinary share capital is owned directly or indirectly by the other company, *and*
- the other company is entitled to at least 75% or more of its profits available for distribution to ordinary shareholders, *and*
- the other company is entitled to at least 75% of the assets in the event of a winding-up of the company.

Example 19.1

A Ltd owns 75% of B Ltd. B Ltd owns 80% of C Ltd.

B Ltd is a direct 75% subsidiary of A Ltd. Therefore, A Ltd and B Ltd *are* in the same group for group relief.

B Ltd owns more than 80% of C Ltd. Therefore, B Ltd and C Ltd *are* in the same group for group relief.

What about A and C?

Is C a 75% direct or indirect subsidiary of A? A's indirect shareholding interest in C is 75% x 80% = 60%. Therefore, C is not either a direct or indirect 75% subsidiary of A and therefore A and C are *not* in the same group.

There are in effect two separate groups for group relief i.e. A and B; and B and C. Thus, A and B can surrender losses to each other and so can B and C. However, C cannot surrender its loss to B which in turn then surrenders it to A.

Note:

For *group* purposes, it is necessary to multiply the percentage share ownership to ascertain whether one company is an indirect subsidiary of another (e.g. A and C above).

Example 19.2

X Ltd owns 75% of both Y Ltd and Z Ltd

X and Y are in the same group for group relief.

X and Z are in the same group for group relief.

In addition, as Y and Z are both 75% subsidiaries of the same third company (i.e. X) then Y and Z are also in the same group (see group definition above).

Therefore, X, Y and Z are all in the same group for group relief.

Example 19.3

A Ltd

75%	60%	75%
B Ltd	C Ltd	D Ltd

A and B are in a 75% group.
A and D are in a 75% group.
B and D are in the same group as both are 75% subsidiaries of A.

Therefore A, B and D are in the same group for group relief.

A and C are *not* in a group (C is *not* a 75% subsidiary of A).
B and C are *not* in a group (as both are not 75% subsidiaries of the same company).
C and D are *not* in a group (as both are not 75% subsidiaries of the same company).
C is simply not part of any group as it is not a 75% subsidiary of any company.

Group relief allows one group company to surrender all or part of current year losses to other group companies to reduce their taxable profits.

Brought forward trading losses may also be surrendered as group relief. However, in this case, a claim under s45A, against its own profits, must first be made as far as possible by the surrendering company.

Current year trading loss surrender

The surrendering company can surrender its current year trading loss for an accounting period either in full or in part to another group company and does not first need to use the trading loss itself (note, however, that in the case of surplus QCD and property business losses the surrendering company must have first tried to itself obtain relief for these two items before they can be surrendered).

The trading loss may be surrendered simply to one other group company or may be split amongst any number of group companies.

Example 19.4

PRT Limited owns 90% of the ordinary share capital of RTU Limited. For the year to 31 March 2027, PRT Limited has a trading loss of £205,000. For the same accounting period, RTU Limited has trading profits of £180,000 and paid QCD of £6,000.

Show how PRT Limited can surrender losses as group relief to RTU Limited without wasting any relief for QCD.

Answer

PRT Limited should surrender trading losses of £174,000 to RTU Limited by way of group relief:

	PRT Limited	RTU Limited
Trading profits	0	180,000
Less: QCD		(6,000)
Less: Group relief		(174,000)
TTP	nil	nil

PRT Limited has trading losses remaining of £31,000 (£205,000 less £174,000). This loss can be carried forward under s45A or claimed under s37 by PRT Limited.

From 1 April 2017 – Expansion of relief to include losses brought forward

The reformed loss relief rules applying from 1 April 2017 expand claims with the introduction of group relief for carried forward losses. This only applies to losses arising from 1 April 2017.

Before brought forward losses can be surrendered, a company must first maximise the loss against its own profits under s45A as far as possible.

Limitation on loss relief for brought forward losses for groups

When considering relief for brought forward losses after 1 April 2017, the deductions allowance applies of £5 million, as detailed in Chapter 18. This allowance must be shared between members of the same group, broadly following the rules for group relief. Group companies must nominate a company to formally claim the £5 million allowance for the entire group. The nominated company will be required to submit a statement within 12 months of the end of its accounting period setting out how the £5 million group deductions allowance has been allocated within the group.

Change of ownership

Where there is a change of ownership, the surrender of brought forward losses as group relief is not available for pre-acquisition losses in the following five years.

Example 19.5

On 31 May 2026, two companies IJ Limited and KL Limited are in the same group and are both eligible to surrender losses brought forward to the other. On 1 June 2026, both companies were acquired by XYZ Limited.

For the five years from 1 June 2026 IJ Limited and KL Limited will be unable to surrender losses incurred before 1 June 2026 to XYZ Limited.

However, they are still able to surrender losses incurred before the change to each other.

Use by claimant company of group relief

The claimant company deducts the group relief against its own TTP (i.e. after QCD).

This, therefore, means that before the claimant company can use the trading loss claimed from another group company it must deduct any QCD of the current accounting period. If the claimant company has its own current year trading losses these do not need to be claimed under section 37 but an assumed claim must be deducted to calculate the maximum group relief that can be claimed.

Group relief is, however, utilised before deductions of any reliefs from a *subsequent* accounting period (e.g. trading loss carried back under section 37).

A claimant company cannot claim an amount of trading loss from a surrendering company that exceeds its own TTP against which the trading loss is to be offset. In other words, the maximum group relief a claimant company can claim is the *lower* of its own TTP and the loss available for group relief.

Example 19.6

A Ltd has a 100% wholly owned subsidiary B Ltd. Both companies prepare their accounts to 31 March.

For the year ended 31 March 2027, A Ltd has a trading loss of £250,000 and no other profits.

For the same accounting period, B Ltd has a trading profit of £90,000; interest income of £25,000; property business income of £45,000; and chargeable gains of £60,000; and makes a qualifying charitable donation of £30,000. B Ltd also has a trading loss brought forward from an earlier accounting period of £25,000.

Show how A Ltd might use its trading loss under the group relief provisions.

Answer

Adopting the pro-forma from Chapter 16 for B Ltd (the claimant company) for the accounting period to 31 March 2027:

Trading profit	90,000
Property business profit	45,000
Interest income	25,000
Chargeable gains	60,000
Total profits	220,000
Less: Trading loss b/f	(25,000)
Less: QCD	(30,000)
	165,000
Less: Group relief	(165,000)
TTP	nil

Notes

1. Only £165,000 of A Ltd's trading loss of £250,000 should be surrendered by A Ltd to B Ltd as B Ltd only had a TTP of £165,000.
2. The balance of the trading loss of (250,000 - 165,000) i.e. £85,000 can be carried forward by A Ltd under s45A or claimed by A Ltd under section 37.

Corresponding accounting periods

As indicated above a trading loss of an accounting period can be offset against the TTP of another group company. However, for the whole of the trading loss to be potentially available for surrender and offset against the other group company's TTP for an accounting period both companies' accounting periods must coincide exactly (coterminous accounting periods).

In Example 19.6 this occurred as both companies' accounting periods ended on 31 March each year.

Where the companies involved in the group relief claim do not have coterminous accounting periods (i.e. their respective accounting periods end on different dates), any trading loss surrendered may only be used by the claimant company against its TTP for the *corresponding accounting period* i.e. that part of the accounting period of the claimant company which falls in the accounting period of the surrendering company's accounting period.

In fact, both the trading losses surrendered and the corresponding TTP are time apportioned.

Example 19.7

Parent Ltd has a wholly owned subsidiary, Sub Ltd. Parent Ltd makes a trading loss of £24,000 for its year ended 30 June 2026.

Sub Ltd has TTP of £36,000 and £20,000 for the years ended 30 September 2025 and 2026 respectively.

How can the group relief provisions be used?

Answer

Parent Ltd and Sub Ltd do not have coterminous accounting periods. Some apportionment is therefore necessary.

Parent Ltd		*1.7.25*	(24,000)		*30.6.26*	
Sub Ltd	*1.10.24*	36,000	*30.9.25*	20,000		*30.9.26*

Sub Ltd year ended 30 September 2025

Only the three months from 1.7.25 to 30.9.25 fall within Parent Ltd's accounting period ended 30 June 2026.

Therefore, Sub Ltd can potentially claim Parent Ltd trading loss attributable from 1.7.25 to 30.9.25, i.e. 3/12 x (24,000) = (6,000) for offset against its TTP for this corresponding period, i.e. Sub Ltd's TTP for this period is 3/12 x £36,000 = 9,000.

As Sub Ltd's TTP for this corresponding period exceeds the available trading loss of Parent Ltd the whole £6,000 loss may be claimed by Sub Ltd.

Sub Ltd year ended 30 September 2026

Sub Ltd can also potentially claim Parent Ltd's trading loss attributable to 1.10.25 to 30.6.26, i.e. 9/12 x (24,000) = (18,000).

Sub Ltd's TTP for this period is 9/12 x £20,000 = 15,000.

In this case, Sub Ltd's TTP is smaller than the trading loss of Parent Ltd available for relief.

Therefore, for its accounting period ended 30.9.26 Sub Ltd can only claim the lower of the trading loss potentially available i.e. £18,000 and its TTP for the corresponding period i.e. £15,000. The loss claimed is restricted to £15,000.

In total, therefore, of Parent Ltd's trading loss for the accounting period ended 30 June 2026 of £24,000, some £6,000 + £15,000 = £21,000 is available for group relief as shown above.

The balance of the trading loss of £3,000, which cannot be used for group relief, can be used by Parent Ltd against its current and prior year's profits under section 37 or be carried forward under section 45A.

Optimising group relief

Where a group comprises more than two companies and one company incurs a trading loss then the question arises as to how group relief should be claimed for the loss. In other words, against which of the other companies' TTP in the group should the loss be surrendered?

The amount of the loss surrendered to any company should be the claimant's TTP after deducting any QCD, to prevent the loss of relief for the QCD. Unlike some loss relief claims, the group relief claim is for a specified amount.

As group companies may pay different rates of corporation tax, the group relief claims may need careful consideration to reflect the most beneficial overall allocation. In addition, as noted above, care should be taken where year ends do not correspond.

Example 19.8

J, K and L are three UK resident companies that form a 75% group for group relief purposes. All companies prepare accounts to 31 March annually and have no other associated companies.

The results for the year ended 31 March 2027 for each company are as follows:

	J	K	L
Trading profit	200,000	(250,000)	80,000
Property business profit	5,000	15,000	20,000
Interest income	20,000	nil	10,000
Chargeable gains	24,000	3,000	2,000
QCD paid	(5,000)	(2,000)	(15,000)

Show how the losses of K may be used.

Answer

First, calculate the position without any section 37 loss or group relief claims

	J	K	L
Trading profit	200,000	nil	80,000
Property business profit	5,000	15,000	20,000
Interest income	20,000	nil	10,000
Chargeable gain	24,000	3,000	2,000
Less:			
Section 37	nil	nil	nil
Less: QCD	(5,000)	(2,000)	(15,000)
TTP	**244,000**	**16,000**	**97,000**

Care needs to be taken with the Group relief claims as different rates of corporation tax may apply based on TTP.

Initially, we will assume that K would like to reduce its CT liability as far as possible in priority to other group companies.

K does not have to make a claim under section 37 before group relief. Therefore, it may make a group relief claim to maximise the section 37 claim. By surrendering losses as group relief, the section 37 relief claim can be restricted to 16,000, K's TTP. Any higher claim by K Ltd will result in the loss of relief for QCD.

Therefore, of K's trading loss of 250,000, some 16,000 should be left after any group relief claim for K to claim under section 37. Therefore 234,000 is available for surrender as group relief.

The corporation tax limits will be divided as there are three associated companies:

Lower limit 50,000/3	=	16,667
Marginal relief limit 250,000/3	=	83,333

It may be necessary to try several options to find the most beneficial group relief claim.

First, the TTP of L should be reduced to 16,667 so that the Small profits rate of 19% will fully apply. This will require a group relief surrender of £80,333

The balance of K's loss, 234,000 less 80,333, can be claimed by J Ltd.

J is still subject to tax on its post-group relief profit at the main rate but avoids any company in the group being subject to the marginal rate.

Therefore, of K's loss of 250,000, 80,333 is claimed as group relief by L and 153,667 by J. The remaining loss of 16,000 is claimed under section 37 by K.

The revised TTP for all group companies can now be computed:

	J	K	L
Trading profit	200,000	nil	80,000
Property business profit	5,000	15,000	20,000
Interest income	20,000	nil	10,000
Chargeable gain	24,000	3,000	2,000
Less:			
Section 37	nil	(16,000)	nil
Less: QCD	(5,000)	(2,000)	(15,000)
TTP before Group relief	**244,000**	**nil**	**97,000**
Group relief	(153,667)		(80,333)
TTP after Group relief	**90,333**	**nil**	**16,667**

Corporation tax payable

J Ltd 90,333 @ 25% = 22,583
K Ltd Nil
L Ltd 16,667 @ 19% = 3,166

Total Corporation tax payable by the group £25,749

Alternatively, the full balance of the loss could be surrendered to J Ltd rather than leaving the Section 37 claim for K Ltd.

Corporation tax payable

J Ltd 74,333 @ 25% =	18,583	
Less Marginal relief	(135)	(3/200 x (83,333-74,333)
K Ltd 16,000 @ 19% =	3,040	
L Ltd 16,667 @ 19% =	3,166	

Total Corporation tax payable by the group £24,654

Overall, this gives a lower total Corporation tax liability for the group but K Ltd may not be happy with this outcome! A similar result could be achieved by increasing the group relief for J Ltd leaving it with a TTP of 16,667 increasing the TTP of L Ltd to 74,333.

Notes

Normally a claim under section 37 must be for the full amount of profits before the deduction of QCD. However, in this example by surrendering losses to other group companies, the loss remaining available for K to claim under section 37 has been reduced to £16,000, therefore preserving tax relief for the QCD in full.

In many cases, several "what if" calculations may be required to find the optimal group relief allocation. The claims should be structured to avoid the loss of relief for QCD and the lowest overall CT burden on the group. Also, group relief may be targeted to remove a company from the requirement to pay CT by instalments.

If the claimant company makes a payment for the group relief, this is ignored for corporation tax purposes by both companies involved in the claim.

Chargeable gains group

For group chargeable gains reliefs to apply a group is defined differently from that applicable for group relief.

For this purpose, a chargeable gains group is a principal (or top) company plus its 75% subsidiaries plus the subsidiaries' 75% subsidiaries and so on, subject to the principal company itself also possessing an effective interest of more than 50% in each company. A company can only be a member of one chargeable gains group.

Example 19.9

Using the structure of Example 19.1:
A Ltd owns 75% of B Ltd. B Ltd owns 80% of C Ltd.
A is the principal or top company.
B is a direct 75% subsidiary of A. Therefore, A and B *are* in a chargeable gains group.
C is a direct 75% subsidiary of B. Therefore, B and C and indeed A *are* all in the same chargeable gains group if, in addition, A possesses a greater than 50% shareholding in C. A's effective shareholding in C is 75% x 80% = 60%.

A, B and C, therefore, form a chargeable gains group even though they do not form a group for group relief purposes (see Example 19.1).

It should, therefore, be noted that a group for group relief purposes may be a different group than one for chargeable gains purposes as shown in the above example.

However, the groups may also be the same (see below).

Example 19.10

A Ltd owns 75% of both B Ltd and C Ltd.
A is the principal or top company.
B and C are 75% subsidiaries of A and therefore A, B and C are in a chargeable gains group and are also in the same group for group relief purposes.

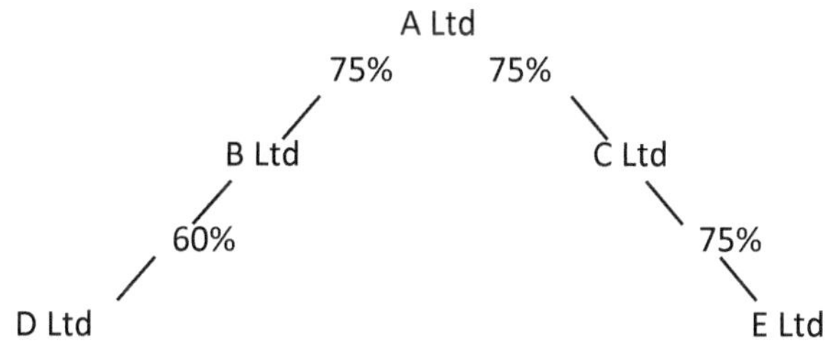

A is the principal company.
B and C are 75% subsidiaries of A and therefore A, B and C form a chargeable gains group.
D is not a 75% subsidiary of B. Therefore, D is not part of a chargeable gains group.
E is a 75% subsidiary of C. In addition, A indirectly holds 75% x 75% = 56.25% of E. Therefore, E is also a part of the A, B and C chargeable gains group.

(Note that for group relief purposes A, B and C form a group, and C and E form a separate group).

The benefits of a chargeable gains group

The existence of a chargeable gains group allows three forms of relief to apply:

- assets may be transferred within the group without gains or losses arising;
- chargeable gains and allowable losses may be transferred to another group company; and
- rollover relief may apply as if all the group companies were a single company.

Intragroup chargeable gains relief

Chargeable gains relief refers to the ability of a chargeable gains group of companies to transfer chargeable assets amongst themselves at no gain and no loss thus avoiding a corporate tax liability on the transfers. Typically, this will legally transfer an asset no longer used by one company to another group company that can use the asset. The asset is deemed to have been transferred at the original cost plus indexation allowance to the date of the transfer (up to December 2017).

As and when the chargeable asset is eventually sold outside the group a gain or loss will arise at that time and will then be subject to corporation tax.

One advantage of this facility is that it enables the capital gains of one group company to be offset against the capital losses of another group company. This is achieved by the transfer of the asset from one company to the other before sale to a third party so that the same company makes the gain and the loss.

Note, however, that any capital losses carried forward within a company must remain within that company. Therefore, if one company is about to sell an asset at a gain then the asset on which the gain arises must be transferred to the company with the capital loss carried forward if these losses are to be used.

Example 19.11

JKL Ltd acquired a chargeable asset in January 2012 for £100,000. It transferred it to ABC Ltd a chargeable gains group company in January 2014 when its market value was £175,000. ABC Ltd subsequently sold the asset outside the group in May 2026 for £300,000. Both companies prepare their accounts to 31 March each year.

Assume the indexation allowances for Jan 2012 to Jan 2014 and Jan 2014 to May 2025 (frozen at December 2017) are £31,400 and £11,169 respectively.

Show the position of both companies.

Answer

Transfer on January 2014

JKL Ltd is deemed to have transferred the asset to ABC Ltd at no gain and no loss i.e. at its original cost to JKL Ltd plus indexation to January 2014:

Asset transferred at £100,000 + £31,400 = £131,400

Therefore, the base cost of the asset to ABC Ltd = £131,400

Sale May 2026

Sale proceeds	300,000
Less: Cost	(131,400)
	168,600
Less: Indexation (Jan 2014 to Dec 2017)	(11,169)
Indexed Gain	157,431

Note

The market value of the asset at the date of the inter-group transfer (i.e. £175,000) is irrelevant.

It should be noted that to prevent the use of tax avoidance involving the transfer of assets to a chargeable group company prior to the recipient company leaving the group, a so-called degrouping charge can apply when a company ceases to be a member of a group owning an asset acquired from another group member within the previous six years. Effectively a gain is triggered based on the market value of the asset at the time of the intra-group transfer.

Election to transfer chargeable gains and allowable losses

Alternatively, members of a capital gains group may make a joint election simply to transfer current year gains and losses to another group company without legally transferring the asset. Therefore, for example, a company with losses brought forward may "receive" gains from another group company to utilise the losses and reduce the overall tax burden of the group. Both companies must be members of the group at the time that the gain or loss is made and the election must be made within two years after the end of the accounting period in which the disposal occurs. This means that the claim can be made retrospectively after the sale. This election can, therefore, reduce the administrative cost of legally transferring assets within a chargeable gains group.

Intragroup chargeable gains replacement of business assets relief (rollover relief)

On the sale of certain business assets (i.e. land and buildings and fixed plant and machinery) *and* subject to satisfying certain conditions (i.e. reinvestment of the sale proceeds from the sale of the old asset in another new business asset must occur within one year before and three years after the sale of the old asset) a company may claim rollover relief on the gain on the sale of the old asset (see Chapter 15 for full details).

Rollover relief applies by allowing the company to defer a gain by reducing the base cost of the replacement asset by the indexed gain on the sale of the old asset.

However, where a chargeable gains group exists it is also possible for the indexed gain on the sale of a business asset by one company to be rolled over against the acquisition cost of a business asset by another group company subject to satisfying the above conditions.

Example 19.12

HIJ Ltd sells a factory in January 2023 for £250,000 which cost £75,000 in March 2012. In March 2027 JKL Ltd a chargeable gains group company purchased another factory for £350,000.

Assume the indexation allowance for March 2012 to December 2017 is £29,475 (The indexation allowance is frozen at 31 December 2017).

What is the position for each of the two companies if rollover relief is claimed?

Answer

As the replacement asset was acquired by a company within the chargeable gains group within three years of the disposal, rollover relief is available.

HIJ Ltd

Sale proceeds	250,000
Less: Cost	(75,000)
	175,000
Less:	
Indexation allowance	(29,475)
Indexed gain	145,525
Rolled over gain	(145,525)
Chargeable	Nil

JKL Ltd

The base cost of the factory acquired by JKL Ltd is £350,000 – £145,525 = £204,475 (i.e. the actual cost reduced by the rolled-over gain).

Where the full amount of the sale proceeds received by one company on the sale of a business asset are not reinvested by another member of the chargeable gains group, only a partial rollover of the gain is available and a balancing chargeable gain immediately arises.

Example 19.13

If in Example 19.12 above JKL Ltd had bought a business asset for £225,000 then the position for each company would be as follows:

HIJ Ltd

Indexed gain (as above)		145,525
Less:		
Excess of sale proceeds over reinvestment	(250,000 – 225,000)	(25,000)
Gain eligible for rollover		120,525
Gain immediately chargeable on HIJ Ltd		25,000

(this gain will be subject to corporation tax in the accounting period in which the sale by HIJ Ltd occurred).

JKL Ltd

The base cost of the asset acquired by JKL Ltd is £225,000 – £120,525 = £104,475.

SUMMARY

- Groups of companies may benefit from various tax reliefs:
    - group relief allowing relief against TTP for current year losses and brought forward losses surrendered by other group companies;
    - tax free transfer of chargeable assets between group companies;
    - the transfer of chargeable gains and allowable capital losses between group companies; and
    - chargeable gains business asset roll-over relief within a group.
- The definition of a group for group relief purposes is different to the definition of a capital gains group.

Questions for students

See Appendix 2 for practice questions relating to Chapters 16 to 19. Answers are available online at https://spiramus.com/uk-taxation-for-students-20267-answers.

CHAPTER 20

National Insurance Contributions (NICs)

Introduction

National Insurance Contributions (NICs) may be payable on earned income, in addition to income tax. Certain NICs give entitlement to state benefits. In particular, entitlement to a full State Retirement Pension requires a minimum number of years of NICs.

NICs are paid on employment income and self-employed profits including partnership trading profits. NICs are not payable on income from holding investments. The amount of NICs payable is determined by the Class of NIC applying.

Classes of contributions

There are four classes of NIC applicable to individuals: Classes 1, 2, 3 and 4. In addition, employers are also required to pay Class 1 and Class 1A NICs where appropriate.

Class 1

NICs under this class are paid on earnings by both employees *and* employers.

Employee

There is no employee's (*or Primary*) Class 1 NIC liability on earnings up to the annual primary threshold of £12,570 (£242 per week). Employee's Class 1 NIC are calculated at 8% on earnings above the primary threshold up to the upper earnings limit of £50,270 (£967 per week), with a rate of 2% on earnings above this.

Earnings for Class 1 NIC includes any remuneration (wages, bonuses etc.) from an employer, paid in money or vouchers readily convertible to cash or goods (but note also included are certain other readily convertible assets, e.g. wine, gold bars). No deductions are allowed for contributions to an employer's approved pension scheme, charitable donations under the payroll giving scheme or any expenses borne by the employee.

Excluded from gross earnings are mileage allowance payments to an employee who uses their own car on business (see Chapter 10) where such payments are up to 45 pence per mile for business mileage (any payments over this allowable limit are subject to both primary and secondary Class 1). Certain other cash benefits which may be paid to an employee (e.g. relocation expenses within the tax-free limit; reimbursement of business expenses) are also excluded, as are tips received directly from a customer.

The employee must be 16 years or older to be liable to NICs. No Class 1 contributions are payable by an employee who reaches pensionable age but an employer is still liable for secondary contributions (see below).

Employer

Employers pay Class 1 Employers or *Secondary* NICs on their employees' *gross earnings* at the rate of 15% above the threshold of £5,000 per annum (£96 per week) with no upper limit.

Example 20.1

Mark is an employee and for the tax year, 2026/27 earns £400 per week. What is the weekly Class 1 NIC liability on his pay?

His own (primary) Class 1 NICs

(£400 – £242) x 8% = £12.64

His employer will also have a liability to (secondary) NICs = (£400 – £96) x 15% = £45.60.

Example 20.2

Tracy is an employee and for the tax year, 2026/27 earns £1,000 per week. What is the weekly Class 1 NIC liability on her pay?

Her own (primary) Class 1 NICs

(£967 – £242) x 8% plus (£1,000 - 967) x 2% = £58.66

Her employer's (secondary) NICs = (£1,000 – £96) x 15% = £135.60

An employment allowance of £10,500 applies to most employers, to be deducted from the total employer's (secondary) Class 1 NIC liability for 2026/27. This allowance is not available where a director is the only company employee.

Finally, employers' secondary Class 1 NIC are not payable for employees under the age of 21 or apprentices under 25 on earnings up to the upper threshold of £50,270.

Contribution periods

Both employer and employee Class 1 NICs are calculated for a contribution period.

A contribution period is a week or a month, or another such period, matching how the employee is regularly paid. Gross earnings for a contribution period then form the amount on which NIC is payable. Throughout the tax year, each contribution period is treated separately, i.e. gross earnings are not cumulated throughout the tax year.

To avoid potential abuse by directors of companies, such individuals are deemed to have an *annual* earnings period (rather than a weekly or monthly period for employees).

The aim is to stop directors from paying themselves a low weekly/monthly salary and a large bonus in one single week/month to avoid NIC.

Example 20.3

Kevin is paid a monthly salary of £3,000. In March 2027, a £10,000 bonus is paid to Kevin.

What are the primary Class 1 NICs payable by Kevin in 2026/27 if
(a) Kevin is an employee?
(b) Kevin is a director?

Answer

a) As an employee

For the eleven months up to February 2027, Kevin's primary NIC will be
8% x (£3,000 – £1,048*) = £156.16 per month

*£12,570/12 = £1,048 per month

For March 2027 Kevin's primary NIC will be based on his pay and bonus, totalling £13,000 (£3,000 + £10,000 bonus)

8% x (£4,189*-£1,048) + 2% x (£13,000-£4,189) = £251.28 + £176.22 = £427.50

Kevin's total primary NIC liability will therefore be
(11 x £156.16) + (1 x £427.50) = £2,145.26

*£50,270/12 = £4,189 per month

b) As a director

In this case, the NICs must be calculated on an annual basis. Kevin's total pay and bonus for the year is 12 months at £3,000 plus a bonus of £10,000 giving total pay of £46,000. Kevin's primary NIC will be

8% x (£46,000 - £12,570) = £2,674.40

Class 1A

Class 1A NICs are only paid by employers (i.e. not employees) and are payable at the rate of 15% on the taxable value of any benefits in kind provided to employees (e.g. company cars; car fuel; etc.; see Chapter 10).

Example 20.4

For the tax year 2026/27, Adam receives, in addition to his salary, the use of a company car which has a taxable benefit of £4,050 and private fuel paid for by his employer which has a taxable benefit of £3,795. What NICs are payable?

Answer

No employee's NICs are payable by Adam on the benefits (Adam will, of course, pay the normal Class 1 NICs on his salary and income tax on the salary plus benefits in kind).

However, his employer is required to pay Class 1A NICs of
15% x (£4,050 + £3,795) = £1,176.75

Class 1A NICs also apply to any taxable termination payments in excess of £30,000. Class 1A NIC liability at 15% will apply to the balance above £30,000.

Class 2

Class 2 NIC are no longer applicable for most individuals.

Up until 5 April 2024, Class 2 NICs were paid by self-employed individuals at a flat weekly rate. From 6 April 2024, Class 2 NICs are not required for most self-employed individuals. Self-employed individuals with profits below £7,105 can pay voluntary Class 2 NIC at the rate of £3.65 per week, for the tax year to qualify for State Retirement Pension purposes.

A sole trader must be 16 years or older to be liable to Class 2 NICs. Class 2 NICs are not payable after reaching pensionable age.

In this textbook, it will generally be assumed that Class 2 NICs are not payable.

Class 4

Class 4 NICs are paid by the self-employed at the rate of 6% on *taxable profits* assessed to income tax for the tax year above £12,570 up to profits of £50,270 and at 2% on *taxable profits* above £50,270.

Taxable profits are arrived at for NIC purposes after allowing a deduction for any available trading losses.

Example 20.5

Annie is self-employed and prepares her accounts to 31 March each year. For the tax year 2026/27, Annie's adjusted trading profit is £65,000. What are Annie's NIC liabilities for 2026/27?

Answer

Annie's Class 4 NICs = 6% x (£50,270 - £12,570) + 2% x (£65,000 - £50,270) = £2,262 + £294.60 = £2,556.60.

Class 3

These are voluntary payments of NIC and are made at the weekly rate of £18.40. Such payments may be made voluntarily where an individual's NIC contribution record is insufficient to provide for full State benefits.

Tax deductibility of NICs

The self-employed may *not* deduct either Class 2 or 4 NICs in arriving at taxable trading profits.

Similarly, an employee cannot deduct Class 1 NICs in arriving at net taxable employment income.

However, employers (sole trader, partnership or company) may deduct their Class 1 and 1A employer contributions made in respect of employees in arriving at taxable trading profits.

Administration

An employee's Class 1 NICs are collected by their employer by deducting the appropriate amounts from the employee's salary each week or month as appropriate.

The employer is responsible for paying both the employee's and employer's contributions to HMRC no later than 14 days (i.e. by 19) after the end of each PAYE month (ending on day 5 of every month).

Employers can claim an employment allowance of up to £10,500 per tax year. This amount is deducted from the total employer's Class 1 NICs only. If the employer's NIC liability is £10,500 or less, then no employer's NICs are payable. The allowance is not available where a director is the sole employee. The employment allowance cannot be used against the employee's NIC or Class 1A NIC.

In the case of Class 1A, the employer pays over the relevant amount to HMRC in one lump sum by 22 July (19 July if not paid online) after the end of the tax year.

Class 4 NICs are paid by the self-employed at the same time as their income tax payments are due (see Chapter 21) which, generally, means that Class 4 NICs due for a tax year are paid by way of two equal payments on account on 31 January within the tax year and on 31 July after the end of the tax year with a balancing payment due on the 31 January following the end of the tax year.

Optional Class 2 NICs are paid with the balancing payment, therefore by 31 January following the end of the tax year.

SUMMARY

- NICs are payments made by employees, employers and the self-employed to HMRC. In return employees and the self-employed receive entitlement to certain state benefits including state retirement pension on reaching pensionable age.
- NICs are not tax deductible either by employees or the self-employed; however, NICs payable by employers on behalf of their employees are tax deductible in computing the trading profits of employers.
- The rates of NIC are higher for an employee than for the self-employed.

Questions for students

See Appendix 2 for practice questions relating to Chapter 20. Answers are available online at https://spiramus.com/uk-taxation-for-students-20267-answers.

CHAPTER 21

Tax Administration for Individuals

Introduction

This chapter explains the administrative provisions for individual taxpayers and the penalties that HMRC may charge for failure to comply with the requirements of current tax legislation. In particular, it should be noted that HMRC may charge penalties for failure to notify liability, failure to make a return on time and failure to make a tax payment on time.

HM Revenue and Customs

The UK tax system is managed by HM Revenue and Customs (HMRC).

HMRC is a non-ministerial department, established by Act of Parliament in 2005, combining the Inland Revenue with Customs and Excise. It has the responsibility for the administration and collection of both direct and indirect taxes in the UK.

UK tax law

UK tax legislation is comprised of many specific tax acts, supported by annual Finance Acts which put into law the announcements made by the Chancellor of the Exchequer in the, usually, annual Budget statement to the House of Commons. As the tax laws are set out by the political party in power at the time, a change of government following a General election may herald significant changes in tax law.

In addition to the statute law, as a result of disputes between taxpayers and HMRC, there is also a growing body of tax case law that can be useful to expand upon or clarify the meaning of the legislation.

HMRC provide technical guidance via the gov.uk website, although it must be noted that this only represents HMRC's view of the law!

Individuals – income tax and capital gains tax

PAYE, Self-Assessment or Making Tax Digital

Most individuals in the UK are not required to complete an annual tax return, with the correct amount of income tax and NIC being deducted by their employer under PAYE.

Self-employed individuals, property landlords and individuals with more complicated tax affairs are required to complete an annual self-assessment tax return.

Self-employed individuals and property landlords who meet certain thresholds test must file quarterly digital statements under Making Tax Digital ("MTD") in addition to a final online annual overall tax return.

Notifying chargeability

An individual who has not received a notice to complete a tax return must notify HMRC that they are chargeable to income tax or capital gains tax within six months of the end of the tax year, therefore by 5 October 2026 in respect of the tax year to 5 April 2026. This will typically apply when an individual commences a business, has a one-off capital gain or expects to have an underpayment of tax, for example, due to higher rate tax on savings and dividends. Failure to meet this deadline will result in a tax geared penalty as detailed later in this chapter.

Self-assessment tax return

Every April, HMRC issues a notice to complete a self-assessment tax return to those taxpayers who are likely to need one (i.e. taxpayers who receive income which has not been taxed at source, e.g. sole traders; those receiving rental income and/or capital gains etc). Most taxpayers will have had their tax correctly deducted under PAYE and are not required to complete a tax return.

The information requested in the return relates to the tax year just ended. Tax return notices issued in April 2027 require information concerning the taxpayer's income and gains for the tax year to 5 April 2027 (2026/27) and in addition, the return enables the taxpayer to claim allowances and reliefs for the year.

Tax return filing date

The Self-assessment tax return needs to be filed electronically online by 31 January following the tax year to which the return relates. Therefore, for the tax year ending 5 April 2027, the filing date is 31 January 2028. If the taxpayer wishes to complete a paper return, then this must be submitted sooner, by 31 October following the end of the tax year. In either case, the deadline may be later if, having been notified of liability to tax on time, HMRC is late issuing a notice to complete a return. In this case, the deadline is three months from the date of issue of the notification, if later than the normal deadline.

Automatic penalties apply for tax returns submitted late.

Late filing penalties

If a Self-Assessment tax return is filed after the dates stated above, then an initial penalty of £100 will be imposed, regardless of the tax liability or even if a refund is due.

Additional penalties apply if there are further delays as follows:

- 3 months late – daily penalties of £10 per day for a maximum of 90 days
- 6 months late – 5% of the tax outstanding with a minimum penalty of £300
- 12 months late – a further 5% of the tax outstanding with a minimum penalty of £300

In the case of returns that are 12 months late, additional tax geared penalties may be charged if the delay is considered deliberate or is concealing a tax liability.

Example 21.1

Andy, having received a notice to submit a tax return in good time, submitted his tax return for the year ended 5 April 2026 to HMRC on 16 October 2027. His return shows an outstanding tax liability of £1,100. What is the total penalty that HMRC may impose for late filing?

Answer

Normal due date for submission is 31 January 2027

Initial Penalty	£100
Daily penalty (£10 x 90 days)	£900
Penalty for 6 months late	£300 (Minimum penalty)
Total penalties	£1,300

Notes

1. The penalty after six months is the minimum amount. Based on 5% of the unpaid tax this would be £55.
2. Interest and penalties would also be charged for any late payment of the tax liability.

HMRC has the discretion to reduce a penalty if there are reasonable grounds for the late return.

Amendments and corrections to tax returns

Normally, an individual has 12 months from 31 January following the end of the tax year to make amendments to their tax return. HMRC may correct any obvious errors or omissions on a tax return up to nine months after they receive a return. An individual has 30 days to reject any such correction.

Making Tax Digital ("MTD")

Introduced from April 2026, Making Tax Digital for income tax ("MTD") is a new fully digitalised way that certain sole traders and landlords are required to use to create, store and report their tax information to HMRC. According to HMRC, MTD will "make it easier for taxpayers to get their tax right first time, help reduce scope for error and enhance customer experience" by providing taxpayers with more up-to-date online information and tax estimates.

From 6 April 2026, MTD applies to sole traders and landlords who had a total combined income from their businesses and rents above £50,000 on their Self-Assessment tax return as submitted for the tax year ended 5 April 2025. As most individuals in this category will be using the cash basis, this basically means receipts above £50,000, regardless of profit.

Example 21.2

Altaf runs a small catering business and also lets two properties. His receipts and profits for the year to 5 April 2025 were as follows:

Year to 5 April 2025	Receipts	Taxable profit
Catering business	36,500	11,800
Property business	15,200	6,300
Total	51,700	18,100

Will Altaf be required to submit quarterly MTD returns from 6 April 2026?

Answer

As Altaf's total income from self-employment and his property business exceeded £50,000, he must register for MTD from 6 April 2026. His profit is irrelevant.

For subsequent years, the registration limit is reduced. From 6 April 2027, registration will be required if receipts for the year ended 5 April 2026 exceeded £30,000; from 6 April 2028 registration will be required if receipts for the year ended 5 April 2027 exceed £20,000.

MTD record keeping and quarterly returns

Individuals within MTD are required to maintain digital records of income and expenditure from their self-employment and property businesses. This can be using dedicated accounting software or on spreadsheets using appropriate bridging software to submit to HMRC. Separate quarterly digital returns are required for each business. For example, a sole trader with a let property is required to make two submissions each quarter.

Cumulative returns of total income and expenditure are required each quarter. Separate quarterly returns are required for each business carried on by the individual. The standard quarter ends and filing deadlines for 2026/27 are:

Update period	Filing deadline
6 April to 5 July 2026	7 August 2026
6 April to 5 October 2026	7 November 2026
6 April 2026 to 5 January 2027	7 February 2027
6 April 2026 to 5 April 2027	7 May 2027

The cumulative returns will be submitted digitally to HMRC by compatible accounting software. Manual updates will not be accepted. An option to submit to the end of the calendar quarters (i.e. to 31 March rather than 5 April) is available but this does not change the filing deadlines.

On submission of each return, HMRC will provide an updated online estimate of the individual's tax liabilities.

MTD Final return

To support the quarterly submissions, under MTD, an online final return will also be required. This will include any "tax adjustments" to the self - employment and property business details, for example capital allowances claims and will also require details of any income not within MTD, such as employment, partnerships and investment income and claims for reliefs. The MTD final return will also include any capital gains for the year. It is envisaged that over time much of this additional detail will be pre-populated based on information already held by HMRC. This final return must be submitted online by 31 January after the tax year end (i.e. the same deadline as a Self-assessment return).

MTD filing penalties

For 2026/27, HMRC have advised that there will be no penalties for late filing of quarterly returns.

A points-based penalty system will apply to late submission of the MTD final return to 5 April 2027 and subsequent submissions. The points-based system will be the same as that which applies to VAT, as detailed in Chapter 23.

Record keeping

HMRC may impose a penalty of up to £3,000 for failure to meet the Self-assessment or MTD record keeping requirements. These rules require an individual to keep all records relating to the preparation of their tax return for 22 months from the end of the tax year concerned (for the tax year to 5 April 2026 this would be 31 January 2028). If the tax return includes trading or property income this is extended to five years and 10 months.

Tax return enquiries

By submitting an annual tax return, individuals provide HMRC with details of their income, gains and claims for reliefs. HMRC accept most returns without question but may issue a notice (under TMA 1970 section 9A) that they are to make an enquiry (or compliance check) into a tax return. Officially, HMRC needs no reason to select a return for such a review but the enquiry will often be triggered by information held by HMRC that suggests an issue. Such an enquiry may be limited to a single item on the return or may cover all entries. HMRC has until 12 months from the date that the tax return is submitted to open such an enquiry. Where the return is submitted late, HMRC has 12 months after the end of the quarter in which the return is submitted to make enquiries. If, as a result of the enquiry, it is discovered by HMRC that the individual has underpaid tax, then in addition to interest for late payment, penalties may apply to the additional tax charged (see Tax geared penalties below).

If the individual does not agree with the findings of HMRC then they may, within 30 days of the decision, appeal the case to the independent First-tier

Tribunal (or direct to the Upper Tribunal for some complex appeals) or request that the case be reviewed by another HMRC officer (and then if not satisfied appeal to the First-tier Tribunal). If the decision is not resolved, then it may be appealed, by either party, to the Upper Tribunal and ultimately if not resolved at this point, on a point of law, to the Court of Appeal. The decisions of such cases make up the case law that supplements and supports UK tax statute law.

Discovery assessments

Although the time limit for a compliance check may have passed, HMRC has the power to re-examine earlier years' tax returns if they "discover" the non-disclosure of items leading to the loss of tax. The normal time limit for such a discovery assessment is four years, extending to six years if the taxpayer is considered careless and 20 years in the case of a deliberate error.

Equally, if a taxpayer "discovers" that they have omitted a claim for tax relief, whether on a return or not, they can make such a claim for repayment up to four years after the end of the tax year involved.

Payment of income tax, capital gains tax, Class 2 and Class 4 NIC

Payments on account

Under both Self-assessment and MTD, two payments on account ("POA") of a tax year's income tax and Class 4 NIC liability are required to be made by *31 January in the tax year, and 31 July following the tax year.*

Example 21.3

Samantha is self-employed and submits an annual Self-assessment tax return. When are her payments on account for 2026/27 due for payment?

Answer

She will be required to make POA on 31 January 2027 and 31 July 2027 in respect of the tax year 2026/27.

Relevant amount

As the first POA falls due before the end of the tax year that it relates to, the actual liability will not be known. Therefore, POA are estimated based on the liability of the previous tax year.

Each POA is calculated as an amount equal to 50% of the aggregate of the income tax and Class 4 NIC liabilities of the *previous* tax year less any tax deducted at source, for example, under PAYE.

The income tax liability for the previous tax year plus Class 4 NIC liability less tax deducted at source is referred to as the "relevant amount". Thus, each POA is equal to 50% of the relevant amount.

However, no POAs are required where:

- the relevant amount is less than £1,000; *or*

- if more than 80% of the taxpayer's income tax liability plus Class 4 NIC for the previous tax year is satisfied by deduction of tax at source; *or*
- if no relevant amount exists for the previous tax year (for example the taxpayer was not required to file a return for the previous tax year).

It is possible to submit a claim to reduce POA if information is held to suggest that they will be excessive, for example when self-employment has ceased.

Balancing payment

When the actual income tax payable for the tax year is finally known, a balancing payment (or repayment) may be due on the 31 January following the tax year end equal to the income tax, capital gains tax and Class 4 NIC (and potentially optional Class 2 NIC) payable for the tax year less the total POAs which have been made. Therefore, for 2026/27, any balancing payment is due by 31 January 2028.

Where any balancing payment and/or POA are paid late and/or are insufficient, interest will be charged and penalties may also apply if the balancing payment is late.

Example 21.4

For the tax year 2025/26, Suki's total income tax and Class 4 NIC liability was £38,000. Income tax of £8,000 was deducted under PAYE.

For 2026/27, Suki's income tax and Class 4 NIC liability is £42,000 of which £5,000 is paid at source, under PAYE, leaving a balance of £37,000.

State the dates on which Suki is required to pay her 2026/27 income tax and NIC liabilities and the amounts payable.

Answer

Suki's income tax and Class 4 NIC liability for 2025/26 was £38,000. Suki paid income tax of £8,000 at source.

Relevant amount = (£38,000 - £8,000) = £30,000

2026/27

POA on 31 January 2027: £15,000 (i.e. 50% of 2025/26 relevant amount)
POA on 31 July 2027: £15,000 (i.e. 50% of 2025/26 relevant amount)
The balancing payment due by 31 January 2028 is £7,000

The balancing payment represents the total income tax and class 4 NIC for 2026/27 less tax deducted at source and the payments on account already made (i.e. £42,000 - £5,000 - £15,000 - £15,000).

Note: It should be noted that the first payment on account for 2027/28, of £18,500, will also fall due by 31 January 2028 and the whole cycle commences again!

Example 21.5

Duncan's income tax liability and Class 4 NICs for 2025/26 were £20,500 of which £19,500 was paid at source.

For 2026/27, his income tax and Class 4 NIC liability is £20,000 of which £16,000 was paid at source.

What amount of tax is Duncan to pay and on what dates in respect of the 2026/27 tax year?

Answer

More than 80% of Duncan's income tax and Class 4 NIC liability for 2025/26 was paid by way of tax deducted at source, i.e. 19,500/20,500 = 95.1%.

Therefore, no POAs are required for 2026/27.

Duncan's remaining tax and NIC liability of £4,000 (£20,000 - £16,000) for 2026/27 is payable on 31 January 2028 in one single amount.

Interest

Interest is charged on all late payments of income, capital gains tax and NIC due under Self-assessment and MTD.

Interest is also charged where a claim to reduce POAs has been made and the POAs that in the event should have been paid are greater than those actually made following the claim.

The interest charge is calculated as simple interest at the rate prescribed by HMRC from the due date until the date of payment. This will apply to both POAs and the balancing payment. Where an excessive claim has been made to reduce POAs, interest will run from the normal due date on any underpayment.

Example 21.6

Patrick paid his POA on 20 March 2026 and 15 September 2026 in respect of the tax year 2025/26 with a balancing payment on 15 February 2027.

From and to what dates will interest be charged?

Answer

Interest will be charged for the following periods:

First POA	31 January 2026 to 20 March 2026
Second POA	31 July 2026 to 15 September 2026
Balancing payment	31 January 2027 to 15 February 2027

Late payment penalties

Late payment penalties are payable *in addition* to any interest which may be charged.

Penalties do not apply to POA dates; only to balances outstanding after the due date of the balancing payment.

Where all or part of the tax and NIC liability for a year remains unpaid for more than 30 days after the balancing payment due date an initial penalty of 5% of the unpaid amount will be charged.

Any tax that remains unpaid more than six months after the due date (i.e. by 31 July) is subject to a further 5% penalty and a further 5% penalty will apply after 12 months (i.e. by the following 31 January).

These penalties are in addition to the tax itself and to any interest charged in relation to that tax.

Example 21.7

Greg has a balancing payment of £7,000 due on 31 January 2027 for 2025/26 but only £4,250 is actually paid on time. The balance is eventually paid on 14 June 2027.

What penalties will arise?

Answer

A balance of £2,750 is outstanding on 2 March 2027, 30 days after the normal due date. Therefore, a penalty of (5% x £2,750) = £137.50 will also be due in addition to the tax liability and interest.

As the balance was paid before 31 July 2027 a second 5% penalty is avoided.

A new system of late payment penalties is introduced starting with the balancing payment for 2026/27 payable on 31 January 2028. The penalties for 2026/27 are as follows:

Payment up to 15 days late	No penalty
Payment 16 to 30 days late	3% of tax owed at 15 days or no penalty if first year.
Payment 31 days or later	Additional 3% of taxed owed at day 30 plus an annual penalty rate of 10% per year on the balance outstanding.

Interest on overpaid income tax

Repayments to a taxpayer of overpaid income tax attract interest calculated at a lower rate than the interest rate charged on overdue income tax.

Interest on any repayment runs from the later of the date that the tax was due or the date HMRC received the payment, until the date of repayment.

Interest paid on tax repayments is exempt from income tax.

Deductibility of interest payments and late payment penalties

Any interest and penalties payable by an individual in respect of late payments of income tax etc. are not tax deductible.

Mitigation of penalties

HMRC may, at their discretion, mitigate any penalty where they are satisfied that an individual can prove that they had a reasonable excuse for not meeting a tax obligation. For example, the death of a spouse shortly before a deadline may be considered reasonable. However, simply having insufficient funds available at a payment date would not be considered to be a reasonable excuse.

Capital gains tax (CGT)

As mentioned above CGT is normally payable with the balancing payment on the 31 January following the end of the tax year to which the tax relates (e.g. 31 January 2028 for the tax year 2026/27).

POAs are never required for CGT. However, as mentioned in Chapter 13, CGT on residential property sales is payable within 60 days of the completion of the sale.

Interest and penalties on late payments and any repayment supplement are the same as those for income tax (see above).

National insurance contributions

As indicated in Chapter 20, Class 4 NICs which are payable by the self-employed are to be paid at the same time and in the same manner as an individual's income tax liability.

As a consequence, in any tax year, POAs are required and these can include Class 4 NIC.

POAs are not required for Class 2 NIC.

Example 21.8

Joe is self-employed and his tax and NIC liabilities for 2025/26 were as follows:

Income tax	£3,700
Class 4 NIC	£1,966
CGT	£4,800

Calculate Joe's payments on account for 2026/27.

Answer

Income tax and Class 4 NIC

Income tax liability for 2025/26		3,700
Class 4 NIC liability for 2025/26		1,966
Relevant amount		5,666
Payments on account for 2026/27:		
31 January 2027	5,666 x 50%	2,833
31 July 2027	5,666 x 50%	2,833

Notes

CGT is not included in the calculation of the "relevant" amount (i.e. is not included in POA).

Joe's balancing payment will be due on 31 January 2028.

There is no requirement to make POA for the CGT. This is due on 31 January following the end of the tax year as part of any balancing payment or earlier in respect of residential property gains.

Tax geared penalties

As mentioned above, in certain circumstances, such as failure to notify or where a tax underpayment is identified following an enquiry, a tax geared penalty may be imposed on an individual. The maximum penalties that can be charged and the minimum that HMRC may reduce them to, in the particular circumstances for each case are as follows:

Type of behaviour	Unprompted disclosure	Prompted disclosure
Reasonable care	No penalty	No penalty
Careless	0% to 30%	15% to 30%
Deliberate error	20% to 70%	35% to 70%
Deliberate and concealed	30% to 100%	50% to 100%

As can be seen, the penalties are set based on the behaviour of the taxpayer. An unprompted disclosure would be, for example, a case where the taxpayer voluntarily discloses an undeclared source of income.

HMRC have a "name and shame" policy for deliberate tax defaulters owing more than £25,000.

(See https://www.gov.uk/government/publications/publishing-details-of-deliberate-tax-defaulters-pddd).

SUMMARY

- Most individuals pay income tax and NIC under PAYE and are not required to submit an annual tax return.
- The self-assessment system requires certain individuals, typically self-employed individuals and property landlords, to meet specific deadlines for filing tax returns and making tax payments.
- Under Making Tax Digital, from 6 April 2026 certain sole traders and property landlords are required to use compatible accounting software to record, store and submit their tax information with quarterly returns plus a final tax return.
- Under both self-assessment and MTD, individuals may be required to make two payments on account of their income tax and Class 4 NIC liability plus a balancing payment which will also include any capital gains tax.
- There are separate penalty regimes that apply for late filing and late payment.
- HMRC have the power to make enquiries into a tax return for up to 12 months from the date a return is submitted.
- Penalties may apply if a tax liability increases because of HMRC enquiries.

CHAPTER 22

Tax Administration for Corporation Tax and Employers

Introduction

This chapter examines the administrative provisions relating to corporation tax and the penalties that HMRC may charge for failure to comply with the regulations. Again, it should be noted that HMRC may charge penalties for failure to notify liability, failure to make a return on time and failure to make a payment of tax on time.

In addition, this chapter also looks at the obligations of employers under PAYE, whether incorporated or not.

Notifying chargeability

A company may be charged a tax geared penalty (see Chapter 21) based on the amount of tax paid late if it fails to notify HMRC that it is chargeable to corporation tax within three months of starting any business activity or receiving taxable income.

Corporation tax return

Companies, like individuals, must self-assess their tax liability in respect of each accounting period and submit a tax return.

A corporation tax return must be submitted within 12 months of the end of the period of account to which it relates. Where financial statements are prepared for more than 12 months, two tax returns will be required but both will be due by the same date, 12 months after the end of the accounting date.

HMRC requires companies to submit returns online using the iXBRL format. A complete corporation tax return must include the tax return with accompanying financial statements and tax computations.

Tax return enquiries

As for individuals, HMRC has the right to make an enquiry into a corporation tax return. HMRC has 12 months from the date that the tax return is submitted to open such an enquiry. Where the return is submitted late, HMRC has 12 months after the end of the quarter in which the return is submitted to make enquiries. A tax geared penalty may apply to any additional corporation tax arising as a result of the enquiry based on the company's behaviour as detailed in Chapter 21.

Interest and penalties

Interest is chargeable where corporation tax is paid late, running from the date that the liability was due to the date of actual payment and unlike the position for individuals, any such interest is a deductible expense in arriving at the net interest income under the loan relationship rules. Similarly, HMRC will pay interest on tax overpaid and this will similarly be treated as taxable interest income (see Chapter 16).

Failure to submit a return by the due date gives rise to a penalty of £200 with an increase to £400 if the return is three months or more late. Where the return is more than six months late, an additional tax geared penalty equal to 10% of the corporation tax unpaid is charged, which rises to 20% if the return is more than 12 months late. The fixed penalties increase to £1,000 and £2,000 respectively if the two preceding returns were also late.

In addition, HMRC may charge a penalty of up to £3,000 for failure to keep the required records. All records required for the preparation of a CT return must be retained for six years after the end of the accounting period.

Payment of corporation tax

Any corporation tax liability for a chargeable accounting period must be paid within nine months and one day after the end of the accounting period unless the company is large. Where accounts are prepared for more than 12 months each chargeable accounting period will have a separate payment date.

Example 22.1

FGH Limited prepares its accounts for the 12 months ended 31 March 2027. FGH Ltd is not a large company. What are the filing and payment deadlines for FGH Ltd for the accounting period to 31 March 2027?

Answer

The corporation tax liability is due for payment on 1 January 2028 (nine months and one day after the end of the accounting period).

The corporation tax return must be filed online by 31 March 2028 to prevent a filing penalty.

Instalment basis

As indicated above, most companies are required to pay their corporation tax liability nine months and one day after the end of the accounting period. However, where a company is considered to be large, then an alternative, instalment based payment system applies.

A company is large if it has augmented profits of £1,500,000 or more for an accounting period. Augmented profits are calculated as TTP plus non-group dividends received.

If the accounting period is less than 12 months, the limit mentioned above is time apportioned.

For a 12-month accounting period, the instalment basis requires a company to pay four equal instalments of corporation tax payable on the 14th day of months 7, 10, 13 and 16 following the start of the accounting period.

Unlike the position of individuals, the corporation tax instalments for an accounting period are based upon estimates of the corporation tax liability for the accounting period and not on the liability for the previous accounting period.

Example 22.2

JS Ltd, a large company, prepares its accounts to 31 March 2027.

Its corporation tax liability will, therefore, need to be settled in four equal instalments due on 14 October 2026, 14 January 2027, 14 April 2027 and 14 July 2027.

Notes

The first two instalments are due before the end of the accounting period and should be best estimates based on the accounting information to date.

If the accounting period is for less than 12 months, there may not enough be time to fit in all four instalments. In this case, the rule for setting the first instalment date remains unchanged, with the next following after three months. However, the last instalment is due three months and 14 days after the end of the accounting period. In addition, the instalments are calculated based on the length of the accounting period.

Example 22.3

FG Ltd is a large company and prepares its accounts for the eight months to 31 August 2026. When are its instalment payments of CT due?

Answer

The accounting period commences on 1 January 2026. Therefore, the first instalment will be due on 14 July 2026, the next instalment will be due by 14 October 2026 and the final will be due on 14 December 2026, three months and 14 days after the end of the accounting period.

As the accounting period is for eight months, the first two instalments will be for 3/8th of the CT liability with the final payment being the remaining 2/8th.

In the case of an accounting period of three months or less, the CT is due in a single payment three months and 14 days after the end of the period.

The instalment basis does not apply for an accounting period if the company was not a large company for the previous accounting period *and* the profits for the current period do not exceed £10 million (or pro rata reduced if associated companies exist). In addition, the instalment basis does not apply where the CT liability does not exceed £10,000.

It should be appreciated that the requirement to pay in instalments can have a significant impact on the cash flow of a company.

For accounting periods beginning on or after 1 April 2019, very large companies (profits exceeding £20 million) will be required to make instalment payments four months earlier, on the 14th day of months 3, 6, 9 and 12 of their accounting periods.

Associated companies

The various thresholds for determining Corporation tax rates and liability for instalment payments must be divided equally between associated companies. For this purpose, a company is associated with another company if one is under the control of the other or both are under the control of the same person or persons at any time during the accounting period. Control usually requires more than 50% of share capital or voting power. Dormant companies are excluded but overseas companies are included.

Example 22.4

Rainbow Ltd owns 55% of the ordinary share capital of Red Ltd, Blue Ltd and Green Inc. Red Ltd owns 100% of the ordinary shares of Pink Ltd. All of the group companies are active except for Blue Ltd which is dormant. Green Inc is incorporated in the USA.

What are the revised profit thresholds for Rainbow Ltd?

Answer

The profit thresholds must be divided equally between 51% group companies.

Rainbow Ltd has three 51% associated companies – Red Ltd, Pink Ltd and Green Inc. Blue Ltd is ignored as it is dormant.

Therefore, the thresholds are divided by 4 for Rainbow Limited as follows:

Small profits rate limit	£50,000/4 = £12,500
Marginal relief limit	£250,000/4 = £62,500
Large Company Profit threshold	£1,500,000/4 = £375,000

Tax geared penalties

If as a result of an enquiry by HMRC additional CT liabilities arise, tax geared penalties may arise. These will be calculated on the same basis as applicable to individuals as detailed in Chapter 21.

PAYE and Real Time Information

Pay As You Earn (PAYE) is designed to enable employers to deduct income tax and NIC from their employees' salaries over a tax year and pay it to HMRC. In effect, every employer acts as a tax collector!

PAYE applies to wages and salaries, round sum allowances and readily convertible assets (i.e. assets readily convertible into cash). It does not, however, apply to allowable reimbursed business expenses.

PAYE does not normally apply to benefits in kind. Benefits will, however, usually restrict the amount of the PAYE code.

PAYE Tax Code Number

If an employee's sole source of income in a tax year is a salary, by applying the correct PAYE tax code number (see below) to the employee's salary, the employer by the end of the tax year will have deducted an amount of income tax from the salary which equals the employee's income tax liability. In principle, the employee will then have no further income tax liability for that tax year.

An individual's PAYE tax code number is issued by HMRC and takes into account various factors. It will depend upon the level of personal allowances to which the individual may be entitled (e.g. personal allowance; marriage allowance; etc.); whether any further deductions are due (e.g. a deduction for allowable professional subscriptions); whether that individual receives any benefits (e.g. a company car); whether that individual receives any minor amounts of untaxed income or has any unpaid income tax from prior tax years.

Example 22.5

John, an employee, earns a salary of £30,000, paid monthly, for 2026/27. His taxable company car benefit is £6,200. He pays allowable professional subscriptions of £480.

John is single, aged 35, and a basic rate taxpayer.

Show John's PAYE code for 2026/27.

Answer

Personal allowance	12,570
Benefits	(6,200)
Professional subscriptions	480
	6,850

John's PAYE code is therefore 685L.

John's employer will be notified by HMRC that his code is 685L without any details of its calculation. A detailed calculation will be provided to John by HMRC.

Note

To create an individual's PAYE code, HMRC simply removes the last digit and replaces it with a specific letter. Thus, to get John's code requires that the '0' be removed to get 685 and replaced with a letter, usually "L".

An employer is notified of an employee's PAYE tax code number for a tax year but the employer does not know the breakdown of the code, just the final amount, maintaining the confidentiality of the employee's personal details.

The employer then, each week or month (depending upon how an employee is paid), applies 1/52 or 1/12 of the employee's allowances (against the weekly or monthly salary). In this manner, over the tax year, the employee will have discharged their income tax liability for that tax year. Similarly, the rate bands will be divided by 1/52 or 1/12 etc.

The application of the code is on a cumulative basis. Thus, after the first three tax months of the tax year, an individual would have received one quarter of their annual personal allowance entitlement. For an individual who starts to work for the first time, say from 6 September 2024, when they are paid on, say 30 September 2024, they will receive six months' worth of annual allowances as they had not prior to September used any of them. Thereafter, they will receive an additional one month's allowance each month and their cumulative position for the tax year to date will be recalculated, taking into account income tax already deducted in previous months. If after the end of the tax year, it is established that the PAYE tax code number was insufficient and an underpayment of tax has arisen, this will be a matter between the individual and HMRC.

NIC will be calculated by the employer as detailed in Chapter 20.

Any tax and NIC deducted by an employer must be paid online to HMRC by the 22nd of the following month (or 19th if paid by cheque).

Forms/returns

A variety of information is required to be supplied by an employer to their employees and HMRC each tax year. This information is supplied on various forms as follows:

- *Form P60* (deadline 31 May after the end of the tax year). This form, provided to each employee, shows their total taxable earnings for the tax year, total tax and NIC deducted, code number, national insurance number, and the employer's name and address.
- *Form P11D* (deadline 6 July after the end of the tax year to be provided to employees and submitted to HMRC). This form shows the taxable value of all benefits and expenses provided to each employee. From April 2027 most benefits in kind will be taxed via PAYE and will not be included on the P11D.
- *Form P45* (given to an employee who leaves employment). This form shows the employee's PAYE code, the income of the employee and the income tax paid to the date of leaving.

RTI (Real Time Information)

Under the PAYE reporting system, certain information must be reported to HMRC in "real time". It is not possible to operate PAYE manually. Details of employees' pay and deductions must be reported to HMRC using payroll software **on or before the day** employees are paid.

The payroll software must provide the following information:

- The amount paid to each employee, including lower-paid employees below the NIC limit.
- Deductions, e.g. income tax and national insurance contributions (NICs)
- Starter and leaver dates, if applicable.

This Real Time information is intended to provide other government departments with up to date details to adjust any income-dependent state benefits etc.

SUMMARY

- Companies must not only file an annual tax return containing information about profits, income and chargeable gains arising but also provide their financial statements and calculation of corporation tax liabilities. The return must be filed by 12 months from the end of the period of account.
- If a company fails to meet its submission deadlines penalties will apply.
- Large companies are required to pay corporation tax in quarterly instalments, with other companies making a single payment nine months and one day after the end of the accounting period.
- Interest may be charged where tax liabilities are settled late and/or are of an insufficient amount.
- Employers are required to calculate and deduct income tax and NIC from each employee's wages under the PAYE system.
- PAYE tax code numbers are used by employers to calculate the income tax liability arising on each employee's monthly or weekly pay.
- Employers are required to provide HMRC with their payroll details under RTI on or before the date any wages etc. are paid and pay any PAYE tax and NIC deductions to HMRC monthly.

Questions for students

See Appendix 2 for practice questions relating to Chapters 21 to 22. Answers are available online at https://spiramus.com/uk-taxation-for-students-20267-answers.

CHAPTER 23

Value Added Tax

Introduction

Value Added Tax (VAT) is a tax on consumer expenditure. It is an indirect tax and its calculation is very different from income tax, capital gains tax and corporation tax. VAT is not a tax on profits or gains and generally, there is no distinction between revenue and capital items. It is administered by HMRC and can apply equally to sole traders, partnerships and limited companies.

How it works

VAT is charged on the supply of *taxable goods or services* when made in the UK by a *VAT registered trader* in the course of a business carried on by them.

At its simplest, a VAT registered trader must pay HMRC the difference between the VAT that they *charge* on sales to their customers (Output tax) and the VAT that they *pay* to their suppliers on purchases and expenses (Input tax), so on the value that they have added, hence it's a tax on value added tax.

Output tax

The VAT charged *by* a taxable person on supplies made *by* them to another person is known as output tax. This output tax less any deductible input tax must be paid over to HMRC by the trader periodically.

Input tax

Input tax is the VAT charged *on* a taxable person on goods and services supplied *to* them by a taxable VAT registered business. Input tax charged can usually be recovered by a VAT registered business from HMRC, by deduction from any output tax payable.

Example 23.1

Over a three-month period, Nigel, a VAT registered trader, charges VAT of £3,500 on services supplied by him and pays his suppliers VAT of £1,500 on purchases.

Nigel will owe £2,000 VAT to HMRC, calculated as £3,500 (output) - £1,500 (input) = £2,000.

Example 23.2

During the quarter to 30 September 2026, BCD Ltd, a VAT-registered trading company, charges VAT of £1,500 on goods supplied and pays their suppliers' VAT of £2,700 on purchases.

BCD Ltd will therefore obtain a VAT refund from HMRC for:
£1,500 (output) - £2,700 (input) = £1,200.

Supplies of goods

Goods are supplied in the UK if the goods are located in the UK and the ownership of the goods passes to another elsewhere in the UK (i.e. sold to a UK based customer) or overseas.

In addition to a simple sale of goods, a supply of goods also includes, for example, a supply of power or heat, or the application of a treatment or process to another person's goods. A supply of goods also arises where a gift of goods is made or where goods are taken out of the business for private use. Finally, the sale of capital items, for example, a machine no longer required by the business, will also be subject to the normal rules for charging output tax.

Supplies of services

Business-to-customer services are supplied in the country where the service provider belongs, where they are performed is irrelevant. However, business-to-business services are treated as taking place where the customer is established. Supplies of services include anything done for consideration that is not a supply of goods.

Value of supply

VAT is charged on the value of the supply of goods or services, which is generally the money paid, after any discounts.

In the case of gifts replacement cost (usually market value) is used. However, small gifts to the same person up to £50, excluding VAT, in a 12-month period are exempt. Where services are provided for no consideration, no supply for VAT is assumed to have been made and thus no VAT is chargeable.

Where goods are taken by a trader for their own use, VAT must be charged on the replacement value of the goods at the time that they are taken.

Standard rated, reduced rated, zero rated and exempt supplies

The type of supply will determine the applicable VAT rate. Although in many cases, a taxable person will only make one type of supply, sometimes, a mixture of the different rated supplies may be made.

Standard rated

The general rule is that supplies are subject to VAT at the standard rate, currently 20%.

Reduced rated

A lower rate of 5% applies to a small number of supplies including supplies of domestic fuel and power.

Zero rated

Zero rated supplies are subject to VAT but at 0%. This applies to items generally considered essential and examples of zero rated supplies include most food, books (including digital downloads from 2020), newspapers and children's clothing and footwear.

Exempt

An exempt supply is one where no VAT is charged as the supply is not a taxable supply.

Input tax cannot be recovered where the input tax relates to an exempt supply.

A trader that only makes exempt supplies may not register for VAT.

Examples of exempt supplies include supplies of land, insurance, education and healthcare.

Rates of VAT

VAT is charged at 20% on the VAT exclusive value of standard rated goods/supplies.

A supply taxed at the zero rate is still a taxable supply but at the rate of 0%.

VAT fraction

VAT is normally calculated at the appropriate percentage of the sale price. But sometimes VAT must be calculated from a price in which it is already included, the VAT inclusive amount. Where the total value of the supply includes VAT then to calculate the amount of standard rated VAT, the VAT inclusive amount is multiplied by the VAT fraction, currently, 20/120, which can be simplified to 1/6.

Example 23.3

Julie charges a customer £300 for a supply of goods including VAT charged at the standard rate.

How much VAT is charged on the sale?

Answer

The VAT included in this amount is = 300 x 1/6 = £50
(Reconciliation: £250 + (20% x £250) = £300)

Care should always be taken to carefully note if outputs and inputs are stated *exclusive* of VAT (20% for standard rate) or *inclusive* of VAT (1/6 for standard rate) to ensure that the VAT element is correctly calculated.

Taxable supplies

Standard, reduced and zero rated (but not exempt) supplies are referred to as taxable supplies.

Example 23.4

Greg is VAT registered. His business makes the following supplies of goods, exclusive of VAT:

Standard rated	£30,000
Zero rated	£20,000
Exempt	£10,000

Calculate Greg's total taxable supplies and output tax

Answer

Greg's standard rated and zero rated supplies are taxable supplies. He, therefore, has taxable supplies of 30,000 + 20,000 = 50,000
Greg's total output VAT is charged on his *taxable* supplies as follows

Standard rated	30,000 x 20%	6,000

Zero rated	20,000 x 0%	0
Total output tax		6,000

Mixture of supplies/Partial exemption

If a business makes taxable supplies (i.e. standard and zero rated) and exempt supplies it is referred to as a partially exempt supplier. In this case, the input VAT which is directly attributable to taxable supplies is recoverable whereas that directly attributable to the exempt supplies is irrecoverable. If any input VAT cannot be directly attributable to a particular type of supply then it may be apportioned between taxable and exempt supplies and partially recovered. If the total unrecoverable input tax is below a *de minimis* level, it will also be recoverable and an annual adjustment may also be required.

Registration

VAT must be charged on sales by a VAT registered business. There are two types of registration: compulsory and voluntary.

Compulsory registration

There are two circumstances when a trader must register for VAT.

The Historic Test

Where a trader makes taxable supplies such that at the end of any month the total value of taxable supplies of the previous 12 months (or a shorter period since the commencement of trading) exceeds £90,000 (exclusive of VAT) then compulsory registration is required (the "historic" test).

Under the historic test, the trader must notify HMRC within 30 days of the end of the month in which turnover exceeds the annual registration limit. In this case, registration is then effective from the start of the month following this 30 day period.

The Future Test

If at any time there are reasonable grounds for believing that in the next thirty days alone the value of supplies will exceed £90,000 (exclusive of VAT), then compulsory registration is also required (the "future" test).

Under the future test, HMRC must be notified by the end of the 30-day period from the date on which the grounds for registration arose. Registration is effective from the start of the 30-day period.

Example 23.5

Des commenced trading in November 2025. All of his sales are of standard rated goods. His monthly turnover was as follows

November 2025	5,500
December 2025	6,200
January 2026	5,800
February 2026	5,500
March 2026	6,300

April 2026	7,000
May 2026	7,100
June 2026	6,900
July 2026	8,600
August 2026	7,500
September 2026	8,600
October 2026	9,300
November 2026	11,700

In which month does Des' turnover exceed the registration limit and by what date must he notify HMRC?

Answer

Des' cumulative turnover must be checked at the end of each month against the registration limit of £90,000 throughout his first year of trading. His total turnover for the first 12 months, to October 2026 is 84,300 and at this point, he is not required to register.

He must then review his total turnover for the previous 12 months at the end of each subsequent month.

Des' total turnover for the 12 months ending 30 November 2026 is 90,500 calculated as follows:

12 months sales to October 2026	84,300
Less Sales November 2025	(5,500)
Add Sales November 2026	11,700
12 months to 30 November 2026	90,500

Therefore, Des' turnover exceeds the registration limit in November 2026 and he must notify HMRC by 30 December 2026 (within 30 days of the end of the month). His registration will be effective from 1 January 2027.

Example 23.6

Tina started her business on 1 August 2025. She has noted that her total taxable supplies since the start of her business have exceeded £90,000 by the end of April 2026.

By what date should she notify HMRC and when will registration be effective from?

Answer

Tina will need to notify HMRC of her requirement to register by 30 May 2026. Her registration will then be effective from 1 June 2026.

Example 23.7

Jeff started trading on 1 August 2026. In his first three months of trading, turnover of taxable supplies was £9,000 per month. On 5 November 2026, he received an order for £95,000 for delivery by 30 November 2026.

By what date should Jeff notify HMRC of his need to register for VAT?

Answer

Under the future test, on 5 November, Jeff expects his turnover to exceed the registration limit in the next 30 days (Only look at the next 30 days and ignore any earlier turnover). Therefore, he must notify HMRC within 30 days of knowing this, so by 5 December 2026. Registration will be effective from 5 November 2026.

Disposals of capital assets should be ignored in calculating the value of taxable supplies for registration purposes.

It is the *person* who is liable to be registered, not the business, and therefore in ascertaining if the registration limits are exceeded by any person all taxable supplies made by the person in all of their businesses must be aggregated.

It is important to note that a person making only exempt supplies cannot be registered because such a person is not making taxable supplies.

If a supply is made before liability to registration arises but payment is made after registration, no VAT is due.

Voluntary registration

Where a person is not required to compulsorily register they may still register voluntarily if they are making taxable supplies in the course of a business or are carrying on activities intending to then make taxable supplies.

Voluntary registration enables any input VAT to be recovered which otherwise would not be the case i.e. unless registration is made no input VAT can be recovered. However, of course, from registration, VAT will need to be charged on sales.

Voluntary registration may be helpful when a trader is worried that they may miss the compulsory registration deadlines and may also help to disguise the size of a small business.

Consequences of registration

Once registration is effective, VAT, at the appropriate rate, must be charged on all taxable supplies. If the business only supplies other VAT registered businesses, this is likely to have very little impact on sales. However, if most sales are to the general public, this will create an immediate 20% increase in the total sales price of standard rated supplies. The trader may, therefore, decide to reduce their pre-VAT prices, reducing their gross profit. However, the trader will benefit from the recovery of input tax on purchases.

After registration, the trader must comply with all administrative requirements of the VAT legislation, for example, providing VAT invoices, submitting quarterly VAT returns etc. as detailed later in this chapter.

Deregistration

Where a person ceases to make taxable supplies, HMRC must be notified within 30 days of cessation. Also, where a person expects taxable turnover to fall below £88,000 (the deregistration threshold) in the next 12 months voluntary deregistration may be made.

The effect of deregistration is that no further input VAT may be recovered and no further output VAT may be charged.

On deregistration, the trader must charge output VAT on the value of any trading stock and current assets held at that date, although this is waived if the VAT due is £1,000 or less.

Penalties for late registration

Where a person has failed to notify HMRC of the need to compulsorily register, a penalty may be charged, based on the amount of VAT that should have been paid had the registration been made at the correct time.

The penalty will be tax geared based on the taxpayer's behaviour as detailed in Chapter 21. The penalty will be between 30% to 100% of the VAT outstanding but may be reduced for unprompted disclosure.

Example 23.8

Josh started to trade on 1 February 2026 and over the first few months his supplies are as follows:

February	£23,000	June	£30,000
March	£26,000	July	£16,000
April	£20,000	August	£10,000
May	£24,000		

He realises in late August that he should have notified HMRC of the requirement to register by 30 June as the £90,000 limit was exceeded during May (23,000 + 26,000 + 20,000 + 24,000= 93,000) and notifies them on 27 August 2026.

Josh is, therefore, two months late in notifying HMRC. He should have notified HMRC by 30 June 2026.

A penalty is thus chargeable based on the net VAT which should have been paid, which is VAT on the July and August supplies (as 1 July 2026 is the date from which his VAT registration should have been effective) less any input tax for these months.

The level of penalty will be determined based on the reason for late notification and whether Josh notifies HMRC before they discover his error. In addition to the penalty, any outstanding VAT for the two months (Output tax less input tax) would also be payable.

Transfer of a Business as a Going Concern

If a business is sold as a going concern, the transfer is not a taxable supply and no VAT is charged.

For this to occur:

- the transferor and transferee must both be VAT registered and the business concerned must continue to be carried on as a going concern;
- the assets transferred must be used by the transferee in the same kind of business as that of the transferor; and
- there must be no significant break in business activities.

If the transferee takes over the VAT number of the transferor they also take over any outstanding VAT compliance obligations and VAT liabilities of the previous owner.

Where the above conditions are not satisfied then VAT is due on the transfer (i.e. the sale of business assets).

Pre-registration VAT

Where, prior to registration, VAT is incurred on the purchase of goods and/or services this VAT may be recoverable once the person registers. VAT is recoverable:

- on *goods* including capital goods and trading stock provided:
  - they are still owned at the date of registration, *and*
  - they were purchased within the four years before registration;
- on *services*, if they were supplied within six months before registration.

The goods or services must have been used for business purposes and must meet the usual rules for recovery of input VAT.

Time of the supply: tax point

The time of supply whether of goods or services, referred to as the tax point, determines the period into which the supply falls (important for timing on VAT returns or the rate of VAT to be charged if there is a change of rate).

The basic tax point for goods is when they are removed by the customer or made available to them.

The basic tax point for services is the time when the services are performed.

The above general rules are overridden in the following situations:

1. if an invoice is issued or payment is received *before* the basic tax point; the tax point becomes the earlier of the date of invoice and receipt of payment.
2. if an invoice is issued within 14 days after the basic tax point date, the invoice date becomes the tax point.

Therefore, to determine the tax point for any supply or receipt it is necessary to work through the following steps. First, establish the basic tax point. Then consider if it can be moved to an earlier date (1. above) in which case that becomes the actual tax point. If it cannot be moved earlier then check if it can be moved later (2. above), in which case that becomes the actual tax point. If it cannot be moved then the basic tax point applies.

If goods are taken on sale or return, the tax point is the earlier of when the customer accepts them or 12 months after the date of despatch.

On a continuous supply of services (e.g. electricity; tax advice) paid for periodically the tax point is the earlier of receipt of such payments and the date of issue of the invoice.

Separate tax points can apply to a deposit and final payment.

Example 23.9

During his VAT quarter to 30 June, Stuart sold goods to the total value of £24,000, exclusive of VAT, to one of his customers. The goods were not in stock and Stuart had to place an order with his suppliers. The customer was asked to pay a deposit of £6,000 on 25 June.

The goods were delivered to the customer on 2 September. Stuart raised an invoice on 30 September and the balance of the monies owed was paid on 10 October.

Show the tax points for this transaction.

Answer

The basic tax point for both parts of the transaction is 2 September.

Deposit monies

The deposit monies were received on 25 June. This date becomes the tax point for the deposit as it was prior to the basic tax point.

The deposit monies are assumed to be inclusive of VAT.

Therefore, Stuart needs to account for output VAT for the quarter ended 30 June of 1/6 x 6,000 = 1,000.

Balance of payment

The goods were made available to the customer on 2 September.

Stuart issued an invoice on 30 September with payment by the customer on 10 October.

The invoice was not issued within 14 days after the basic tax point (i.e. 2 September) and payment was not made before 2 September. Therefore, 2 September remains the tax point.

Stuart will therefore need to account for output VAT in the quarter ended 30 September of 20% x 24,000 = 4,800 less VAT on deposit (1,000)] = £3,800

Miscellaneous computational points

Discounts

Where a trade discount is offered VAT is chargeable on the discounted amount. Where a settlement discount is offered VAT is initially chargeable on the full amount. If the customer takes advantage of the discount, then the VAT is calculated on the discounted price. It may be necessary to raise a credit note to balance this in the trader's accounting records.

Assets for personal use

If goods or services are purchased specifically for private use, no VAT can be recovered (i.e. the VAT payable cannot be treated as input VAT). If, however, there is both business and private use of goods purchased then the input tax can be apportioned (i.e. only the business element is deducted).

As detailed above if goods are withdrawn from a business for personal use, output tax must be accounted for on the replacement value of the goods at the time that they are taken.

Motor cars

No recovery of input tax can be made on the purchase of a motor car unless the car is used wholly for business purposes (which is generally most unlikely!).

Consequently, no VAT is chargeable on the sale of a used car on which input tax was not recovered.

Leased cars

The recovery of input tax on car lease charges is restricted by 50% where the car has any private use.

Accessories

VAT cannot be recovered on the cost of accessories fitted when the car is bought unless there is 100% business use. It is, however, normally possible to recover VAT on accessories fitted subsequently despite potential private use.

Repairs, maintenance

Provided that there is some business use, a taxable trader can recover *all* the VAT on repair and maintenance costs even if the car is used partly for private use.

Car fuel

If fuel is provided for a car which includes private use by an individual (i.e. proprietor, employee or director) then the business may recover the input VAT on the total cost of the fuel but it must also account by way of *output* VAT an amount calculated according to the fuel scale rate provided by HMRC.

This fuel scale charge is based on the car's CO_2 emissions with the lowest rate band covering cars with emissions up to 120g/km or less, working up through various bands until the highest band for cars with emissions of 225 g/km or greater.

The amount of output VAT will be determined by taking 1/6 of the appropriate fuel scale charge.

Example 23.10

Jackie, a sole trader, purchases a motor car, with emissions of 200g/km, which she uses partly for business and partly for private purposes. The fuel scale charge for a car with this level of emissions is £436 per quarter. Her car fuel bills for the quarter totalled £750 (VAT inclusive).

What is the net VAT recoverable for the quarter?

Answer

No VAT can be recovered on the purchase of the car.
Jackie can recover VAT on the inclusive cost of the fuel £750 x 1/6 = £125

However, she must also account for the output tax on the scale charge calculated as £436 x 1/6 = £72.

Jackie's net overall position will be £53 input tax increase (£125 - £72).

Note

Strictly, there is an increase in output tax of £72 and recoverable input tax of £125, which gives a net position of £53 recoverable.

A business can opt not to recover any input VAT on any fuel for any of its vehicles. This would be advantageous if the additional output tax would create an overall increase in VAT payable. Alternatively, the scale charge will not apply if only VAT on fuel used for business mileage is recovered, supported by accurate mileage records.

Vans

VAT can normally be recovered on the purchase of vans and their running costs, including fuel without the restriction applicable to cars.

Where a registered business recovered input VAT on the purchase of a van, they must charge VAT on the full selling price when it is sold.

Accommodation

No VAT can be recovered on the costs of providing residential accommodation for a director or a person connected with him or her.

VAT on staff removal expenses is normally recoverable.

Bad debts

Output tax is usually charged based on the invoiced amount and not the receipt of payment. If a debt becomes bad or irrecoverable, a claim for repayment of output VAT can be made if the following conditions are satisfied:

- the debt has been written off as a bad debt, *and*
  at least *six months* have elapsed since the debt was due and payable, *and*
- the VAT charged on the supply has been paid to HMRC, *and*
- the appropriate accounting records have been maintained by the supplier.

If a payment on account of the debt has been made it will be allocated on a FIFO basis unless the debtor has attributed it to a specific debt or debts.

The claim for bad debt relief must be made within four years and six months from the due date of payment.

Entertainment

VAT on business entertainment of suppliers or UK customers cannot be recovered whereas VAT on entertaining staff or overseas customers is recoverable. All VAT can be recovered on the costs of hotels and subsistence incurred by a taxable trader or its staff for business purposes.

Calculation of VAT liability

VAT is usually calculated for a three-month period. The following example illustrates how the VAT due for a quarter would be calculated by deducting recoverable input tax from the output tax due.

Example 23.11

Luke is a VAT registered trader and is preparing his VAT return for the quarter to 31 October 2026. During the quarter he made the supply of standard rated services of £36,500, exclusive of VAT.

Luke purchased goods costing £5,040 inclusive of VAT during the quarter. In addition, he incurred various other expenses and has identified the following amounts of input tax:

VAT on petrol	£150
VAT on entertaining suppliers	£30
VAT on mobile phone	£10

It has been established that the scale charge for the car is £296 and that 50% of the use of the mobile phone is for private purposes. Calculate Luke's VAT payable for the quarter.

Answer

Output tax:			
Sales	36,500 x 20% =		7,300
Fuel scale charge	296 x 1/6 =		49
Input tax:			
Purchases	5,040 x 1/6	840	
Petrol		150	
Entertaining – Blocked		0	
Mobile phone – 50%		5	
			(995)
VAT Payable			6,354

Administration and penalties

VAT returns

VAT on the supply of goods and services must be accounted for on a quarterly basis. However, the relevant quarters are determined by HMRC. Therefore, some traders will have quarterly return periods of, say, 31 March, 30 June, 30 September and 31 December; others may have 28 February, 31 May, 31 August and 30 November etc.

The return, which is completed online by the trader, shows the total input and output VAT for the period and the net VAT that needs to be accounted for. HMRC must receive the completed return and the VAT due within one month and seven days following the relevant quarter period.

Where a trader is likely to receive VAT refunds rather than having to make VAT payments, as may occur where a registered trader is making primarily zero rated supplies, monthly returns may be submitted.

Making Tax Digital

Under Making Tax Digital, VAT registered businesses are required to maintain digital accounting records and submit their VAT return generated directly from within their own functionally compatible accounting software. The accounting software will be required to record details of individual sales and purchases and preserve digital records. It is hoped that this digital process will prevent many common errors that arise in VAT returns.

VAT invoices

If a taxable person makes a taxable supply, a VAT invoice must be issued to the purchaser. This enables the recovery of any input VAT by a VAT registered purchaser. Without a valid VAT invoice, input tax cannot be recovered. The invoice must show all of the following:

- the supplier's name, address and VAT registration number;
- the name and address of the customer;
- the invoice number, its date of issue and the tax point;
- the type of supply and a description of the goods supplied; and
- the VAT exclusive amount, the rate of VAT, the amount of VAT payable and any cash discount offered.

Less detailed invoices can be issued where the VAT inclusive amount does not exceed £250. There is no requirement to issue a VAT invoice for retail supplies to unregistered businesses or individuals. A retailer may assume that no VAT invoice is required unless the customer asks for one when an invoice should be issued using the rules detailed above.

Late returns or payments – New Points-based penalty system

From 1 January 2023, a new points-based penalty system replaces the previous default surcharge and will apply to both late VAT returns and payments.

Penalties for late submission work on a point-based system, with one point each time a return is late. For quarterly returns, once four points have been accumulated a £200 penalty will be charged and a further £200 penalty for each subsequent late return. The penalties will apply even if there is no VAT liability or a VAT refund is due.

Once the penalty threshold is reached, to clear all accumulated points, all outstanding returns must be submitted and there must be no late quarterly returns for the next 12 months. If the penalty threshold is not breached, any points will automatically clear after two years.

Example 23.12

Gemma has fallen behind with her VAT returns. Her VAT returns for the quarters ended 30 April 2026 and 31 July 2026 were both submitted late.

What is her current penalty position and what will happen if the next three returns are all submitted late?

Answer

With two late quarterly returns, Gemma has accumulated two points. As she has not yet reached four points, she will not receive any penalty.

If the next return, to 31 October 2026, is late, her points total will increase to three, so still below the penalty threshold.

If the subsequent return to 1 January 2027 is late, she will have accumulated four points and a penalty of £200 will be imposed.

If Gemma then submits the return to 30 April 2027 late, as she has already breached the penalty threshold, a further £200 penalty will apply.

Notes

Gemma will be required to submit all of the next four quarterly returns on time to reset the penalty points to Nil, otherwise, subsequent late returns will each attract a £200 filing penalty.

For late payments, there will be an initial penalty of 3% of the VAT outstanding for 15 days with an additional 3% penalty for any VAT outstanding at 30 days after the due date. If any VAT remains unpaid after 30 days, an additional penalty accrues daily at a rate of 10% per annum on the outstanding balance.

In addition, late payment interest will apply to any VAT paid late.

Minor errors and corrections

If a trader discovers an error on a previous VAT return, they may simply adjust the next return to account for this within certain limits. This only applies if the net adjustment is within the greater of £10,000 and 1% of the quarter's turnover, subject to a maximum adjustment of £50,000.

HMRC may impose a penalty if they believe that the error is deliberate or careless.

Larger errors must be notified to HMRC and interest will be charged on the late paid VAT. Again, HMRC may also impose a tax geared penalty.

VAT visits and inspections

HMRC has the right to request to visit a business' trading premises and inspect its business records.

If following an inspection an underpayment of VAT is discovered, HMRC may raise an assessment to collect this, together with interest. In addition, a tax geared penalty may be imposed as detailed in Chapter 21.

VAT Records

Records used to prepare a VAT return must be retained for six years. In particular, this must include copies of all VAT invoices issued and invoices used to support a claim for input tax.

Special Schemes

Many small businesses find VAT administration very time-consuming. Three optional special schemes have been introduced to help businesses by reducing the administrative burden.

The three schemes are:

- annual accounting;
- cash accounting; and
- flat rate scheme.

Annual accounting

Where a business has an anticipated annual taxable turnover (i.e. standard plus zero rated supplies) not exceeding £1,350,000 (excluding VAT) then instead of completing four quarterly returns, a business may elect for Annual accounting and make a single annual return for the previous 12 months.

The business must be up to date with all of its VAT returns and must not have committed a VAT offence in the previous 12 months.

Although only one return is necessary, the business is required to make nine equal monthly payments of VAT based on the net VAT liability for the previous year (i.e. each payment equals 10% of the previous year's net VAT liability). These payments are due in months 4 to 12 inclusive.

A final balancing payment for the year must be made within two months of the end of the year at which time the annual return must also be lodged.

A trader must leave the scheme where taxable turnover for the last annual accounting period exceeds £1,600,000. The trader must notify HMRC with a view to leaving the scheme where they anticipate that their turnover will exceed these limits in the current accounting period.

Cash accounting

As discussed above VAT is calculated for each quarter based on invoices issued and received; basically, the accruals basis.

However, where annual taxable turnover does not exceed £1,350,000, a trader may elect to prepare VAT returns on the cash basis, again provided that their VAT position is up to date. This basis simply requires that output and input VAT for a quarter is calculated on a cash received and cash paid basis.

This basis has the advantage that any output VAT which is normally accounted for in the quarter in which an invoice has been raised need not be accounted for until the trader receives settlement of the invoice. Therefore, this means that automatic relief for bad debts is obtained. On the other hand, until the trader settles invoices on their purchases, input VAT cannot be recovered.

A trader must leave the scheme if annual taxable turnover exceeds £1,600,000 at the end of a VAT period.

Flat rate scheme

Under the flat rate scheme, small businesses may calculate their VAT liability as a flat rate percentage of total turnover (i.e. inclusive of VAT, and including standard, zero rated and exempt supplies) thus avoiding the need to keep detailed records of input and output tax.

The scheme is available to small businesses with a taxable turnover which is not anticipated to exceed £150,000 in the next 12 months. A trader must leave the scheme if their annual total VAT inclusive turnover exceeds £230,000.

Under the scheme, a trader charges the customer the normal amount of VAT (i.e. output VAT) on sales and is charged VAT as usual on purchases (i.e. input VAT). However, the output VAT is not paid over to HMRC nor is the input VAT recoverable. Instead, in each VAT period, a flat rate is charged on the VAT inclusive turnover plus any exempt supplies and this amount of VAT is then payable to HMRC as normal.

The flat rate varies according to the type of business or trade sector. Rates vary, and by way of example, the flat rate percentage for accounting is 14.5%; for advertising 11%; estate agencies 12%; legal services 14.5%; food manufacturing 9%; and tobacco or newspaper retailing 4%.

This scheme cannot be used in conjunction with the cash accounting scheme (see above) but can be used with the annual accounting scheme (see above).

Example 23.13

Connor, a self-employed barber, uses the flat rate scheme (applying the appropriate flat rate for his business activity of 13%) and makes annual standard rated sales (VAT excluded) of £90,000 and zero rate sales of £2,000. Connor's purchases amount to £8,800 (all relating to standard rate supplies, VAT inclusive).

Calculate VAT payable under the normal and flat rate methods.

Answer

On the normal basis, Connor would account for

Output tax	Standard rate sales	90,000 x 20% =	18,000
	Input tax	8,800 x 1/6 =	(1,467)
			16,533

Under the flat rate scheme, Connor would account for:

Output VAT = 13% x (90,000 + (90,000 x 20%) + 2,000) = 14,300

HMRC became aware that many traders were using the scheme as a way to reduce their VAT liability, as illustrated by the above example, rather than the intended reason of reducing administration. Therefore, a flat rate of 16.5% applies to all 'limited cost business' rather than the normal business specific rates. A limited cost business is one with total purchases less than either 2% of turnover or £1,000 a year.

Substantial traders

If a trader has an annual VAT liability exceeding £2,300,000 then monthly payments on account of each quarter's liability must be paid over to HMRC thereafter.

These monthly payments on account are deducted when calculating the net VAT payable for the quarter. Each monthly payment is based on the previous year's VAT liability and equals 1/24 of this annual amount.

VAT – imports and exports

As VAT is a tax charged on supplies consumed in the UK, when goods are exported they are 'consumed' outside the UK and to impose VAT on such goods would be against the purpose of the tax. Therefore, a supply of goods to a destination outside the UK (i.e. the export of goods) is zero-rated. The business making the export must retain evidence of export to support the zero rate applied.

If a UK business imports goods from outside the UK (or from outside the EU to Northern Ireland) the business will have to pay import VAT on goods under the reverse charge procedure whereby the purchaser must calculate and pay the VAT. VAT is normally charged at the same rate as if the supply had been supplied in the UK.

A VAT registered business can account for this import VAT on their VAT Return by using postponed VAT accounting which allows the business to both declare import VAT and reclaim it as input tax on their next VAT Return. The VAT incurred on the imported goods can be reclaimed as input tax subject to the normal rules.

Alternatively, a business can choose to pay import VAT directly to HMRC at the point of importation. Again, this VAT incurred on the imported goods can be recovered on the next VAT return, subject to the normal rules.

A UK trader not registered for VAT will still have to pay VAT on the import of goods but will not be able to reclaim it.

Interaction of VAT and the other taxes

Generally speaking, VAT is excluded from income tax and corporation tax calculations of VAT registered businesses.

Thus, all calculations are performed net of VAT if the business is VAT registered. The simple reason is that in most cases, VAT charged as output VAT on sales and input VAT payable on purchases is offset giving rise to a VAT net payment or net recovery. In other words, VAT does not impact a business other than from a cash flow perspective.

However, sometimes VAT may be irrecoverable by a trader (e.g. on the purchase of motor cars or if only exempt supplies are made). In such cases some form of relief is in principle available as follows:

Income and corporation tax

Irrecoverable VAT may be deducted as a business expense in computing trading profit where it relates to an allowable expense. However, if such VAT relates to the purchase of a capital item and is irrecoverable it may form part of the cost of the item for capital allowance purposes instead.

Capital gains tax

VAT paid on the purchase of a chargeable asset is excluded from any subsequent capital gain computation if the VAT is recoverable. However, where the VAT is irrecoverable the purchase price will be the VAT inclusive price. Note, however, that on a future sale any VAT that may be charged on the sale price should be excluded in computing any capital gain.

SUMMARY

- VAT is a consumption tax applied to the supply of goods and services.
- Other than from a cash flow perspective, VAT is generally cost neutral for a VAT registered business.
- VAT charged on sales (output VAT) is offset by VAT paid on purchases (input VAT) and the balance is either paid over to or recovered, from HMRC, normally for a three month period.
- There are some restrictions on the input VAT that may be recovered.
- Failure to file a VAT return and/or make the appropriate payment on time may lead to penalties.
- For small businesses, certain schemes are available to make the administration of VAT easier, including annual accounting, cash accounting and the flat rate scheme. Various conditions must be satisfied before any of these schemes may be adopted.

Questions for students

See Appendix 2 for practice questions relating to Chapter 23. Answers are available online at https://spiramus.com/uk-taxation-for-students-20267-answers.

CHAPTER 24

Inheritance Tax: an introduction

Introduction

The calculation of Inheritance Tax (IHT) is very different from the other taxes detailed in this book. The chapter will look at the basics of how an individual's IHT liabilities are calculated both during their lifetime and on death.

Basic principles

IHT is a tax on the transfer of value, most commonly on the death of an individual. Only individuals and trusts are liable to IHT. This book will not consider the IHT charges that can apply directly to a trust.

Technically speaking, liability to IHT arises when a chargeable person (e.g. an individual or trust) makes a chargeable transfer (e.g. a gift) of chargeable property (e.g. cash, shares etc.). For IHT to be applicable, there must be an element of gift (gratuitous benefit). Therefore, a genuine arm's length commercial transaction cannot give rise to an IHT liability.

IHT always applies to UK assets. Normally, IHT also applies to a UK resident's worldwide assets. However, this does not apply until the individual is considered a UK long-term resident. An individual is a long-term resident once they have been resident in the UK for at least ten years out of the twenty tax years before the year of the IHT event. There are special rules that can apply when a long-term resident leaves the UK.

As regards chargeable property this includes almost all property of any type, with few exempt items. An ISA, for example, is exempt from income tax and capital gains tax but is chargeable for IHT. A very generous relief, known as business property relief, can apply to business interests held for at least two years.

Lifetime transfers

For gifts to other individuals, there is no immediate charge to IHT. However, if the individual making the gift dies within the following seven years, then potentially the gift is subject to IHT and must be considered when reviewing the IHT position on death. Therefore, such gifts are referred to as potentially exempt transfers or PETs.

Gifts to most trusts can create an immediate IHT charge and in these cases are referred to as chargeable lifetime transfers (CLT). In addition, where a CLT is made within seven years of death, the CLT will also be reviewed on death with potentially additional IHT payable.

A number of exemptions can apply to lifetime transfers.

First, and perhaps most importantly, any transfers between spouses or civil partners are exempt from IHT, whether during lifetime or on death. Gifts to registered charities and political parties are similarly exempt.

During each tax year, an individual may make gifts totalling £3,000 completely exempt from IHT. If this annual exemption is not fully used, it may be carried forward and utilized in the following tax year only, after the current year exemption has been used in full. If there are multiple transfers during a year, whether PETs or chargeable, the annual exemption must be used against the earliest transfer in a tax year and in chronological order against further transfers.

In addition, small gifts totalling no more than £250 per individual recipient each tax year are also exempt.

Example 24.1

Albert made no gifts during the tax year to 5 April 2026. During the year to 5 April 2027, he gave £8,000 to his son and £200 to each of his five grandchildren on their birthdays. All of the gifts were made in cash.

What is the value of the potentially exempt transfers?

Answer

The gifts to each of his grandchildren were below £250 per individual in total during 2026/27 and are therefore exempt.

As Albert did not make any gifts in the previous tax year, he has the annual exempt amount of £3,000 for the current tax year 2026/27 and the unused allowance of the previous year 2025/26. The gift to his son for IHT is £8,000 - £3,000 - £3,000 = £2,000. This is a potentially exempt transfer or PET.

Therefore, if Albert dies within seven years of the date of making the gift to his son, the PET of £2,000 is potentially subject to IHT.

Gifts made in consideration of marriage are exempt up to specific limits. For gifts from a parent, the exemption is £5,000, reduced to £2,500 for gifts from grandparents and remoter ancestors or from a party to the marriage. Finally, a gift of up to £1,000 by anyone else on marriage is also exempt. This exemption also applies to civil partnerships.

As IHT is charged on capital, a further exemption applies to gifts that constitute normal expenditure out of income. There is no financial limit on this exemption but it must be able to be demonstrated that the gifts are habitual, are made from excess income and do not affect the donor's standard of living.

Value Transferred – Loss to the donor

In the above example, simple cash gifts were referred to. However, a gift could be of property or shares. For IHT purposes the value transferred is based on the reduction in the donor's estate and not the value received by the recipient.

Example 24.2

Reisha owns 70% of the shares in her family investment company and decides to give a 25% shareholding to her daughter. The gift will reduce Reisha's shareholding to 45%.

It has been established that a 70% shareholding is valued at £500,000, a 45% shareholding £225,000 and a 25% shareholding £100,000. What is the value of the shares gifted for IHT purposes?

Answer

Before the gift, Reisha's 70% shareholding was valued at £500,000 and after the gift, her remaining 45% shareholding has a value of £225,000. The value of the 25% transfer for IHT is the loss to Reisha's estate calculated as £500,000 - £225,000 = £275,000.

Notes

The transfer will be a PET and will fall out of any IHT charge if Reisha survives seven years from the date of the gift.

If the £3,000 annual exemption has not already been used, this will be available to reduce the value of the PET.

IHT on the death estate

On death, IHT is charged on the basis that the deceased made a transfer of all of their assets immediately before death. This calculation will require all assets to be valued and any liabilities at death to be deducted to arrive at the total estate. Also, any reasonable funeral costs, including the provision of a headstone, may be deducted.

The annual exemption and small gifts exemptions do not apply on death. However, any legacies to a surviving spouse, civil partner, charity or political party are exempt.

Example 24.3

Jed died on 24 August 2026. Jed had never married and lived in a rented property. On his death, he had the following assets and liabilities:

Quoted shares	150,000
Bank deposits	185,000
ISA	18,000
Household items	3,500
Motor car	6,000
Outstanding gas bill	120

Jed's funeral cost £3,900.

Jed had not made any lifetime gifts and under his will, all assets are left to his niece.

Calculate the value of Jed's death estate for IHT.

Answer

Quoted shares	150,000
Bank deposits	185,000
ISA	18,000
Household items	3,500

Motor car	6,000
Less:	
Outstanding gas bill	(120)
Funeral cost	(3,900)
Gross chargeable estate	358,480

Note

Note that the ISA, although exempt from income tax and capital gains tax, is subject to IHT. Similarly, the motor car would be exempt from capital gains tax but again is chargeable to IHT.

The rate of IHT on the death estate

IHT is charged at a flat rate of 40% on the death estate above the nil rate band of £325,000. However, where there are chargeable lifetime transfers or PETs within seven years before death, the full nil rate band may not be available.

In addition, a residence nil rate band: (RNRB) of up to £175,000 is also available if the estate at death leaves a residence (for example a house) of the deceased to their direct descendants. The available RNRB is limited to the value of the residence less any outstanding repayment mortgage if lower. The amount of RNRB is reduced for estates above £2 million. The reduction is £1 for every £2 exceeding £2 million before deducting certain reliefs and exemptions.

Example 24.4

Continuing from Example 24.3 above, calculate the IHT payable on Jed's death.

Answer

As Jed had not made any lifetime gifts, the full IHT nil rate band will be available. Jed's estate did not include a residence; therefore, the residence nil rate band is not available.

IHT payable

325,000 @ 0%	0
33,480 @ 40%	£13,392
358,480	£13,392

If the deceased was married or in a civil partnership, any unused nil rate band and/or residence nil rate band may be claimed on the death of the survivor. This is based on the proportion of the unused rate band rather than the actual amount. The transferred unused nil rate band may be used against the death estate and any lifetime gifts taxable as a result of death. The transferred residence nil rate band may only be used against the death estate.

Example 24.5

Hilda died in May 2007 leaving £120,000 to her children and the remainder of her estate to her husband, Stan. Stan died on 14 May 2026 leaving his entire estate to his children. The estate comprised his house (i.e. his residence) valued at £280,000 and other assets of £550,000 giving a total estate value of £830,000. The IHT Nil rate band available in May 2007 was £300,000. Stan and Hilda made no lifetime gifts. Calculate the IHT liability on Stan's death.

Answer

Hilda's estate used £120,000 of the £300,000 IHT nil rate band in 2007. This represents 40% (120,000/300,000) of the band, leaving 60% to be claimed on the death of Stan.

On his death, Stan's estate will have available his IHT nil rate band of £325,000 plus £195,000 (60% of £325,000) transferred from Hilda, giving a total of £520,000.

Stan's estate will also benefit from the residence nil rate band of £175,000 and can claim Hilda's unused RNRB, for a total of £350,000. As this is higher than the value of the residence, £280,000, it is restricted.

The IHT on Stan's estate is therefore calculated as follows:

Nil rate band	325,000 @ 0%	
Transferred Nil rate band	195,000 @ 0%	
RNRB (Capped)	280,000 @ 0%	
Balance	30,000 @ 40% =	£12,000
	830,000	

These rate bands are frozen until the end of 2030/31.

Reduced rate of IHT

A reduced rate of inheritance tax was introduced in 2012 to encourage charitable giving. The IHT rate is reduced from 40% to 36% for estates where at least 10% of the taxable estate is left to charity. For this relief, taxable estate means the value of the deceased's net assets after deducting the available nil rate band, and any reliefs or exemptions other than the value gifts to charity and the residence nil rate band.

IHT on chargeable lifetime transfers

A lifetime transfer to a trust is referred to as a chargeable lifetime transfer (CLT) as it may create a lifetime IHT charge. The nil rate band of £325,000 still applies but IHT is charged at the lifetime rate of 20%. If the donor agrees to meet the IHT charge then this creates a further loss to the estate. In these cases, the chargeable transfer is effectively grossed up. IHT is charged at 20/80 or 25% and the gross transfer includes both the transfer and associated IHT.

Example 24.6

Erica transfers £400,000 into a trust on 1 December 2026. She has not previously made any lifetime gifts. What is the IHT liability and loss to Erica's estate if:

a) Erica bears the cost of the IHT liability, or
b) the IHT is paid from the trust?

Answer

Erica will be entitled to deduct the annual exemption for both the current year 2026/27 and the previous year 2025/26. The chargeable transfer is therefore £400,000 – 3,000 – 3,000 = £394,000.

a) If Erica pays the IHT the liability will be:

325,000 @ 0%	
69,000 @ 25% (20/80)	17,250

The loss to the estate is the net transfer of £394,000 plus the IHT of £17,250, giving a gross chargeable transfer of £411,250.

b) If the trust bears the IHT liability:

325,000 @ 0%	
69,000 @ 20%	13,800

The loss to the estate is the net transfer of £394,000 only.

If further chargeable lifetime transfers are made within seven years, then only the balance of the nil rate band will be available.

Example 24.7

Following on from Example 24.6 above, Erica transfers £100,000 into another trust on 1 June 2030 and again agrees to bear the IHT cost. She had made no other lifetime transfers since 1 December 2026. What is the IHT liability and loss to Erica's estate?

Answer

Erica will be entitled to deduct the Annual exemption for both 2029/30 and 2030/31. The chargeable transfer is therefore £100,000 – 3,000 – 3,000 = £94,000.

Next, we must look at the available nil rate band. This will be £325,000 less any chargeable lifetime transfers made within the previous seven years, at this point, PETs are ignored.

As Erica made a chargeable lifetime transfer on 1 December 2026 in excess of £325,000, there is no remaining nil rate band available. The IHT liability on the chargeable lifetime transfer on 1 June 2030 will, therefore, be £94,000 @ 25% (20/80) = £23,500, with the loss to the estate of £117,500 (£94,000+£23,500)

Note

If Erica had waited until after 30 November 2033 to make the second chargeable lifetime transfer, then the transfer on 1 December 2026, would be ignored as it would be more than seven years ago, and the full nil rate band would again be available.

If the trust agreed to pay the IHT on the transfer on 1 June 2030, the IHT payable by the trust would be £94,000 @ 20% = £18,800 and the loss to the estate £94,000.

Lifetime transfers – additional IHT on death

As mentioned above where a lifetime transfer, whether a PET or CLT is made within seven years of death, the transfer will come into charge to IHT at death rates.

Each transfer must be considered in chronological order and may utilise the IHT nil rate band before the death estate. Credit is given for any lifetime IHT paid. If the IHT liability on death is less than the lifetime charge, the excess cannot be refunded.

Example 24.8

Henry made a gift of £120,000 to his daughter in May 2020 and a subsequent gift into a trust of £50,000 in June 2024. Henry died on 12 August 2026 leaving an estate of £300,000. Henry was unmarried, did not make any other lifetime transfers and his death estate did not include a residence. Calculate the lifetime IHT payable by Henry. Calculate any IHT liabilities arising as a result of Henry's death.

Answer

Lifetime transfers

May 2020 Transfer to daughter	120,000	
Annual exemption CY 2020/21	(3,000)	
Annual exemption PY 2019/20	(3,000)	
PET	114,000	– PET No lifetime IHT liability
June 2024 Transfer to trust	50,000	
Annual exemption CY 2024/25	(3,000)	
Annual exemption PY 2023/24	(3,000)	
CLT	44,000	
IHT 44,000 @ 0%	0	

IHT on death 12 August 2026

Nil rate band available	325,000
PET May 2020	(114,000)
CLT June 2024	(44,000)
Balance of Nil rate band	167,000
Estate on death	300,000
IHT 167,000 @ 0%	
133,000 @ 40%	£53,200

Notes

The IHT position of each lifetime transfer is calculated first in chronological order. The IHT position of each gift within seven years before death is then reviewed to consider any additional IHT payable.

In this case, as the lifetime transfers are below £325,000 in total, there is no IHT payable on the lifetime transfers. However, the lifetime transfers utilise part of the IHT Nil rate band increasing the IHT payable on the death estate.

If as a result of death any IHT is payable on lifetime transfers, the resulting tax liability may be reduced by taper relief. The taper relief increases as the time from the date of the gift to the date of death increases according to the following table:

Years before death	Taper relief
0-3	0%
3-4	20%
4-5	40%
5-6	60%
6-7	80%

It should be noted that it is the IHT liability that is tapered and not the transfer. In effect, this means that taper relief can only apply where lifetime transfers are in excess of the nil rate band.

Example 24.9

Dorothy made a gift of £100,000 to her son on 17 January 2016. She then made a transfer of £400,000 to a trust on 1 May 2023 agreeing to pay any IHT arising. Dorothy died on 10 June 2026 with a taxable estate of £600,000. Dorothy had 10% of her late husband's nil rate band available and her estate did not include a residence. Calculate any IHT liabilities arising in Dorothy's lifetime and as a result of her death.

Answer

IHT on Lifetime transfers

17 January 2016 Transfer to son		100,000	
Annual exemption CY 2015/16		(3,000)	
Annual exemption PY 2014/15		(3,000)	
PET		94,000	PET – No lifetime IHT liability
1 May 2023 Transfer to trust		400,000	
Annual exemption CY 2023/24		(3,000)	
Annual exemption PY 2022/23		(3,000)	
CLT		394,000	
IHT	325,000 @ 0%	0	
	69,000 @ 25% (20/80)	17,250	

As Dorothy agreed to pay the IHT, the gross transfer (or loss to Dorothy's estate) is:

CLT	394,000
IHT	17,250
Gross transfer	411,250

IHT on death 10 June 2026

Nil rate band available	325,000
Transferred nil rate band (10%)	32,500
Nil rate band	357,500

PET 17 January 2016 (more than seven years before death) no additional IHT liability

CLT 1 May 2023		411,250
IHT	357,500 @ 0%	0
	53,750 @ 40%	21,500
Less: taper relief @ 20%		(4,300)
		17,200

Less IHT paid on CLT	(17,200)	(Actually paid £17,250)
Additional IHT payable	0	
Balance of Nil rate band	0	
Estate on death	600,000	

The entire available nil rate band has been fully utilised by the CLT on 1 May 2023. Therefore, the whole death estate is subject to IHT at 40%.

IHT	600,000 @ 40%	240,000

Notes

1. The IHT position of each lifetime transfer is calculated first in chronological order.
2. The IHT position of each transfer within seven years before death is then reviewed to consider any additional IHT payable.
3. The gift to Dorothy's son in January 2016 occurred more than seven years before death and is completely exempt.
4. The gift into trust occurred between three and four years before death. Therefore, the additional IHT liability on death is reduced by 20% taper relief.
5. The IHT paid during the lifetime on the transfer into the trust in May 2023 is deducted from the additional liability arising on death. As the lifetime tax exceeds the additional tax on death, no further IHT is payable. However, there can be no repayment of lifetime tax.
6. As the IHT nil rate band has been fully utilised by the lifetime transfer into trust, the estate on death is fully charged at 40%.

When considering the additional IHT on transfers in the seven years before death, any chargeable lifetime transfers or PETs that have become chargeable in the seven years before each transfer must also be taken into account. Although in the case of a chargeable lifetime transfer this may be more than seven years before the date of death, it can still impact the IHT liability.

Example 24.10

Peter died on 12 May 2026 leaving a death estate of £510,000 including a residence valued at £300,000. His entire estate is left to his daughter. Peter was unmarried. In his lifetime Peter had made the following transfers, after deducting any available allowances:

16 July 2017	Transfer to trust	150,000
5 September 2021	Gift to daughter	200,000

The trust agreed to pay any IHT arising on the transfer on 16 July 2017.

Calculate the IHT payable as a result of Peter's death.

Answer

Chargeable transfer July 2017– more than seven years before death – no further IHT liability on death.

PET 5 September 2021			200,000
Nil rate band		325,000	
Less CLT 16 July 2017		(150,000) (within seven years of PET)	
Balance available		175,000	
IHT payable	175,000 @ 0%	0	
	25,000 @ 40%	10,000	

Taper relief (4 -5 years) @ 40%	(4,000)	
IHT payable	6,000 (Payable by daughter)	
Estate on death 12 May 2026		510,000
Nil rate band	325,000	
Less PET 5 September 2021	(200,000)	
Balance available	125,000	
NRB 125,000 @ 0%	0	
RNRB 175,000 @ 0%	0	
210,000 @ 40%	84,000 (payable from the estate)	
510,000		

Notes

1. Although the transfer to a trust in July 2017 is more than seven years before death when considering the IHT of the PET on 5 September 2021 any chargeable transfers in the seven years before that date must be considered.
2. As the PET was to Peter's daughter, she will be responsible for the payment of the IHT liability arising as a result of Peter's death.
3. The available nil rate band on the death estate is reduced by any transfers within the seven years prior to death, both chargeable lifetime transfers and PETs. In addition, the RNRB is available.
4. If Peter had lived until 5 September 2028, the PET would have become fully exempt.

Business Property Relief

Business property relief (BPR) is a valuable inheritance tax relief for business owners whether making a lifetime transfer or on death. Significant changes to these rules are introduced from 6 April 2026 with full relief capped and reduced relief applying above a £2.5 million limit.

When "relevant business property" is transferred, relief may reduce the value of the asset for IHT purposes by either 50% or 100%. Therefore, qualifying relevant business property may be passed on completely free of IHT, provided the relevant conditions and limits are met.

For lifetime transfers within seven years of the donor's death, BPR is only available if the recipient still owns the property at the date of death. BPR is also available for qualifying business property within the death estate.

To qualify for BPR two key conditions must be satisfied:

1) The property must be 'relevant business property'; and
2) The asset must have been held for a least two years.

Relevant business property qualifying for the 100% relief allowance is:

1) A sole trader's business assets or an interest in a trading partnership;
2) Shares in an unquoted trading company.

The 100% relief allowance applies to qualifying assets up to a cumulative value of £2.5 million transferred in a seven-year allowance period, including in lifetime and on death. Once the 100% relief allowance is fully utilised, 50% relief will apply to the remaining qualifying value.

Other relevant business property assets qualifying for 50% relief only are as follows:

1) Quoted shares or securities in a trading company of which the transferor has voting control;
2) Unquoted shares that are traded on a recognised stock exchange, including AIM.
3) Land, buildings, plant and machinery owned by an individual and used either in a trading partnership in which they are a partner or a trading company which they control.

The 100% relief allowance period "resets" every 7 years, in a manner similar to the nil rate band. Any unused allowance may be transferred to a spouse or civil period on death.

Example 24.11

Abe made a gift of shares valued at £1,400,000 to his daughter June in March 2024, after deducting any other allowances. Abe died on 4 August 2026 at which date he still held shares valued at £3,000,000 in his trading company. The shares qualify for BPR and June still held the shares gifted to her on her father's death.

What BPR is available on Abe's death?

Answer

Abe had a BPR 100% relief allowance of £2,500,000 in the seven-year period to his death on 4 August 2026. The lifetime gift in March 2024 utilises £1,400,00 of this, reducing the value of the PET to June to £Nil.

This leaves a balance on death of £1,100,000. The remaining transfer on death receives BPR at 50%:

Value of shares on death	£3,000,000
Balance of 100% allowance	(1,100,000)
Balance	1,900,000
BPR @ 50%	(950,000)
Remaining value included in estate	£950,000

Detailed rules can restrict the extent of the relief where a company owns non-trading assets.

Agricultural Property Relief (APR) provides a similar exemption from IHT for qualifying farming assets. The £2.5 million 100% relief allowance applies to the combined value of qualifying BPR and APR assets.

IHT Administration

Any IHT liability arising as a result of death is payable by the end of the sixth month after the person dies. For example, if the person died in January 2027, the IHT would be payable by 31 July 2027. The IHT return (Form IHT400) must be filed with HMRC within 12 months of the date of death to avoid a penalty.

For IHT on lifetime transfers (CLT) made between 6 April and 30 September, IHT is due by 30 April in the following year, otherwise by six months after the end of the month of transfer and normally the IHT return is due by the same date.

SUMMARY

- Inheritance tax (IHT) is charged on transfers of value.
- The value of the transfer is based on the principle of the loss to the estate.
- IHT can apply in lifetime for transfers to trusts, but it more commonly applies on death.
- Lifetime gifts to another individual are potentially exempt, assuming that the donor survives seven years from the date of the gift.
- Transfers to trusts can give rise to a lifetime IHT charge at 20% (or 20/80 if the transferor bears the tax). If the transferor pays the IHT liability arising, then this increases the loss to the estate.
- Any lifetime transfers within seven years before death may come into charge to IHT at death rates, but credit is given for any lifetime IHT paid.
- IHT on death is charged at 40% on the estate above the available nil rate band.
- Transfers between spouses and civil partners are exempt from IHT, whether in lifetime or on death.
- An additional residence nil rate band applies where a residence is left on death to lineal descendants.
- For each chargeable transfer, both lifetime and on the death estate, you need to work through the following steps:
    1. Calculate the value of the transfer.
    2. Deduct any available reliefs.
    3. Deduct any exemptions.
    4. Calculate the cumulative total of all of the transfers in the previous seven years.
    5. Calculate the remaining Nil rate band.
    6. Apply IHT to the new transfer value at the appropriate rate.
    7. If applicable, deduct taper relief.
    8. If applicable, deduct any lifetime tax already paid on the transfer.

Questions for students

See Appendix 2 for practice questions relating to Chapter 24. Answers are available online at https://spiramus.com/uk-taxation-for-students-20267-answers.

APPENDIX 1

Some practical tips to help you to study taxation

Introduction

Taxation is something of a "Marmite" topic for many accountants – they either love it or hate it! Tax is a dynamic subject with rules, rates and allowances changing every year. However, this book attempts to simplify the tax rules as much as possible to help you to find studying tax interesting and enjoyable.

The rules of UK taxation can be logical, but often they are not! Don't worry, therefore, if you have difficulty understanding a particular issue because it doesn't seem logical; it probably isn't!

For example, the UK's income tax year runs from 6 April to the next 5 April (e.g. 6 April 2026 to 5 April 2027). It does *not* operate on a calendar year i.e. 1 January to 31 December basis.[2]

The taxes which you will usually study as part of your course are:

- income tax;
- capital gains tax;
- corporation tax;
- national insurance contributions;
- value added tax; and
- inheritance tax.

*Income tax is **very** important* and an understanding of income tax (the tax paid by individuals) is recommended before moving on to corporation tax (the tax paid by companies).

Computational approach

The tax syllabus, whether for undergraduates or as part of a professional qualification, primarily involves the ability to perform and understand computations i.e. working out an individual's taxable income and income tax liability or a company's corporation tax liability.

Usually, a detailed knowledge of the UK's tax case law or its legislation is not needed (although reading some tax cases can be surprisingly entertaining!). Students do not, therefore, need to be able to recite details of tax cases heard by the courts or section numbers from the tax legislation (i.e. the various Acts of Parliament) until studying for ATT or CIOT.

---

[2] Well, there is a logic but we need to go into the difference between Julian and Gregorian calendars and understand why the new year was celebrated on Lady Day (25 March).

As the approach is usually computational without doubt one of the keys to passing the examinations is to understand and be able to reproduce the various proforma layouts adopted throughout this book in preparing the various computations.

Proformas

A proforma is simply a standard layout of how a particular computation should be carried out.

The proforma layout not only reflects the order in which a computation needs to be performed but can also effectively be used as a revision aid with the support of your study notes.

One approach to studying tax is, therefore, to ensure that you know and understand the proforma or layout for key calculations and to make your own notes for each proforma.

Key proformas or computational layouts can be found in the following examples earlier in this text:

Income tax calculation	Example 4.6
Adjusted profit – sole trader	Example 6.2
Capital allowances – sole trader	Example 7.9
Corporation tax – TTP	Example 16.1
Adjusted profit – limited company	Example 16.16
Capital allowances – limited company	Example 16.13

Because of the volume of material covered in a taxation course, there is often little time to revise all the elements of the course as you go along, which is, of course, the ideal way to study. A proforma should help in this regard.

Doing questions

When starting to study a new tax (e.g. capital gains tax) or an aspect of it (e.g. use of capital losses) the starting point should be for you to try to understand the theory i.e. an explanation of the underlying concepts. Simply doing questions is *not* the answer. If you understand the principles involved you will not be left stumped if the question is in a different format to any you have previously seen.

Try to understand the underlying concepts *before* attempting any questions. In this book, I have included worked examples in the text which illustrate the points under discussion. Read the text and together with the examples try to understand what is happening. Do not simply try to follow the example without having first tried to understand the theory.

Only when you think you have understood the theory and any related examples does it make sense to try some questions in Appendix 2 for yourself.

In attempting questions, the more you can try the better. If you find difficulty in answering a particular question then *before* looking at the answer, reread the text and try the question again. Do not simply and immediately look at the answer; this should only be done as a last resort when you have really tried to answer the question.

When looking at an answer, do not simply check the numbers; note, in particular, the layout and order in which the various issues are tackled.

Make up your own questions!

In theory, the tax rules laid out in this text would apply to any individual or company regardless of their wealth or profit level. Usually, tax questions consist of unrelated amounts of income and gains and your task is to accurately calculate the income, gains or tax liability. Try taking an existing question and simply change all of the numbers and attempt to recalculate the correct answer. Hopefully, you are studying with other students and can challenge one of your colleagues to calculate the answer as well and together you can discuss any differences in your answers.

Common parts of the syllabus

Some topics are relevant to more than one type of tax and certainly, some are, relatively speaking, more important than others.

For example, capital allowances (basically tax allowable depreciation) are relevant to both income and corporation taxes. Therefore, studying this particular topic means that you may be able to attempt more questions in your exam than where a particular topic can only appear once (e.g. VAT cash accounting scheme).

Similarly, the adjustment of accounts profits (i.e. adjusting accounts profits to taxable profits) is highly relevant to both income and corporation taxes. It is, therefore, a good idea when you see that a topic appears relevant to more than one type of tax or situation to make sure you fully understand it. This will enhance your ability to pass your exams.

SUMMARY

The most important point is to understand the underlying concepts.

Simply practising multiple questions without attempting to understand the underlying theory is not a good idea.

Only when you feel you have a reasonable understanding of an area should you then attempt a variety of questions.

When looking at model answers to questions take note of how the answer is laid out and the order in which it's presented.

When you have finished a particular tax, e.g. income tax, it is a good idea to try to find time to look through the material again before starting the next tax. Your proforma plus attaching notes should be of immense help in this regard.

Don't be frightened to look at other tax sources which may also help.

If you are completely stuck, then looking at an alternative text or website may be the key to unlocking the solution. Each learner has their own particular style and sometimes reading an alternative text may instantly make the "penny drop". However, always ensure that any text matches the Finance Act that you are studying. A FA2022 tax text may not look very different from this FA2026 text, but a huge amount of tax legislation will have changed in that period as well as the tax rates and allowances! Also, be careful of AI as it may not be up to date!

Although not the easiest of websites for the newcomer to UK tax, the official HM Revenue & Customs website at http://www.hmrc.gov.uk/ may also sometimes be of help.

Identify those areas or rules which are relevant to more than one type of tax or situation.

Finally, try to enjoy your studies. Tax can be challenging but could hold the key to your future career. Before my first day of work at HMRC, my only previous contact with tax had been in a game of Monopoly! Even if you do not pursue a career in this field, I hope that at least you will be equipped to check your first payslip!

Good luck with all your studies!

APPENDIX 2

Questions for Students

Answers are available online at https://spiramus.com/uk-taxation-for-students-20267-answers or by using the QR code below:

CHAPTERS 1 TO 4

Question 1

For the year to 5 April 2027, James has the following income:

Employment income	18,000
Bank interest	800
Dividends	2,400

Income tax of £1,050 was deducted under the Pay As You Earn (PAYE) regulations from James' employment earnings.

Calculate the income tax payable for 2026/27.

Question 2

For the year to 5 April 2027, Carol has the following income:

Employment income	26,000
Bank interest	1,600
Dividends	5,500

Income tax of £2,600 was deducted under PAYE from Carol's employment income.

Calculate the income tax payable for 2026/27.

Question 3

For the year to 5 April 2027, Harry has the following income:

Self-employment profits	49,000
Bank interest	1,600
Interest from ISA	300
Dividends	6,800

Calculate the income tax payable for 2026/27.

Question 4

For the year to 5 April 2027, Helen has the following income:

Employment income	35,000
Income from property	5,000
Bank interest	2,600

Dividends	5,200

Income tax of £4,625 was deducted under PAYE from Helen's employment income.

In addition, Helen paid interest of £2,400 on a qualifying loan.

Calculate the income tax payable for 2026/27.

Question 5

For the year to 5 April 2027, Ed has the following income:

Employment income	95,000
Self-employment profits	15,000
Bank interest	1,800
Dividends	5,900

Income tax of £35,100 was deducted under PAYE from Ed's employment income.

Calculate the income tax payable for 2026/27.

Question 6

For the year to 5 April 2027, Ann has the following income:

Property income	85,000
Bank interest	2,600
Dividends	7,100

Ann made donations to charity, under gift aid, of £4,800 during the year.

Calculate the income tax payable for 2026/27.

Question 7

For the year to 5 April 2027, Sid has the following income:

State retirement pension	8,500
Occupational pension	4,800
Bank interest	5,500
Dividends	1,600

Calculate Sid's income tax liability for 2026/27.

Question 8

For the year to 5 April 2027, Tom has the following income:

Employment income	205,000
Property income	15,000
Bank interest	1,600
Dividends	2,800

Income tax of £82,100 was deducted under PAYE from Tom's employment income.

In addition, Tom paid interest of £5,000 on a qualifying loan.

Calculate the income tax payable for 2026/27.

Question 9

For the year to 5 April 2027, Sofie has the following income:

Trading profits	70,000
Property income	25,000
Bank interest	11,600
Dividends	8,000

In addition, Sofie paid personal pension contributions of £2,400 and a donation to charity under gift aid of £800.

Calculate the income tax payable for 2026/27.

CHAPTER 5

Question 10

Roger owns two residential properties which he lets.

Property 1

This property was purchased by Roger on 1 May 2026. Immediate repair work costing £2,300 was carried out on the property before it could be let, the damage to the property had been reflected in a reduced purchase price of the property.

The property was let from 1 July 2026 at an annual rental of £6,300, payable monthly on the last day of each month.

Property 2

The property is let furnished for the entire tax year. The rent received was £8,000. Expenditure comprises property repairs of £300, rent collection fees of £700 and new furniture costing £2,000. The new furniture replaced a similar old item, which was sold for £75.

Other general expenditure:

Other costs relating to the property letting business for the tax year ended 5 April 2027 include loan interest of £2,800 and insurance premiums of £900.

All rent was received on the due date and all expenses mentioned were paid during the tax year.

Calculate Roger's property business income for the year to 5 April 2027.

Question 11

Heather leases a shop to Fahad from 1 November 2026. She grants a 20 year lease to Fahad for a lease premium of £12,000. In addition, Fahad pays rent of £500 per month on the last day of each month with the first rent falling due on 30 November 2026.

Calculate Heather's taxable property business income for 2026/27.

CHAPTERS 6 TO 7

Question 12

Alice started trading on 1 April 2026 and is preparing her first accounts to 31 March 2027. She is preparing her accounts using the cash basis. Her accounting records show the following:

Cash and debit card sales received	26,400
Credit sales recorded	18,500
Outstanding receipts from credit sales	2,800
Cash purchases paid	14,800
Unpaid purchase invoices	970
Bank transfer for the purchase of a new computer	1,100
Direct debits for electricity	600
Direct debits for mobile phone	360
Travel expenses – paid by debit card	880
Cash entertaining suppliers	240
Business insurance paid cash – policy expires June 2027	800

Note: 30% of the use of the mobile phone is for private use

Prepare Alice's profit and loss account to 31 March 2027 using the cash basis.

Calculate Alice's tax adjusted trading profits to 31 March 2027.

Question 13

Explain the main differences to your calculation under Question 12 if the traditional/accruals method of accounting was used.

Question 14

Noah, a sole trader, started carrying on his trade as a sports retailer (under the trading name of "Sports for All") on 1 May 2026 and his first accounts, prepared by his accountant under the cash basis, for the year ended 30 April 2027 show the following:

Income		
Gross profit		115,300
Rental income		15,000
Building society interest received		1,600
		131,900
Expenses		
Telephone	1,200	
Salaries	39,000	
Rent and rates	9,000	
Light and heat	5,000	
Repairs and maintenance	2,500	
Advertising	25,000	
Motor expenses	10,000	
Sundry expenses	8,000	
		(99,700)
Net profit		32,200

Notes

1. The figure for telephone comprises £800 for the landline for the shop used exclusively for business and £400 for Noah's mobile, 40% of the use of which has been agreed as private.
2. Salaries included a salary to Noah's wife of £15,000 as she works in the shop as a sales assistant. The other sales assistants doing the same job receive a salary of £12,000.
3. Noah and his wife live in a flat above the shop. The figures for "rent and rates" and "light and heat" are for both the shop and the flat. The accountant has agreed with the tax authorities that 30% of these expenses relate to the flat.
4. Of the "repairs and maintenance" £250 related to the decoration of the flat and £2,250 related to repairs to the shop.
5. Included in the figure of £25,000 for advertising was £5,000 which related to Christmas presents to his customers of various wines and spirits, and £4,000 which related to diaries sent out to customers which had cost Noah £10 each and had on the front of them Noah's logo and the name of his business "Sports for All". The rest of the expenditure related to advertisements which Noah had placed in newspapers and trade magazines.
6. Noah decided to lease a new car (rather than buy it outright). The car had an annual leasing charge of £6,000. The balance of the expenditure is related to normal running costs (e.g. petrol, repairs etc.). The tax authorities have agreed that 60% of Noah's usage relates to private usage with 40% representing business usage. The car has CO_2 emissions of 140 g/km.
7. Sundry expenses included client entertaining of £2,000; staff entertaining of £450 on a day out in London; a fine of £500 for breach of health and safety regulations; a car park fine of £50 incurred by one of the sales assistants when on business for Noah; a donation to a local charity of £75 and a donation of £50 to his local political party; a subscription of £80 to the Sports Retailers Association; legal fees of £375 in connection with the granting of a brand new lease on the shop; and accountancy fees for accounts preparation of £500.
8. Noah's son wanted a pair of trainers for Christmas. Noah, therefore, took a pair from the shop for his son but did not pay for them. The trainers, if they had been sold to a member of the public, would have a retail price of £135 but their cost to Noah had been £100.
9. Capital allowances on the old car have been calculated at £2,800

Calculate Noah's tax adjusted trading profit to 30 April 2027.

Question 15

Andrew has operated as a self employed consultant for many years. His profit and loss account to 31 March 2027 calculated using the cash basis is as follows:

Fees received		120,000
Add: Bank interest received		55
Less: Expenses		
Motor expenses	6,600	

Donation to a national charity	1,000	
New photocopier	1,500	
Legal fees for grant of a 5-year lease	900	
Other allowable expenses	43,500	
		(56,700)
Profit for the year		63,355

45% of Andrew's motoring was private.

Andrew's capital allowances pools brought forward are as follows

Car used by Andrew (CO_2 emissions 155 g/km) 15,400

Calculate Andrew's adjusted trading profits, after capital allowances for the year to 31 March 2027.

Question 16

Jenny carries on her trade as a sole trader. She prepares her accounts to 30 September each year having started to trade on 1 October 2025.

Her tax adjusted profits were:

Year ended 30 September 2026	12,000
Year ended 30 September 2027	25,000
Year ended 30 September 2028	33,000

Calculate Jenny's assessable profits for each of the first three tax years of trading, identifying the appropriate basis periods for each tax.

Question 17

Nicholae trades as a sole trader plumber. He prepares his accounts to 30 June each year having started to trade on 1 September 2025.

His tax adjusted profits were:

10 months to 30 June 2026	18,000
Year ended 30 June 2027	26,000
Year ended 30 June 2028	35,000

Calculate Nicholae's assessable profits for each of the first three tax years of trade identifying the appropriate basis periods for each tax.

Question 18

Linda has carried on her trade as a sole trader for many years.

Her tax adjusted profits were:

Year ended 31 December 2025	30,000
Year ended 31 December 2026	27,000
Period ended 31 January 2027	2,100

Linda ceased trading on 31 January 2027.

Calculate Linda's assessable profits for each of the two tax years to 5 April 2027.

Question 19

Aamil has traded as a sole trader for many years.

His tax adjusted profits were:

Year ended 30 April 2023	27,000
Year ended 30 April 2024	30,000

Aamil had overlap profits available of £7,600.

Calculate Aamil's assessable profits for 2023/24 under the transitional rules and identify the profits that may be spread over five years.

Question 20

Jane, a sole trader, prepares her accounts using the traditional accruals accounting method. She can therefore claim capital allowances.

Jane prepares her accounts to 31 December each year. As at 31 December 2025, there is a tax written down value of £2,400 on her main pool.

Her purchases were as follows:

Purchases

1 September 2026	Equipment	16,000	
1 August 2026	Motor car	15,000	(emissions 145g/km. Jane uses this car privately 30% of the time)
30 January 2027	Van	8,000	

Calculate Jane's capital allowances for the years ended 31 December 2026 and 2027.

Question 21

Yan commenced trading on 1 November 2025 and bought various capital items all of which qualify for capital allowances.

He prepares his first accounts for the 10 months to 31 August 2026 using the accruals basis. His fixed asset purchases were as follows:

14 December 2025 - Plant and equipment £96,000
20 June 2026 - Motor car (for an employee; CO_2 emissions 145g/km) £18,600
3 August 2026 - Motor car (for an employee; CO_2 emissions 45g/km) £10,400

Calculate Yan's capital allowances for the 10 months to 31 August 2026.
(Note this question would have the same solution if instead of Yan it referred to Yan Limited, a company subject to corporation tax).

Question 22

During the accounting year to 5 April 2027, Harry, a sole trader using the cash basis sold his existing car for £15,000. This car had originally cost £32,000 and had a tax written down value brought forward of £17,644. It was replaced by a new car costing £34,000. This new car had CO2 emissions of 42g/km. Both cars have 25% private use.

Calculate Harry's capital allowances for the year to 5 April 2027.

Question 23

Ellie has been in business for several years preparing accounts annually to 31 March using the traditional accruals method. As at 31 March 2026, she has the following tax written down values:

Main pool	6,400
Private use asset	14,016

The private use asset is a motor car (CO_2 49 g/km) originally purchased for £20,000. The private use of the car by Ellie has been agreed at 40%.

During the year to 31 March 2027, Ellie made the following transactions

Purchases

Plant and machinery	24,000
Motor car	15,500 (for an Ellie, C02 emissions 105g/km)

Sales

Equipment	Proceeds	3,000 (all at below original cost)
Motor car	Proceeds	17,000 (This is Ellie's car at the start of the year)

Calculate Ellie's capital allowances for the year ended 31 March 2027.

Question 24

PHC Limited ceased trading on 16 October 2026 having traded for many years, preparing accounts annually to 31 December.

The WDV brought forward at 31 December 2025 were as follows

Main pool	16,700
Special rate pool	2,400

During the period to 16 October 2026, PHC Limited purchased new equipment for £1,200.

On cessation, all assets were sold for the following amounts

Main pool assets	10,000
Special rate pool assets	2,600

All assets were sold for less than their original cost.

Calculate PHC Limited's capital allowances for the period to 16 October 2026.

(Note this question would have the same solution if instead of PHC Limited it referred to a sole trader eligible for capital allowances).

CHAPTER 8

Question 25

Kelly a sole trader has been trading for many years as an online shop and prepares her accounts to 31 March each year.

Her adjusted trading results for the past few years are as follows.

Year ended 31 March 2025	70,000
Year ended 31 March 2026	(50,000)
Year ended 31 March 2027	125,000

Calculate Kelly's assessable trading profits for each relevant tax year, assuming she makes a loss claim only under ITA2007 section 83.

Question 26

Karim a sole trader has been trading for many years and prepares his accounts to 31 March each year.

His adjusted trading results for the past few years are as follows.

Year ended 31 March 2025	15,000
Year ended 31 March 2026	(65,000)
Year ended 31 March 2027	12,500

His other income for the tax years 2024/25, 2025/26 and 2026/27 is £18,000, £30,000 and £14,000 respectively.

Calculate Karim's net income for each relevant tax year assuming he makes the maximum loss claim under section 64 and identify the amount of the trading loss of £65,000 (if any) which remains available for carry forward under section 83.

Question 27

Julie started to trade on 1 July 2024 as a self employed designer and prepared her accounts to 30 June. Her results were as follows:

Year ended 30 June 2025	(24,000)
Year ended 30 June 2026	36,000
Year ended 30 June 2027	48,000

Calculate Julie's assessable profits for the tax years, 2024/25, 2025/26 and 2026/27, assuming that she carries forward any losses under section 83.

Question 28

Jimmy started in business on 1 June 2025 and prepares his accounts to 31 May each year.

His results were as follows:

Year ended 31 May 2026	(34,000)
Year ended 31 May 2027	15,000

Before he set up in business Jimmy was an employee and received the following employment income:

2022/23	25,000
2023/24	26,500
2024/25	28,000

Calculate Jimmy's net income for the tax years 2022/23 to 2026/27 assuming that he makes a loss claim under section 72.

Question 29

For the tax year 2026/27, Martha, a sole trader, made a trading loss of £40,000.

She also had chargeable gains of £45,000 and a capital loss of £14,000. Martha also had a capital loss available for carry forward from prior tax years of £18,500.

Before any loss claim, Martha's net income for 2026/27 was £25,000.

Calculate the amount of Martha's chargeable gains after the annual exemption and after electing to also use section 71. Quantify the amount of capital loss (if any) available for carry forward to future tax years.

Question 30

Hetta is a self-employed property developer and made a substantial loss for the year to 31 March 2026. Her results for the last two years were as follows:

Year ended 31 March 2026 Loss (92,000)

Year ended 31 March 2027 Profit 25,000

Also, Hetta received income from Property lettings of £72,000 for the year to 5 April 2026 and £30,000 to 5 April 2025.

Calculate Hetta's taxable income for each of the two years to 5 April 2027 maximising any loss claims. Assume that 2026/27 tax allowances apply to all years.

CHAPTER 10

Question 31

Howard is an employee of ABC Ltd. His salary for the tax year 2026/27 was £100,000. Howard was also provided with a petrol engine company car with a list price of £35,000 and CO_2 emissions of 122 grams/km. The car cost ABC Ltd £29,750. The car was first provided on 6 December 2026.

Calculate Howard's employment income for 2026/27.

Question 32

Parla is employed as a sales director. She is provided with a petrol engine company car with a list price of £25,800 and CO_2 emissions of 116 grams/km. The car was provided from 6 April 2026 until 6 November 2026 when it was replaced with a new diesel engine (Not RDE2) car with a list price of £30,000 and CO_2 emissions of 147 grams/km. Parla made a capital contribution of £6,000 towards the cost of the new car.

Calculate the assessable benefit in respect of the cars for 2026/27.

Question 33

Martin is an employee of PQR Ltd receiving a salary for the tax year 2026/27 of £45,000. He was also provided with a hybrid petrol company car with a list price of £22,500 and CO_2 emissions of 42 grams/km, electric range 35 miles. Martin's employer pays for all the petrol for the car. Martin made a contribution for private use of the car of £50/month.

Calculate Martin's employment income for 2026/27.

Question 34

Michelle accepted a job with XYZ Ltd starting on 6 April 2026. Her salary was £40,000 but her employer did not provide her with a company car. Instead, Michelle was expected to use her own car and the company agreed to pay her expenses when on business at 40p per mile for the first 5,000 business miles and 20p per mile thereafter. In the tax year 2026/27, Michelle travelled 30,000 business miles using her car.

Michelle contributes 5% of her salary to the XYZ Ltd occupational pension scheme.

Calculate Michelle's employment income for 2026/27.

Question 35

Rab accepted a job with AB Ltd from 6 April 2026. His annual salary is £54,600. He will also be covered by the company's private medical insurance cover. This will cost AB Ltd £860 per annum.

Rab is expected to use his own car and AB Ltd has agreed to pay him expenses when on business of 50p per mile for the first 10,000 business miles and 35p per mile thereafter. In the tax year 2026/27, Rab drove 17,000 business miles.

Calculate Rab's employment income for 2026/27.

Question 36

Rachel is employed by XY Ltd and as part of her remuneration package is provided with living accommodation. The house in which she lives was purchased by her employer in January 2025 for £450,000. The annual value of the house is £1,500. Rachel pays rent of £100 per month for the provision of the property.

Calculate Rachel's assessable benefit for 2026/27.

Question 37

Malcolm is employed by QR Ltd and as part of his remuneration package is provided with accommodation. The house in which he lives was purchased by his employer in January 2022 for £300,000. Further expenditure was incurred by QR Ltd in improving the house including £50,000 in March 2023, £15,000 in July 2025 and £34,000 in May 2026. The annual value of the house is £1,100. The house was first made available to Malcolm on 6 April 2025. Malcolm contributes £75 per month to his employer in respect of the provision of the accommodation.

Calculate the assessable benefit for 2026/27.

Question 38

If the accommodation referred to in Question 37 above was qualifying job-related accommodation what would then be the benefit taxable on Malcolm for 2026/27?

Question 39

Assuming the same circumstances as set out in Question 37, if in addition, QR Ltd paid various running expenses of the house as set out below, calculate the benefit on which Malcolm will be taxed for 2026/27:

Heating	1,550
Cleaning and maintenance	1,000
Telephone	675*
Structural repairs	7,500
Council tax	1,100

*the telephone costs are made up of £250 for the line rental, business calls £350 and private calls of £75.

Question 40

How would your answer differ if in Question 36 if the accommodation was job-related?

Question 41

James is employed by DE Ltd who has allowed him the private use of some recording equipment which had a market value of £3,500 at the date it was first provided to James on 6 July 2026.

Calculate the benefit on which James will be taxed for the tax year 2026/27.

Question 42

Emma is employed by FG Ltd and has been provided with some photographic equipment for her private use with a market value of £3,000 on the date it was first provided to her on 6 April 2024.

On 5 January 2027, Emma's employer gave the equipment to her which at that time had a market value of £500.

Calculate the total taxable benefit on which Emma will be taxed for the tax year 2026/27 in respect of the photographic equipment.

Question 43

How would your answer differ from Question 42 if instead, Emma had paid £500, the market value at the time, for the photographic equipment in January 2027?

Question 44

Calculate the total taxable value of the following benefits in kind provided to Junaid by his employer in the course of his employment throughout 2026/27:

1. removal expenses on relocation of £8,500
2. a car park space near to where Junaid works, cost to employer £1,040
3. use of a mobile telephone, cost to employer £480
4. an interest free loan of £6,000
5. job-related accommodation with an annual value of £2,400
6. a company van available for unlimited private use, costing £14,000

Question 45

Erin received an interest free loan of £18,000 from her employer on 6 July 2026. On 6 December 2026, she repaid £5,000 to his employer.

Calculate Erin's benefit in kind for 2026/27 in respect of the loan under both the average and precise methods.

Question 46

How would the answers to Question 45 differ if Erin was required to pay interest at 1% per annum on the loan?

CHAPTER 12

Question 47

Tessa is a sole trader. Her trading profit for the tax year 2026/27 was £150,000 and Tessa also received dividends of £10,000 during the year. She paid personal pension contributions during 2026/27 of £75,000 net.

Tessa has paid personal pension contributions of £40,000 net during each of the three previous tax years.

Calculate Tessa's income tax liability for 2026/27.

Question 48

Explain the difference in the way that an employee obtains tax relief for pension contributions that they may make to an occupational pension scheme as compared to how a sole trader obtains relief for personal pension contributions. In addition, can an employee who is a member of a company pension scheme also make contributions to a personal pension scheme?

CHAPTERS 13 TO 15

Question 49

Diane acquired an investment property in February 2010 for £75,000. She improved the property in May 2012 for £14,000. The property was sold in September 2026 for £190,000. Diane paid legal fees of £2,000 and agent's fees of £750 on the sale.

Calculate Diane's capital gain.

Question 50

Rita acquired an investment property in May 2012 for £105,000. In addition, she paid legal fees of £1,500 in connection with the purchase. In November 2014, when the property was valued at £180,000, Rita transferred the property to her husband Bill. Bill subsequently sold the property in June 2026 for £275,000, incurring legal fees of £2,500.

Calculate Bill's capital gain in 2026/27 on the sale of the property.

Question 51

How would your answer to Question 50 be different (if at all) if Rita and Bill were not married?

Question 52

Tara acquired eight hectares of land for £62,000 in July 2009. In October 2026 she sold five hectares of land for £99,800. The market value of the remaining land was valued at £120,000 in October 2025. Calculate the capital gain arising on the sale of the five hectares and state the cost relating to the remaining three hectares.

Question 53

Harry sold a painting in May 2026 for £5,000. He purchased the painting in October 2015 for £3,750. Calculate Harry's capital gain on the sale of the painting.

Question 54

Gwen sold an antique necklace in August 2026 for £8,700, incurring sales commission of £100. She had purchased the necklace for £3,600 in May 2008, Calculate Gwen's capital gain on the sale of the necklace.

Question 55

During 2026/27 Sally sold three paintings. The purchase price and sale proceeds of each were as follows:

Painting 1	Cost	3,000	Sale proceeds	7,000
Painting 2	Cost	7,000	Sale proceeds	12,400
Painting 3	Cost	8,200	Sale proceeds	4,800

Calculate Sally's capital gains or losses on the sale of the three paintings.

Question 56

James has capital gains of £9,000 and capital losses of £6,500 for 2026/27, before deducting his annual exemption. Calculate James' net capital gains for 2026/27. How much, if any, of his loss and /or annual exemption is available to carry forward?

Question 57

For 2026/27 Ravi has capital gains of £22,400 and losses of £8,200. Ravi has capital losses brought forward of £27,600.

Calculate Ravi's net capital gains tax position for 2026/27 and the amount, if any, of capital losses available to carry forward at 5 April 2027.

Question 58

Sarah bought a flat in Birmingham on 1 April 2010 for £75,000 and lived there as her main residence until 30 September 2013 when she moved to Edinburgh in connection with her job. She returned to her flat on 1 October 2016 and lived there until 31 March 2018 when she decided to go overseas backpacking with a friend for two years. She returned on 1 April 2020 and lived in her flat until 30 September 2021, when she moved into her partner's house. Sarah's flat remained unoccupied until it was sold on 31 March 2027 for £185,000.

Calculate Sarah's chargeable gain on the sale of the flat.

Question 59

Heather sold a residential property on 2 June 2026 making a capital gain of £43,000. She also made capital gains of £8,400 on the sale of other assets in 2026/27. Heather had capital losses brought forward of £6,000 and is a higher rate income taxpayer.

Calculate Heather's capital gains tax liability for 2026/27 and state the dates of payment.

Question 60

Mary sold a factory unit, held as an investment property, in September 2026 for £202,000. She had acquired the building for £78,000 in May 2010 and had extended it for £25,000 in July 2014. Mary also disposed of a painting in October 2026 for £18,220, incurring auctioneer's fees of 2%. She had acquired the painting for £40,000 in February 2006. Mary had capital losses brought forward of £5,400. Mary's taxable income in 2026/27 was £33,000.

Calculate Mary's capital gains tax liability for 2026/27 and state the due date for payment.

Question 61

Lilly made the following disposals of capital assets during 2026/27.

(a) In September 2026, she disposed of her classic vintage car for £30,000, which she had bought in 1999 for £10,000.

(b) In May 2026, she sold an antique vase for £8,500. She inherited it from her uncle in September 2008 and the probate value was £4,000. It originally cost her uncle £500.

(c) On 13 January 2026, she sold some antique furniture for £9,000. This was purchased at auction in February 2021 for £6,700. Acquisition costs of £300 were incurred.

(d) In September 2026, she sold a painting at an auction for £5,200. The painting cost £8,100 in August 2023.

Calculate the total net gains and losses arising from the above disposals for 2026/27.

Question 62

Helen made the following acquisitions of ordinary shares in AB plc:

Date	**Number of shares**	**Cost £**
September 2010	600	1,200
May 2015	400	1,000
September 2017	400	1,200
January 2020	1,200	4,800

In September 2022, Helen acquired further shares in AB plc when the company issued a 1 for 4 rights issue at £5 per share.

Helen disposed of 900 shares in July 2026 for £7 per share.

Calculate Helen's chargeable gain in 2026/27 following her disposal of shares in July 2026, assuming that she made no further acquisitions within the next 30 days.

Question 63

John acquired shares in LM plc as follows:

Date	Number of shares	Cost £
1 July 2016	2,600	2,000
11 April 2019	900	7,500
17 July 2026	200	800
10 August 2026	600	2,000

John sold 4,100 shares for £18,000 on 17 July 2026.

Calculate John's capital gain on the sale in July 2026.

Question 64

Chris bought a business in September 2014 for £120,000. There are no non-business assets. He gave it to his daughter Mary in June 2026 when it was worth £400,000. Gift relief was claimed.

Calculate for the tax year 2026/27:

1. the capital gain assessable on Chris, and
2. Mary's base cost of the business for capital gains tax purposes.

Question 65

Susan bought a business in May 2004 for £10,000. She sold the business to her daughter Jo in September 2020 for £28,000 when it was valued at £50,000. Gift relief was claimed. There are no non-business assets. Jo subsequently sold the business for £125,000 in March 2027.

Calculate for the tax year 2026/27:

1. The gain assessable on Susan
2. Jo's base cost for capital gains tax purposes and
3. Jo's capital gains tax on the sale in March 2027.

Question 66

James decided that his business needed a new factory. He sold his existing factory for £900,000 in June 2026 having acquired it in February 2015 for £250,000. His new factory, acquired in March 2027, cost £1.2 million.

Calculate James' chargeable gain on the sale of the factory. What is the base cost of the new factory if rollover relief is claimed?

Question 67

Assume that in Question 66 James had purchased his new factory in August 2025.

How would your answer be different (if at all)?

Question 68

Heather decided to expand her business and needed new premises. She sold her existing showroom for £90,000 in October 2026, having acquired it in May 2015 for £50,000. Heather purchased a new showroom for £80,000 in March 2027.

Calculate Heather's chargeable gains, if any for 2026/27, assuming that she claims the maximum rollover relief.

Question 69

In October 2026, Les decided to give all the shares in his trading company, JK Ltd, to his son, Mark.

The gift comprised 100,000 ordinary shares (100% of the company) worth £750,000. The shares cost Les £25,000 in July 2004.

The company's net value at the date of the gift was as follows:

Freehold factory	500,000
Motor cars	50,000
Investments (shares)	150,000
Current assets	100,000
	800,000
Current liabilities	(50,000)
Net value	750,000

Calculate Les' chargeable gain and identify how much (if any) of the gain may be rolled over if gift relief is claimed. Assuming gift relief to have been claimed as appropriate identify the base cost of the shares for Mark.

Question 70

Rupinder is a director of PR Ltd a trading company and has worked for the company since 2014. Rupinder owns 10,000 shares in PR Ltd that she acquired at £1 per share in May 2016, representing 10% of the ordinary share capital. Rupinder sold her entire shareholding in June 2026 for £1,200,000. PR Ltd owns no non-trading assets. Rupinder has never previously made a chargeable gain and has no other gains during 2026/27. Rupinder is a higher rate taxpayer for 2026/27.

Calculate Rupinder's capital gains tax liability for 2026/27.

Question 71

How would the answer to Question 67 differ if Rupinder's shares only represented a 4% shareholding in PR Ltd?

Question 72

Tim, a higher rate taxpayer, sold shares qualifying for Business asset disposal relief in September 2026 making a gain of £650,000. Tim had previously claimed Business asset disposal relief of £400,000 in respect of another gain in 2016/17.

Calculate Tim's capital gains tax liability for 2026/27.

Question 73

During 2026/27 Claire made the following capital gains and losses

Qualifying for Business asset disposal relief

Gains	150,000
Losses	(25,000)

Other gains

Residential property	75,000
Shares	22,000

Claire has never previously claimed business asset disposal relief and has capital gains losses brought forward of £16,000. Claire's taxable income for 2026/27 was £30,000.

Calculate Claire's capital gains tax liability for 2026/27.

CHAPTERS 16 TO 19

Question 74

JB Ltd's accounting period for the year ended 31 March 2027 shows the following items:

Adjusted trading profit	45,000
Interest income	4,000
Rental income	6,000
Chargeable gain	5,000
Dividends received	10,000
Non trade loan interest paid	1,000
Charitable donations paid	15,000

Calculate JB Ltd's TTP and corporation tax liability for the accounting period ended 31 March 2027. JB Ltd has no associated companies.

Question 75

If in Question 74 JB Ltd also paid dividends of £10,000 how would this affect your answer (if at all)?

Question 76

If in Question 74 JB Ltd had four associated companies how would this affect your answer (if at all)?

Question 77

KL Ltd prepares its accounts to 31 May each year.

For the year ended 31 May 2026, the company's net profit was £3,050,100.

This was arrived at after the following items:

Other income and gains:

Dividends received	12,000
Interest received	40,000
Profit on sale of an office block	350,000

Expenses:	
Entertaining (clients)	15,000
Accountant's fees for preparing accounts	9,000
Health and safety fine	5,000
Depreciation	300,000
Interest payable (trading loan)	400,000
Donation to national charity	20,000

Capital allowances of £120,000 may be claimed (not included in the above) and whilst the office block sale produced a capital profit of £350,000 computed on accounting principles for tax purposes it produced a chargeable gain of £570,000.

Calculate KL Ltd's adjusted trading profit, TTP and corporation tax liability for the year ended 31 May 2025. KL Ltd has no associated companies.

Question 78

MN Ltd's accounting period for the year ended 31 March 2027 shows the following results before taking into account the implications of a lease payment and capital allowances:

Trading profit	145,000
Chargeable gain	12,000
	157,000
Less: Charitable donations	(5,000)
	152,000

On 1 December 2026, MN Ltd was granted a 40-year lease of a commercial property by a third party for a premium of £50,000.

As at 1 April 2026, the main pool for capital allowances had a tax written down value of £60,000. On 3 May 2026, an item of plant was sold for £16,000 (original cost £25,000). New plant and machinery costing £32,300 was purchased during the period and on 1 November 2026 a motor car was purchased for £30,000, CO_2 emissions 105 g/km. The car was used by MN Ltd's managing director and 20% of the use of this car was for private purposes.

Calculate MN Ltd's corporation tax liability for the accounting period ended 31 March 2027. MN Ltd has no associated companies.

Question 79

Identify the accounting periods of GH Ltd in respect of which corporation tax will be charged if accounts are prepared for the period 1 January 2026 to 30 April 2027.

When will the corporation tax liabilities have to be settled and when will the relevant returns need to be filed? GH Ltd is not a large company.

Confirm whether each of the following statements is true or false:

APPENDIX 2

(1) Rental income is apportioned on a time basis.
(2) Trading income is apportioned on a time basis.
(3) Interest income is apportioned on a time basis.
(4) Dividend income is taxable when received.

Question 80

CGC Limited sold two assets during the accounting period ended 30 November 2026:

Asset 1	Purchased	May 2010	Cost	12,500
	Sold	June 2026	Proceeds	24,300
Assets 2	Purchased	January 2015	Cost	14,800
	Sold	October 2025	Proceeds	15,100
Indexation factors		May 2010 to December 2017		0.244
		January 2015 to December 2017		0.089

Calculate the gain for each item and the net gains to be included in the calculation of TTP for CGC Limited to 30 November 2026.

Question 81

EF Ltd's results for the accounting period ended 31 December 2026 were as follows:

Trading profit	410,000
Rental income	60,000
Chargeable gain	150,000
Donation to charity	25,000

For the accounting periods ended 31 December 2024 and 31 December 2025, trading losses of £185,000 and £425,000 respectively arose.

Calculate EF Ltd's corporation tax liability for the period ended 31 December 2026 after the relief for any losses has been claimed and identify any losses remaining to carry forward. EF Ltd has one associated company.

Question 82

LK Ltd's results were as follows:

	Year ended 31/12/25	3 months ended 31/03/26	Year ended 31/03/27
Trading profit	150,000	60,000	(650,000)
Rental income	60,000	35,000	150,000
Interest income	8,000	40,000	90,000
Charitable donations	12,000	10,000	15,000

Calculate LK Ltd's TTP for each of the above periods utilising the trading loss of £650,000 in the most tax efficient manner and identify (if any) the amount of trading loss remaining to carry forward.

Question 83

JB Ltd, MB Ltd and NB Ltd form a group for group relief purposes. Their results were as follows for the accounting period ended 31 March 2027:

	JB Ltd	MB Ltd	NB Ltd
Trading profit	150,000	(250,000)	13,000
Rental income	5,000	15,000	10,000
Interest	20,000	2,500	5,000
Chargeable gains	30,000	4,000	2,000
Charitable donations	5,000	-	15,000

Calculate the TTP for each company assuming that MB Ltd claims any loss relief available and the balance of the loss is surrendered as group relief.

Question 84

During the year to 31 March 2026, GH Ltd made a trading loss of £25 million. During the year to 31 March 2027, GH Ltd has taxable profits before losses brought forward of £18 million, comprised entirely of trading profits.

Calculate the TTP for GH Ltd to 31 March 2027 after claiming the maximum relief for losses brought forward and the balance of the loss, if any.

Question 85

For the year to 31 December 2025, JK Ltd made a trading loss of £40,000. JK Ltd's taxable profits to 31 December 2026 are as follows:

Trading profits	38,000
Chargeable gains	5,000
Interest received	1,000
Qualifying charitable donations paid	8,000

Calculate the TTP for JK Ltd to 31 December 2026, assuming the optimum claim for losses brought forward.

Question 86

BigTree Limited owns 90% of the ordinary share capital of Oak Limited and 80% of Elm Limited.

Oak Limited incurred an adjusted trading loss of £240,000 for the year ended 31 March 2027. The initial TTP for the three companies before loss relief and Group Relief claims is as follows:

	BigTree	Oak	Elm
Adjusted trading profit	510,000	Nil *	15,000
Rental profit		75,000	
Capital gains		10,000	
Less: QCD			(3,000)
Provisional TTP	510,000	85,000	12,000

(* Before loss relief)

Prepare revised calculations of the TTP for each company after claiming relief for Oak Limited's trading losses and calculate the Corporation tax liability payable by each company.

Question 87

CD Ltd and HD Ltd form a group for chargeable gain purposes. Each company prepares its accounts to 31 March 2027.

CD Ltd transferred a factory that it no longer wished to use to HD Ltd in November 2017 – when its market value was £750,000. CD Ltd had originally paid £350,000 for the factory in August 1998.

HD Ltd subsequently sold the factory for £900,000 in July 2025.

Indexation allowances:

August 1998 to November 2017	9,100
November 2017 to December 2017	100

Calculate the chargeable gains (if any) arising on the transfer of the factory to HD Ltd and the chargeable gain arising on the sale of the factory by HD Ltd in July 2026.

CHAPTER 20

Question 88

Sandy is a sole trader and his accounts are prepared to 30 June each year. For the tax year 2026/27, Sandy's trading profit is £57,500. Sandy also received rental income of £8,500.

Calculate the total amount of National Insurance Contributions (NIC) payable by Sandy for 2026/27.

Question 89

James is an employee and received a salary of £50,000 and cash vouchers of £2,000 during 2026/27.

Calculate the employee's and employers' NIC payable in respect of James' salary assuming an annual basis of calculation.

Question 90

Steffi is an employee of CD Ltd. For the tax year 2026/27, Steffi's salary is £25,000 and her taxable benefits (including a company car and an interest free loan) amount to £7,200.

Identify which classes of National Insurance Contributions (NIC) apply to Steff and CD Ltd and calculate the amount(s) payable for 2026/27 assuming an annual basis.

Question 91

How would the answer to Question 85 differ if Steff informed you that she was a member of the CD Ltd approved occupational pension scheme and her personal contributions during 2026/27 were £1,250?

Question 92

State the dates on which Classes 1, 1A and 4 NIC are payable.

CHAPTERS 21 AND 22

Question 93

In the tax year 2025/26 Ben's income tax liability amounted to £10,300. £2,500 of his income tax liability had been deducted under PAYE. In the tax year 2026/27, the corresponding figures were £15,600 and £3,000 respectively.

Calculate the payments on account (if any) Ben is required to make on behalf of his income tax liability for the tax year 2026/27 and the amount of any balancing payment. State the dates on which these payments are due to be paid.

Question 94

In the tax year 2025/26 Gill's income tax liability amounted to £12,800. £11,900 of her income tax liability had been satisfied by way of tax deducted under PAYE. In the tax year 2026/27, the corresponding figures were £15,600 and £2,100 respectively.

Calculate the payments on account (if any) Gill is required to make on behalf of her income tax liability for the tax year 2026/27 and the amount of any balancing payment. State the dates on which these payments are due to be paid.

Question 95

Brian's total tax and national insurance liabilities for 2025/26 are as follows

Income tax	8,400
Capital gains tax	2,100
Class 4 NIC	1,500

What will his payments on account be for 2026/27 and what are the due dates?

Question 96

Hannah paid her balancing payment for the tax year 2026/27 of £8,500 on 21 June 2028.Hannah has made all previous tax payments on time.

Explain the additional charges that Hannah will have incurred as a result of this late payment.

Question 97

Colin submitted his Self-Assessment tax return for the tax year ended 5 April 2026 on 31 March 2027. What penalty (if any) may be charged? If Colin had submitted the return on 31 July 2027 would any additional penalty be due and if so, how much?

Question 98

UV Ltd prepares its annual accounts each year to 31 December. For the year ending 31 December 2026 state the payment date on which its corporation tax liability has to be settled and the deadline for filing the corporation tax return. UV Ltd is not a large company.

Question 99

PM Ltd has TTP of £1,480,000 for the year to 31 March 2027. During the accounting period, PM Ltd received dividends of £150,000. PM Ltd is not a member of a group and was considered a large company in the previous accounting period. PM Ltd has no associates.

State the corporation tax liability of PM Ltd for the year to 31 March 2027, the payment date for the corporation tax liability and the filing date for the Corporation tax return.

Question 100

QRS Ltd has TTP for the 8 months from 1 May 2026 to 31 December 2026 of £852,300. It has two associated companies throughout the period and was previously considered a large company.

Calculate the Corporation tax liability to 31 December 2026 and state the payment dates.

CHAPTER 23

Question 101

Tony is completing his VAT return. He has a purchase invoice for £600 exclusive of VAT and another for £960 inclusive of VAT.

How much input VAT can Tony recover?

Question 102

Julia sells a sculpture for £1,000 plus VAT. She receives a payment on account of £250 on 25 March 2026. The sculpture is delivered on 28 April 2026. Julia's VAT returns are made up to calendar quarters. She issues a VAT invoice on 4 May 2026 and receives payment of the balance outstanding on 27 May 2026.

State the tax point(s) and amounts(s) due.

Question 103

Alan prepared his VAT returns to 31 March, 30 June and 30 September 2026. The submission and payment dates for each of the quarters were as follows:

	Date of payment/ submission	**VAT due**
31 March 2026	10 May 2026	7,000
30 June 2026	12 August 2026	15,000
31 September 2026	18 December 2026	12,000

Explain the consequences for Alan.

Question 104

Victoria commenced trading on 1 May 2025. For the first six months of trading, Victoria made standard rated supplies of £8,000 per month and zero rated supplies of £3,500 per month.

For subsequent months Victoria's turnover was as follows

	Standard rate	Zero rate
November 2025	8,500	4,000
December 2025	9,100	5,300
January 2026	10,500	6,100

In which month did Victoria's turnover exceed the registration limit?

By what date should she notify HMRC and from what date will she be registered?

Question 105

Graham is a sole trader and is registered for VAT. During the quarter to 30 June 2026, the following transactions occurred:

Standard rated sales	60,000
Zero rated sales	35,000
Standard rated purchases	28,000
(This includes £1,500 client entertaining)	
Zero rated purchases	20,000
Purchase of new car	22,500
Purchase of new computer	1,000

All of the above amounts are exclusive of VAT and are standard rated unless otherwise specified.

In addition, Graham has reviewed his outstanding credit sales and has written off as bad debts the following sales:

18 October 2025	1,200
5 March 2026	600
2 April 2026	1,500

All of these amounts were payable 30 days after the date of sale and are shown inclusive of VAT.

Calculate the VAT payable by Graham for the quarter to 30 June 2026.

CHAPTER 24

Question 106

Asha made two gifts during the tax year to 5 April 2027.

On 1 August 2026, she made a cash gift to her daughter Ellie of £17,500.

On 10 November 2026, Asha created a discretionary trust for her grandchildren with an initial gift of £500,000. Asha agreed to settle any IHT on the gift to the trust.

With calculations explain the IHT liability on these two gifts. Asha has not previously made any lifetime gifts.

Question 107

Helen died on 14 June 2026. On that date, she held the following assets:

House and contents (Helen's residence)	495,000

Quoted shares	150,000
ISA investments	95,000
Cash at bank	78,000
Car	6,000

Helen's funeral cost £5,000. Helen's husband had died two years earlier, leaving £227,500 to their daughter and the balance of his estate to Helen. At the time of Helen's husband's death, the IHT nil rate band was £325,000. Helen's estate has been left in her will to her daughter. Helen did not make any lifetime gifts.

Calculate the IHT liability arising on Helen's death.

Question 108

Robert died on 6 May 2026, leaving an estate at the date of death of £600,000 including his main residence, valued at £350,000. The entire estate was left equally to his son and daughter.

In June 2020, Robert had made a gift of £50,000 to his son. In September 2024, Robert made a gift of £400,000 into a trust, with Robert paying any IHT arising.

Calculate the IHT arising on the two gifts, both in lifetime and as a result of Robert's death. Calculate the IHT liability on Robert's estate on death. There is no transferable nil rate band available.

APPENDIX 3
Multiple Choice Questions

This Appendix provides some basic initial questions to test your knowledge after completing most chapters or as a part of your revision before an assessment. Perhaps you could appoint one student on your table as the quiz master and they could go around the table asking the questions!

Chapter 2

1. On which date does the UK tax year commence?

   A. 1 January
   B. 1 March
   C. 6 March
   D. 6 April

2. Which body is responsible for the administration of taxation in the UK?

   A. IRS
   B. Inland Revenue
   C. HM Revenue and Customs
   D. HM Treasury

3. What is the difference between tax planning and tax evasion?

   A. Tax planning involves complex schemes designed to bypass laws
   B. Tax planning involves using the tax laws as designed to reduce a tax liability
   C. Nothing – both are illegal
   D. Tax evasion involves only large businesses

4. When is Making Tax Digital for Income tax introduced

   A. 6 April 2025
   B. 6 April 2026
   C. 6 April 2027
   D. 6 April 2030

5. Which statement is true

   A. An individual only pays tax at one tax rate
   B. The top rate of tax on savings income is 45%

C. Once income exceeds £37,700, income tax is payable at 40% on all income.

D. All sources of income are taxed at the same rates.

6. Which of the following is exempt from income tax?

A. State retirement pension

B. Rent from letting farmland

C. Premium bond winnings

D. Dividends from UK companies

7. What is the usual order to tax sources of income?

A. NSI, then DI, then SI

B. DI, then SI, then NSI

C. NSI, then SI, then DI

D. SI, then NSI, then DI

8. Which of the following is not included in the calculation of NSI?

A. Pensions received

B. Wages from part-time employment

C. Self-employed profits

D. Interest received

9. Dividends falling within the basic rate band are taxed at what rate?

A. 7.5%

B. 8.75%

C. 10.75%

D. 20%

10. If taxable NSI is £25,000 and taxable SI is £10,000, how much of the basic rate band is available to use against DI?

A. £Nil

B. £37,700

C. £2,700

D. £500

Chapter 2 MCQ Solutions: 1D; 2C; 3B; 4B; 5B; 6C; 7C; 8D; 9C; 10C.

Chapter 3

1. Taxable income =

   A. Total income less personal allowance

   B. Net income less reliefs

   C. Net income less personal allowance

   D. Total income less reliefs

2. Interest paid on which one of these loans would be an allowable relief?

   A. Loan to purchase a car for work

   B. Loan to buy a house to be used as a main residence

   C. Loan to introduce capital to a property rental business

   D. Loan to purchase an interest in a partnership

3. What statement is true?

   A. Tax planning is illegal

   B. Tax planning advice can only be provided by an accountant

   C. Intentionally under declaring sales is tax evasion

   D. Tax evasion only applies when the tax loss exceeds £100,000

4. The personal allowance can be reduced when adjusted net income exceeds

   A. £50,000

   B. £100,000

   C. £125,140

   D. £150,000

5. Which statement is true

   A. Married couples and civil partners share personal allowances

   B. 10% of the personal allowance can be transferred to a basic rate taxpaying spouse or civil partner

   C. 10% of the personal allowance can always be transferred to a spouse or civil partner

   D. Any unused personal allowance can be transferred to a spouse or civil partner

6. If an individual has an adjusted net income of £120,000, their personal allowance will be reduced to

A. £Nil

B. £2,570

C. £10,000

D. It will be available in full

7. What is the starting rate for savings for a higher-rate taxpayer?

A. £Nil

B. £100

C. £500

D. £1,000

8. The High Income Child Benefit Charge can apply if adjusted net income exceeds?

A. £37,700

B. £60,000

C. £100,000

D. £125,140

9. The top rate of income tax on NSI is?

A. 20%

B. 40%

C. 45%

D. 50%

10. The UK tax year ends on

A. 31 December

B. 31 January

C. 31 March

D. 5 April

Chapter 3 MCQ Solutions: 1C; 2D; 3C; 4B; 5B; 6B; 7C; 8B; 9C; 10D.

Chapter 4

1. True or false – charitable donations under Gift aid are paid net of 25% income tax

A. True

B. False

2. If a net personal pension contribution of £1,200 is paid, the gross contribution is

A. £900

B. £960

C. £1,440

D. £1,500

3. Which statement is true?

A. The maximum basic rate band is always £37,700

B. The basic rate band may be reduced if income exceeds £37,700

C. The basic rate band is increased by the net gift aid donations and personal pension contributions paid.

D. The basic rate band is increased by the gross gift aid donations and personal pension contributions paid.

4. If an individual has a net income of £130,000 and pays £8,000 net to charity, their available personal allowance will be

A. £Nil

B. £8,000

C. £2,570

D. £1,570

5. Which statement is false?

A. Paying personal pension contributions can increase the available personal allowance

B. The personal allowance can never be reduced below £1,000

C. Paying charitable donations under gift aid can reduce the amount of income taxable at the additional rate

D. Personal pension contributions are paid net of basic rate income tax

6. If an individual pays £400 net to charity under gift aid and £1,200 net to a personal pension, their extended basic rate band will be

A. £38,100
B. £38,200
C. £39,200
D. £39,700

7. The dividend allowance is always

A. £500
B. £1,000
C. £2,000
D. £5,000

8. True or false, when determining the savings starting rate, gift aid donations and personal pension contributions are ignored.

A. True
B. False

9. Which of the following would be taxed as NSI?

A. Dividends from a non-UK company
B. State retirement pension
C. Interest on Gilts
D. Interest on an ISA

10. If an individual has taxable income as follows: NSI of £20,000, SI of £5,000 and DI of £200,000, their savings starting rate taxed at 0% will be

A. £0
B. £500
C. £1,000
D. £5,000

Chapter 4 MCQ Solutions:1B; 2D; 3D; 4C; 5B; 6D; 7A; 8B; 9B; 10A

Chapter 5 Income from a property business

1. True or false – an individual's income from a property business is usually calculated on an accruals basis.

   A. True

   B. False

2. An individual receives rent of £8,000 from a residential letting and incurs allowable property business expenses of £1,500 and mortgage interest of £1,200. Their net taxable property business profits are

   A. £8,000

   B. £5,300

   C. £6,500

   D. £500

3. Which statement is true?

   A. Separate calculations are always required for rents received from residential and commercial properties

   B. Rental income from residential income is taxed as Savings income (SI)

   C. Profits from letting commercial properties are always considered earned income.

   D. Rental income from commercial and residential properties is usually combined to calculate profits from a property business.

4. Which of the following would not be an allowable deduction from property business income?

   A. Rent collection fees

   B. Decorating costs between lettings

   C. Interest on a loan to buy a let residential property

   D. Gardening expenses

5. Rent of £1,000 per month is due during 2026/27. During the tax year, only £9,000 was received with the balance received six months late. Which statement is correct?

   A. Rent of £12,000 is assessable for 2026/27

   B. Rent of £9,000 is assessable for 2026/27

6. If an individual pays £500 net to replace a broken bed that initially cost £300 in their let property, a deduction of how much would be allowable?

A. £500

B. £300

C. £200

D. £Nil

7. Jon purchased a TV for a property that he lets. The TV cost £400. There had never previously been a TV in the property. What is the allowable deduction from Jon's property business income?

A. £Nil

B. £400

C. £40 per year for 10 years

D. £400 spread over the expected usable life of the TV

8. How much rent can be received tax-free per year from letting furnished accommodation in a taxpayer's own home under rent a room relief?

A. £1,000

B. £6,000

C. £7,500

D. £12,570

9. True or false, property business profits are taxed as NSI?

A. True

B. False

10. Which statement is correct?

A. Tax relief is not available on interest paid on a loan to purchase let residential property

B. Interest paid on a loan to purchase let residential property is deducted as an allowable property business expense

C. Interest paid on a loan to purchase let residential property is allowed as a basic rate tax reducer.

D. Interest paid on a loan to purchase let commercial property is allowed as a basic rate tax reducer.

Chapter 5 MCQ Solutions: 1B; 2C; 3D; 4C; 5B; 6A; 7A; 8C; 9A; 10C

Chapter 6 Trading profits

1. True or false – an individual's trading business profits are usually calculated using the cash basis.

   A. True
   B. False

2. Which one of the following is not one of the badges of trade

   A. Profit motive
   B. Additional work
   C. Control
   D. Length of ownership

3. Under the cash basis which of the following capital items would be allowable when calculating taxable profits of a sole trader?

   A. A car used for business
   B. New business premises
   C. Depreciation of all capital items
   D. New office furniture used in the business

4. Which one of the following would be an allowable deduction from a sole trader's trading profits

   A. Fees for acquiring a new shop
   B. Website upkeep costs
   C. A donation to a national charity
   D. Gifts to customers of wine

5. Which statement is true?

   A. Wages for a sole trader are deducted from trading profits but are taxable as employment income.
   B. Wages for a sole trader are not allowable as they are business drawings and should not be included in the profit and loss account

6. Maddie starts trading on 1 November 2025 and prepares her first accounts to 31 October 2026 showing taxable trading profits of £18,600. What are her taxable trading profits for 2025/26?

A. £3,100
B. £7,750
C. £9,300
D. £18,600

7. Jonah has net profits of £46,200 before adjustments. He has established that net profits include £500 dividends received and £7,300 private expenses. What is his tax adjusted trading profit?

A. £46,700
B. £39,400
C. £54,000
D. £53,000

8. True or false – when using the accruals basis, the capital allowances rules are used to calculate deductions for expenditure on all plant and machinery

A. True
B. False

9. The general rule for allowable expenses when calculating taxable trading profits is that the expenses must be incurred

A. Wholly for the benefit of the business owner
B. Wholly and exclusively for the purpose of the trade
C. Wholly, exclusively and necessarily for the purpose of the trade
D. Exclusively and necessarily for the purpose of the trade

10. Which of one the following gifts to a customer would be an allowable deduction from a sole trader's business profits

A. Chocolates costing £25
B. Wine costing £30 with a special label showing the business logo
C. A diary costing £40
D. A pen costing £45 showing the business name.

Chapter 6 MCQ Solutions: 1A; 2C; 3D; 4B; 5B; 6C; 7D; 8A; 9B; 10D

Chapter 7 Capital Allowances

1. True or false – depreciation is always disallowed and added back when calculating tax adjusted trading profits

   A. True

   B. False

2. Which of the following would not be considered plant and machinery

   A. A car for an employee with CO2 emissions of 110g/km

   B. A packaging machine

   C. A new warehouse building

   D. A lift fitted to a new office building

3. Under the cash basis for sole traders which statement is true?

   A. Depreciation is disallowed and capital allowances are deducted

   B. The cost of most plant and machinery is allowed as a deduction from trading profits

4. What is the rate of writing down allowance (WDA) on the main pool?

   A. 6%

   B. 14%

   C. 18%

   D. 40%

5. Which of TWO the following items would be added to the special rate pool?

   A. A car for an employee with CO2 emissions of 110g/km

   B. A packaging machine

   C. A new warehouse building

   D. A lift fitted in a new office building

6. Which TWO of the following items would qualify for 100% FYA?

   A. A new zero-emissions delivery vehicle

   B. A second-hand fully electric motor car

   C. Equipment for gas, biogas and hydrogen vehicle refuelling

   D. Solar (PV) panels

7. Liz has plant and machinery in her main pool of £5,000 and £1,500 in her special rate pool. What would be the maximum capital allowances claim for the accounting period to 5 April 2027

A. £910
B. £790
C. £390
D. £6,500

8. True or false – when the balance on a pool falls below £1,000, the remaining amount can be fully claimed as capital allowances

A. True
B. False

9. Assets with private use by a sole trader are

A. Added to the appropriate pool
B. Added to a separate pool and WDA is claimed at 6%
C. Added to a separate pool and WDA is reduced for the percentage private use
D. Not eligible for capital allowances

10. Which of one the following items could not qualify for AIA

A. A car for a sales manager
B. A van for a decorator
C. A delivery motorbike
D. A helicopter

Chapter 7 MCQ Solutions: 1A; 2C; 3B; 4B; 5A & D; 6A &C; 7B; 8A; 9C; 10A

Chapter 8 Sole trader business losses

1. True or false – if a sole trader's business incurs a loss, they cannot claim capital allowances

   A. True
   B. False

2. Can unused trading losses be carried forward to offset future profits indefinitely?

   A. Yes
   B. No, they expire after four years
   C. Only for businesses in the first four years of trading
   D. Only for businesses in the farming sector

3. Trading losses carried forward must be?

   A. Set against non-trading income of future years
   B. Set against total income of future years
   C. Set against future profits from the same trade carried on by the individual
   D. Set against future profits from any trade carried on by the individual

4. As an alternative to carrying forward losses, current year losses may be claimed against

   A. Total income of the current tax year only
   B. Total income of the previous tax year only
   C. Total income of the current and/or the previous tax year
   D. Trading profits of the previous tax year only

5. When would it be advantageous to carry forward trading losses rather than carry them back?

   A. To improve cash flow
   B. When a higher tax rate is expected to apply in the future
   C. When a lower tax rate is expected to apply in the future
   D. When charitable donations are to be made in the next year

6. The maximum trading loss that can be offset against non-trading income is limited to the greater of

A. £100,000 and 50% of adjusted total income
B. £50,000 and 10% of adjusted total income
C. £50,000 and 25% of adjusted total income
D. 20% of adjusted total income

7. True or false – a loss relief claim can reduce net income, increasing the personal allowance available for a tax year

A. True
B. False

8. True or false – it is possible to claim a trading loss against capital gains

A. True
B. False

9. Which of the following is not a requirement for claiming trading loss relief?

A. The business operates on a commercial basis
B. Losses are correctly declared on a tax return
C. Turnover exceeds £90,000 annually
D. A claim is made within the appropriate time limit

10. Trading losses incurred in the first four years of a new trade can

A. Only be carried forward
B. Be carried back 3 years
C. Be carried back 2 years
D. Be sacrificed for a tax-free grant

Chapter 8 MCQ Solutions: 1B; 2A; 3C; 4C; 5B; 6C; 7A; 8A; 9C; 10B

Chapter 9 Partnerships

1. True or false – a tax return is required to be submitted by a trading partnership

   A. True
   B. False

2. Which statement is correct? When calculating the tax liability for members of a trading partnership

   A. The partnership trading profits are divided equally between the partners
   B. Partnership profits are taxed as dividend income
   C. The partnership trading profits can be allocated unequally in line with the partnership agreement
   D. Partnerships cannot use the cash basis.

3. True or false – Partners can only join or leave a partnership at the start of the tax year?

   A. True
   B. False

4. If a partnership makes a trading loss, which statement is correct

   A. Each partner can decide how to claim relief for their share of the loss
   B. The loss is carried forward against the partnership profits or subsequent years
   C. All partners must agree on how to claim loss relief
   D. Partnerships cannot make a trading loss

5. True or false – each partner is taxed on their share of the partnership profits for a tax year regardless of the amount they draw from the partnership

   A. True
   B. False

Chapter 9 MCQ Solutions: 1A; 2C; 3B; 4A; 5A

Chapter 10 Employment income

1. True or false – an individual can choose for their income to be taxed as employment income or self-employed income

   A. True

   B. False

2. For an employee, when is a bonus taxed?

   A. The date of receipt or availability

   B. The end of the period that the bonus relates to

   C. The date the employer decides to pay a bonus

   D. The following 5 April

3. True or false – a benefit in kind is a form of remuneration not in cash?

   A. True

   B. False

4. Which TWO of the following employer-provided benefits in kind are not taxable

   A. Private use of a motorbike

   B. Private medical health insurance

   C. Car parking near the workplace

   D. Private use of one mobile phone

5. When calculating the taxable benefit in kind for a car provided to an employee, which factor is NOT considered?

   A. The car's CO2 emissions

   B. The car's list price

   C. The car's age

   D. The type of fuel it uses

6. Unless there is a specific rule, the taxable value of a benefit in kind is usually calculated as

   A. The cost that the employee has saved

   B. The marginal cost of the benefit in kind to the employer

   C. The amount agreed with HMRC

   D. 25% of the annual value

7. True or false – the taxable benefit in kind on a loan to an employee is calculated as interest on the loan calculated at the official rate less the rate of inflation.

A. True
B. False

8. When calculating the benefit in kind for a car, the maximum deduction for an employee's capital contribution is limited to the lower of the amount paid and

A. £2,000
B. £3,000
C. £5,000
D. £10,000

9. What is the maximum additional benefit in kind for a diesel car?

A. 1% of list price
B. 2% of list price
C. 3% of list price
D. 4% of list price

10. True or false - all taxable benefits in kind are calculated for the full tax year

A. True
B. False

11. The normal benefit in kind for the private use of an asset is calculated as the market value of the asset when first made available multiplied by

A. 10%
B. 20%
C. 25%
D. 37%

12. True or false – the use of an employee's charging facilities for an electric company car is tax free?

A. True
B. False

13. The additional benefit in kind for employer provided accommodation only applies where

A. The accommodation cost the employer more than £75,000
B. The market value of the property is more than £75,000 when first made available
C. The accommodation has been bought more than 10 years before it is made available
D. The accommodation cost the employer more than £150,000

14. A trivial benefit is kind must satisfy which of the conditions to be tax-free

A. Cost less than £50
B. Is provided to all employees
C. Is in reward for service
D. Must show the employer's name or logo

15. To be allowable, employment expenses must be incurred

A. Wholly and necessarily in the performance of the employee's duties
B. Wholly and exclusively in the performance of the employee's duties
C. Wholly, exclusively and necessarily in the performance of the employee's duties
D. Wholly, exclusively in the performance of the employee's duties and be approved by the employer

Chapter 10 MCQ Solutions: 1B; 2A; 3A; 4C & D; 5C; 6B; 7B; 8C; 9D; 10B; 11B; 12A; 13A; 14A; 15C

Chapter 11 Personal tax: Overseas aspects

1. True or false – a UK resident individual is subject to UK income tax on their worldwide income.

   A. True
   B. False

2. How many days could a previously resident individual visit the UK for without failing the automatic overseas test?

   A. 0 days
   B. 15 days
   C. 45 days
   D. 90 days

3. How many ties would an individual arriving in the UK need to have to be considered UK resident if they visited the UK for 95 days?

   A. 1 tie
   B. 2 ties
   C. 3 ties
   D. 4 ties

4. If a UK individual pays overseas tax on a non-UK income source, what is the limit to Double Tax Relief (DTR)

   A. DTR only applies to companies
   B. Relief for overseas tax paid is unrestricted
   C. Relief for overseas tax paid is limited to the total UK tax liability
   D. Relief for overseas tax paid is restricted to the UK tax liability on that income source.

5. Under the Foreign Income and Gains regime, overseas income and gains can be exempted from UK taxation for how many years?

   A. 2 years
   B. 3 years
   C. 4 years
   D. 5 years

Chapter 11 MCQ Solutions: 1A; 2B; 3C; 4D; 5C

Chapter 12 Pension contributions

1. How is income tax relief provided for occupational pension contributions?

   A. As a deduction from wages
   B. By paying net of basic rate tax
   C. As an increase to the personal allowance
   D. By extending the basic and higher rate bands

2. True or false – occupational pension contributions do not reduce pay for Class 1 NIC.

   A. True
   B. False

3. What is the standard limit of annual pension savings before an annual allowance charge?

   A. £10,000
   B. £37,700
   C. £60,000
   D. £100,000

4. Helen's only income is from property rental and savings. What is the maximum net personal pension contribution that she can make?

   A. Nil
   B. 2,880
   C. 3,600
   D. 10,000

5. Where an annual allowance charge applies, this is charged to income tax

   A. At 20%
   B. As Savings income
   C. At 45%
   D. As the top slice of income after dividends

Chapter 12 MCQ Solutions: 1A; 2A; 3C; 4B; 5D

Chapter 13 Capital gains tax: General principles

1. What is the Capital Gains tax annual exempt amount for 2026/27?

    A. 12,300
    B. 6,000
    C. 3,000
    D. 5,000

2. The sale of which of the following assets is NOT subject to Capital Gains Tax?

    A. Quoted Shares
    B. Motor car
    C. Residential property
    D. Antique furniture

3. True or false – the gift of an asset to anyone is a capital gains tax disposal?

    A. True
    B. False

4. When an asset is inherited, the recipient's base cost is

    A. The deceased's original cost
    B. Nil, as they did not pay for it
    C. The value on the day the deceased died
    D. The value on the date probate of the estate is complete

5. Bas sold 3 hectares of land. This was part of a 10-hectare field which originally cost £20,000. The 3 hectares were sold for £10,000 and at the time, the remaining land was valued at £40,000. What was the cost of the land sold

    A. £4,000
    B. £6,000
    C. £10,000
    D. £16,000

6. True or false – an antique luxury watch is exempt from capital gains tax

    A. True
    B. False

7. A painting was bought for £5,000 and sold for £7,000. What is the capital gain?

    A. Nil
    B. 1,666
    C. 2,000
    D. 3,000

8. Which of the following gaps in occupation could not fully be deemed occupied for main residence relief?

A. A gap of 3 years when working overseas
B. A gap of 2 years when living elsewhere
C. A gap of 5 years when working away from home in the UK
D. A 6-month gap directly before the property is sold

9. Which of the following is correct about reporting a residential property gain for Capital Gains Tax?

A. You have 30 days to report and pay any tax due
B. You have 60 days to report and pay any tax due
C. You report at the end of the tax year
D. The return and any tax are due on 31 January following the tax year end

10. True or false – if the basic rate band is extended, this can also apply to capital gains

A. True
B. False

Chapter 13 MCQ Solutions: 1C; 2B; 3A; 4C; 5A; 6A; 7B; 8C; 9B; 10A

Chapter 14 CGT Shares and securities

1. Which purchase is matched first with a sale of shares by an individual

    A. The share pool
    B. Purchase up to 9 days before the sale
    C. Purchases on the day of the sale
    D. Purchases in the 30 days after the sale

2. True or false – Gilts are exempt from capital gains tax

    A. True
    B. False

3. Gifts of shares between married couples or civil partners are treated as

    A. A sale at market value
    B. A sale at cost

4. True or false – the 30-day after the date of sale rule cannot apply when the purchase takes place in the next tax year?

    A. True
    B. False

5. Which of the following will increase the cost of a shareholding?

    A. A bonus issue
    B. A rights issue
    C. A reorganisation
    D. A takeover

Chapter 14 MCQ Solutions: 1C; 2A; 3B; 4B; 5B

Chapter 15 CGT Business reliefs

1. What is the time limit for acquiring a new asset after a sale for "rollover relief" to be available

   A. 1 year
   B. 2 years
   C. 3 years
   D. 6 years

2. True or false - Rollover relief is available to individuals and limited companies

   A. True
   B. False

3. Glyn sells a factory unit for £60,000 making a gain of £25,000. He reinvests £55,000 in a new factory. How much gain will remain taxable after a rollover relief claim?

   A. Nil
   B. 5,000
   C. 25,000
   D. 30,000

4. True or false - Gift relief can apply on the gift of an investment property to an individual

   A. True
   B. False

5. True or false – Gift relief can apply to the sale of an asset where the sale proceeds are less than the market value

   A. True
   B. False

6. What is the lifetime limit on gift relief

   A. There is no limit
   B. £100,000
   C. £1,000,000
   D. £10,000,000

7. True or false – Business asset disposal relief (BADR) reduces the chargeable gain by 18%

   A. True
   B. False

8. What is the minimum period of ownership of shares for BADR to be available

A. 6 months
B. 1 year
C. 2 years
D. 6 years

9. True or false – BADR can be available to a sole trader when disposing of any business assets while the business continues

A. True
B. False

10. For BADR to apply to shareholdings, what is the minimum percentage holding?

A. No limit
B. 3%
C. 5%
D. 10%

Chapter 15 MCQ Solutions: 1B; 2A; 3B; 4B; 5A; 6A; 7B; 8C; 9B; 10C

Chapter 16 Corporation tax

1. True or false – all companies incorporated in the UK are UK resident for corporation tax?

   A. True
   B. False

2. What is the main rate of Corporation Tax in the UK for the financial year 2024?

   A. 19%
   B. 20%
   C. 25%
   D. 26.5%

3. Which of the following would not be included in the calculation of taxable total profits (TTP)?

   A. Trading profits
   B. Rental income
   C. Capital gains
   D. Dividends received

4. A UK company with augmented profits and TTP of £45,000 for the financial year 2026 will pay Corporation Tax at what rate

   A. 19%
   B. 20%
   C. 25%
   D. Marginal rate

5. The marginal relief for Corporation Tax is available for companies with augmented profits between

   A. £50,000 and £250,000
   B. £100,000 and £500,000
   C. £25,000 and £150,000
   D. £20,000 and £200,000

6. True or false – a chargeable accounting period for Corporation tax cannot exceed 12 months?

   A. True
   B. False

7. Which two of the following statements regarding capital allowances are true?

   A. Sole traders cannot use full expensing
   B. Limited companies cannot claim the Annual Investment Allowance
   C. Limited companies do not restrict allowances for private use
   D. Only Sole traders can claim the Structures and buildings allowance

8. Which of the following would be disallowed and added back in the calculation of tax-adjusted trading profits for a limited company?

A. Private motor expenses of the managing director
B. The expenses of a staff summer party costing £180 per head
C. Employers Class 1 and 1A NIC
D. Gifts to customers of shirts with the company logo costing £60 each

9. True or false - a company controlled by 4 equal shareholders would be considered a Close company?

A. True
B. False

10. True or false – Research and development credit is not available to unincorporated businesses

A. True
B. False

Chapter 16 MCQ Solutions: 1A; 2C; 3D; 4A; 5A; 6A; 7A & C; 8D; 9A; 10A

Chapter 17 Chargeable gains for companies

1. What is the purpose of Indexation allowance?

   A. To reduce tax on trading profits
   B. To adjust gains for inflation up to December 2017
   C. To exempt gains before December 2017
   D. To defer the tax liability on the gain

2. How are excess capital losses treated for Corporation Tax?

   A. They can be deducted from TTP
   B. They are carried forward and offset only against future capital gains
   C. They can be surrendered for a CT repayment
   D. They can be carried back against gains of the previous accounting period

3. Which of the following qualifies for rollover relief in UK Corporation Tax?

   A. Sale of obsolete trading stock
   B. Disposal of depreciating assets only
   C. Proceeds from the sale of a qualifying business asset reinvested into another
   D. Transfer of capital losses between related companies

4. A company sells a building and incurs legal fees for the sale. How are the legal fees treated?

   A. Not deductible
   B. Deductible as trading expenses
   C. Allowable as incidental costs of disposal
   D. Treated as a capital loss

5. What is the correct order of matching for share sales by a company?

   A. Same day purchases, purchases in the next 30 days, then the share pool
   B. All shares in the same company are pooled
   C. Same day purchases, purchases in the previous 9 days, then the share pool
   D. Same day purchased, purchase in the next 9 days, then the share pool

Chapter 17 MCQ Solutions: 1B; 2B; 3C; 4C; 5C

Chapter 18 Company losses

1. True or false – trading losses cannot include claims for capital allowances

   A. True
   B. False

2. How many years can a corporate trading loss be carried forward against TTP of a later accounting period

   A. One year
   B. Three years
   C. Six Years
   D. Indefinitely until it is fully used

3. Which statement is true about a company's trading loss for an accounting period?

   A. Trading losses can only be carried forward
   B. Trading losses may be offset against TTP of the current accounting period only
   C. Trading losses may be offset against TTP of the current accounting period and the TTP of the previous 12 months in any order to maximise tax savings
   D. Trading losses may be offset against TTP of the current accounting period and only then against TTP of the previous 12 months.

4. True or false – trading losses are deducted after qualifying charitable donations when calculating TTP

   A. True
   B. False

5. True or false – a company's trading losses can never be offset against its capital gains.

   A. True
   B. False

Chapter 18 MCQ Solutions: 1B; 2D; 3D; 4B; 5B

Chapter 19 Groups of companies

1. To be part of a group relief group, a parent company must control at least:

   A. 25% of ordinary shares
   B. 75% of ordinary shares
   C. 90% of voting rights
   D. 100% of ordinary shares

2. Group relief allows a company to

   A. Only surrender trading losses to its parent company
   B. Only surrender losses after first claiming against its own TTP
   C. Surrender losses to any company in the group relief group
   D. Only surrender trading losses to its subsidiaries

3. True or false – a non-resident company may surrender losses as group relief

   A. True
   B. False

4. True or false – if a company is a member of a capital gains group, it will always also be a member of a group relief group

   A. True
   B. False

5. Which statement is incorrect about capital gains groups

   A. Member companies may claim rollover relief where one member sells and another member acquires the replacement asset
   B. Member companies may transfer assets without creating a capital gain
   C. Member companies may transfer current year gains and losses
   D. Member companies may transfer brought forward losses

Chapter 19 MCQ Solutions: 1B; 2C; 3B; 4B; 5D

Chapter 20 National Insurance Contributions

1) At what age do individuals in the UK typically start paying National Insurance contributions?

A. 18
B. 16
C. 21
D. There is no age limit

2) Which Class of NICs apply to benefits in kind?

A. Class 1A
B. Class 1 Employee's contributions
C. Class 1 Employer's contributions
D. Class 2

3) What would the Class 1 Employee's NIC liability be on an annual salary of £30,000?

A. £1,394
B. £2,400
C. £2,614
D. £3,750

4) True or false – the employment allowance reduces an employer's total Class 1 employer's NIC and Class 1A NIC liability

A. True
B. False

5) Which Class of NICs apply to profits from self-employment?

A. Class 1
B. Class 1A
C. Class 3
D. Class 4

Chapter 20 MCQ Solutions: 1B; 2A; 3A; 4B; 5D

Chapter 21 Tax Administration for individuals

1. True or false – most UK individuals are required to submit an annual self-assessment tax return

   A. True
   B. False

2. If an individual commences self-employment during the tax year to 5 April 2027, by what date must they notify HMRC?

   A. Within 30 days of commencement
   B. 5 April 2027
   C. 5 October 2027
   D. 31 January 2028

3. By what date must a self-assessment tax return for the year to 5 April 2027 be submitted online to HMRC to avoid a late filing penalty?

   A. 5 April 2027
   B. 31 October 2027
   C. 31 January 2028
   D. 5 April 2028

4. True or false – MTD applies only to sole traders

   A. True
   B. False

5. What is the maximum penalty for failing to keep tax records for the required time?

   A. £100
   B. £1,000
   C. £3,000
   D. £10,000

6. What is the normal time limit for HMRC to open an enquiry into a self-assessment tax return?

   A. 1 month from submission
   B. 1 year from submission
   C. 5 April following the tax year end
   D. 4 years from submission

7. Payments on account of the tax liability for the year to 5 April 2027 are due on which dates?

   A. 31 January 2027 and 31 July 2027
   B. 31 July 2027 and 31 January 2028
   C. 31 October 2026 and 31 January 2027
   D. 5 April 2027 and 5 October 2027

8. An individual's tax liabilities to 5 April 2026 were income tax £12,000 and capital gains tax £2,000. What are each of their payments on account for 2026/27?

A. Nil
B. £1,000
C. £6,000
D. £7,000

9. True or false – Class 4 NICs are included in the calculation of payments on account?

A. True
B. False

10. Which of the following income sources counts towards the MTD ITSA qualifying income threshold?

A. Employment income taxed under PAYE
B. State Pension
C. Property rental income
D. Dividends from a close company

Chapter 21 MCQ Solutions: 1B; 2C; 3C; 4B; 5C; 6B; 7A; 8C; 9A; 10C

Chapter 22 Tax Administration for Corporation tax

1. What is the usual filing date for a Corporation tax return?

   A. 31 January after the end of the accounting period
   B. 30 days after the end of the accounting period
   C. 9 months and one day after the end of the accounting period
   D. 12 months after the end of the accounting period

2. What is the usual tax payment date for a company that is not large?

   A. 31 January after the end of the accounting period
   B. 30 days after the end of the accounting period
   C. 9 months and one day after the end of the accounting period
   D. 12 months after the end of the accounting period

3. For a large company, when is the first quarterly tax payment due?

   A. 6 months and 14 days after the start of the accounting period
   B. 31 March after the start of the accounting period
   C. 6 months and 14 days after the end of the accounting period
   D. 3 months after the start of the accounting period

4. What is the annual summary of pay and tax that must be provided to all employees?

   A. P11D
   B. P45
   C. P60
   D. SA100

5. On what form are employers required to provide details of benefits in kind to HMRC

   A. P11D
   B. P45
   C. P60
   D. SA100

Chapter 22 MCQ Solutions: 1D; 2C; 3A; 4C; 5A

Chapter 23 Value Added Tax

1. What is the historic turnover test threshold for VAT registration?

   A. Taxable turnover in the previous 12 months exceeds £50,000
   B. Taxable turnover in the previous 12 months exceeds £90,000
   C. Taxable turnover in the previous 12 months exceeds £150,000
   D. Taxable turnover in the next 30 days exceeds £75,000

2. When must a business notify HMRC that the historic threshold test has been met?

   A. 30 days after the end of the month
   B. 1 month after the end of the month
   C. 3 months after the end of the month
   D. 3 months and 7 days after the end of the month

3. Which rate of VAT applies to most essential food products?

   A. Standard rate (20%)
   B. Reduced rate (5%)
   C. Zero rate (0%)
   D. It is usually exempt from VAT

4. When can businesses claim VAT bad debt relief?

   A. On the next VAT return
   B. When the debt is at least 3 months old
   C. When the debt is at least 6 months old
   D. When the debtor business enters liquidation

5. Which scheme allows businesses to pay VAT as a percentage of gross turnover?

   A. Cash Accounting Scheme
   B. Annual Accounting Scheme
   C. Flat Rate Scheme
   D. Retail Margin Scheme

Chapter 23 MCQ Solutions: 1B; 2A; 3C; 4C; 5C

Chapter 24 Inheritance Tax

1. Which of the following is a potentially exempt transfer (PET) for IHT purposes?

   A. A gift of £50,000 to a discretionary trust
   B. A gift of £1,000,000 to a child
   C. A gift of £10,000 to a UK charity
   D. A gift of £5,000 to a political party

2. What is the main consequence if the donor dies within seven years of making a PET?

   A. The gift becomes exempt from IHT
   B. The gift becomes chargeable to IHT
   C. The recipient must return the gift
   D. The gift is taxed at 10%

3. What is the IHT rate on a chargeable lifetime transfer (CLT) above the nil-rate band where the donee agrees to bear any tax?

   A. 10%
   B. 20%
   C. 25%
   D. 40%

4. Which of the following is not an IHT exempt lifetime transfer?

   A. Gifts to UK charities
   B. Gifts of £3,000 per tax year
   C. Gifts to a UK-resident spouse
   D. Gifts to a discretionary trust

5. True or false – A transfer is exempt from IHT if a donor survives seven years after making a PET?

   A. True
   B. False

6. What is the effect of taper relief on lifetime transfers?

   A. It reduces the value of the gift
   B. It reduces the additional IHT liability on gifts made between 3 and 7 years before death
   C. It reduces the IHT rate on the death estate
   D. It only applies to gifts to spouses or civil partners

7. Which of the following qualifies for the Residence Nil-Rate Band (RNRB)?

   A. Leaving a £600,000 home to a grandchild
   B. Leaving a £500,000 home to a niece
   C. Leaving a £4 million residence to children.
   D. Leaving a home valued at £400,000 to a sibling.

8. A single person's estate is valued at £600,000 and does not include a residence? What is the IHT liability assuming no lifetime transfers?

A. Nil
B. £110,000
C. £120,000
D. £240,000

9. What is the maximum total combined nil-rate bands for a married couple leaving a home to their children?

A. £325,000
B. £500,000
C. £650,000
D. £1,000,000

10. Who typically arranges the payment of IHT from an estate?

A. The executor or administrator of the estate
B. The deceased's next of kin
C. The beneficiaries of the will
D. HMRC automatically deducts it

Chapter 24 MCQ Solutions: 1B; 2B; 3B; 4D; 5A; 6B; 7A; 8B; 9D; 10A

Index

www.ingramcontent.com/pod-product-compliance
Lightning Source LLC
LaVergne TN
LVHW050759061126
851857LV00012B/618
9781913507350